Hot Thought

Hot Thought

Mechanisms and Applications of Emotional Cognition

Paul Thagard

in collaboration with Fred Kroon, Josef Nerb, Baljinder Sahdra, Cameron Shelley, and Brandon Wagar

A Bradford Book
The MIT Press
Cambridge, Massachusetts
London, England

MIT Press books may be purchased at special quantity discounts for business or sales promotional use. For information, please email special_sales@mitpress.mit.edu or write to Special Sales Department, The MIT Press, 55 Hayward Street, Cambridge, MA 02142.

This book was set in Sabon on 3B2 by Asco Typesetters, Hong Kong, and was printed and bound in the United States of America.

Library of Congress Cataloging-in-Publication Data

Thagard, Paul.
Hot thought : mechanisms and applications of emotional cognition / Paul Thagard ; in collaboration with Fred Kroon . . . [et al.].
    p. cm.
"A Bradford book."
Includes bibliographical references and index.
ISBN-13: 978-0-262-20164-3 (hc : alk. paper)
ISBN-10: 0-262-20164-X (hc : alk. paper)
1. Emotions and cognition. I. Kroon, Fred. II. Title.

BF311.T416 2006
152.4—dc22   2006041979

10 9 8 7 6 5 4 3 2 1

To five fine friends, from days in Cambridge, Toronto, Ann Arbor, Princeton, and Waterloo: Dan Hausman, Mark Golden, Steve Bank, Michael Ranney, and Joanne Wood.

Contents

Preface

This book is a collection of articles on emotional cognition—hot thought—produced since the 2000 appearance of my book, *Coherence in Thought and Action*. The articles are concerned with mental mechanisms that explain how cognition and emotion interact to produce many kinds of human thinking, from everyday decision making to legal reasoning to scientific discovery to religious belief. Part I of the book describes cognitive, social, neural, and molecular mechanisms that interact in ways that provide explanations of many kinds of human thinking that crucially involve emotion. Part II goes into greater depth in particular domains, showing the application of emotional cognition to the understanding of thinking in law, science, religion, and other areas. The last two chapters address philosophical questions about the normative status of emotional cognition, especially when and how thinking and reasoning *should* be emotional. The final chapter also provides pointers to related current and future work on the nature and significance of emotional cognition.

The chapters reprint the relevant articles largely intact, but I have done some light editing to coordinate references and remove redundancies. Origins of the articles are indicated in the acknowledgments.

Acknowledgments

While I was writing and revising this text, my research was supported by the Natural Sciences and Engineering Research Council of Canada. I have benefited from discussions with many people about the role of emotions in cognition. I am particularly grateful to the coauthors of articles included in this collection: Fred Kroon, Josef Nerb, Baljinder Sahdra, Cameron Shelley, and Brandon Wagar. Please note that Baljinder and Brandon were first authors of their respective articles. For comments on particular chapters, I am indebted to Allison Barnes, Barbara Bulman-Fleming, Peter Carruthers, Mike Dixon, Chris Eliasmith, Christine Freeman, David Gooding, Usha Goswami, Ray Grondin, Tim Kenyon, Patrick Lee, James McAllister, Elijah Millgram, Josef Nerb, Stephen Read, Baljinder Sahdra, Cameron Shelley, Jeff Shrager, Craig Smith, Eliot Smith, Steve Smith, Marcia Sokolowski, Rob Stainton, Robin Vallacher, Chris White, and Zhu Jing.

I am grateful to the respective publishers and to my coauthors for permission to reprint the following articles:

Sahdra, B., and P. Thagard (2003). Self-deception and emotional coherence. *Minds and Machines* 15: 213–231.

Thagard, P. (2001). How to make decisions: Coherence, emotion, and practical inference. In E. Millgram (ed.), *Varieties of Practical Inference*, 355–371. Cambridge, Mass.: MIT Press.

Thagard, P. (2002). Curing cancer? Patrick Lee's path to the reovirus treatment. *International Studies in the Philosophy of Science* 16: 179–193.

Thagard, P. (2002). How molecules matter to mental computation. *Philosophy of Science* 69: 429–446.

Thagard, P. (2002). The passionate scientist: Emotion in scientific cognition. In P. Carruthers, S. Stich, and M. Siegal (eds.), *The Cognitive Basis of Science*, 235–250. Cambridge: Cambridge University Press.

Thagard, P. (2003). Why wasn't O. J. convicted? Emotional coherence in legal inference. *Cognition and Emotion* 17: 361–383.

Thagard, P. (2004). What is doubt and when is it reasonable? In M. Ezcurdia, R. Stainton, and C. Viger (eds.), *New Essays in the Philosophy of Language and Mind. Canadian Journal of Philosophy*, supplementary volume 30, 391–406. Calgary: University of Calgary Press.

Thagard, P. (2005). How to be a successful scientist. In M. E. Gorman, R. D. Tweney, D. C. Gooding, and A. P. Kincannon (eds.), *Scientific and Technological Thinking*, 159–171. Mahwah, N.J.: Lawrence Erlbaum.

Thagard, P. (2005). The emotional coherence of religion. *Journal of Cognition and Culture* 5: 58–74.

Thagard, P. (forthcoming). Critique of emotional reason. In C. de Waal (ed.), *Susan Haack: The Philosopher Replies to Critics*. Buffalo: Prometheus Books.

Thagard, P., and F. W. Kroon (forthcoming). Emotional consensus in group decision making. *Mind and Society*.

Thagard, P., and J. Nerb (2002). Emotional gestalts: Appraisal, change, and emotional coherence. *Personality and Social Psychology Review* 6: 274–282.

Thagard, P., and C. P. Shelley (2001). Emotional analogies and analogical inference. In D. Gentner, K. H. Holyoak, and B. K. Kokinov (eds.), *The Analogical Mind: Perspectives from Cognitive Science*, 335–362. Cambridge, Mass.: MIT Press.

Wagar, B. M., and P. Thagard (2004). Spiking Phineas Gage: A neurocomputational theory of cognitive-affective integration in decision making. *Psychological Review* 111: 67–79.

I am grateful to Todd Nudelman for astute copyediting, and to Abninder Litt for help with the proofreading and index.

I Mechanisms

1 | Mental Mechanisms

Emotional Cognition

Emotional cognition is thinking that is influenced by emotional factors such as particular emotions, moods, or motivations. Here are some examples of situations where people are strongly influenced by their emotions, for good or bad:

A jury member reviews the evidence that an accused man is guilty of murder, but discounts much of it because he seems like a nice guy.

A scientist is told by advisors that her planned research is pointless, but she pursues it because she finds it exciting, and goes on to win a Nobel prize.

An entrepreneur decides to start a novel kind of business because his gut instinct tells him that it will be highly successful, and it is.

A voter wavers over what political candidate to choose, then opts for one with enormous charisma.

A person overcome with anxiety and guilt because of family disasters finds comfort in becoming a born-again Christian.

The primary descriptive aim of this book is to increase understanding of how emotional cognition works in such situations. The secondary normative aim is to suggest ways of improving thinking by appreciating the difference between cases where emotions foster good decisions and those where emotions get in the way. Reasoning is a particular kind of thinking in which decisions are made or beliefs are acquired as the result of the comparative evaluation of different options with respect to various kinds of evidence. Contrary to standard philosophical assumptions, reasoning is often an emotional process, and improving it requires identifying and assessing the impact of emotions.

Accomplishing both the descriptive and normative aims requires an appreciation of the mental mechanisms that underlie mental cognition. Part I of

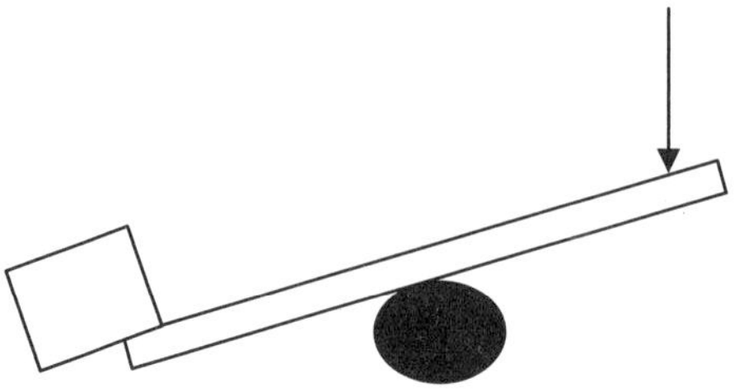

Figure 1.1
A simple machine, the lever.

this book describes some of the cognitive, social, neural, and molecular mechanisms that are crucial for emotional thinking. These mechanisms provide explanations of how emotions often influence people's decisions and other inferences. Part II shows how such mechanisms operate in emotional reasoning in law, science, and religion, and discusses the difference between desirable and undesirable kinds of emotional thinking. Before getting into details, however, it is necessary to say what mechanisms are and how they contribute to explanation.

Machines and Mechanisms

Humans invented simple machines such as levers and wedges long before the beginning of recorded history. Consider the basic lever shown in figure 1.1. It consists of only two parts, a stick and a rock. But levers are very powerful and enabled people to build huge structures such as the Egyptian pyramids. In general, a machine is an assemblage of components that transmit force, motion, and energy to each other to accomplish some task. To describe a machine and explain its operation, we need to specify its components, their properties, and their relations to other parts. Most important, we need to describe how changes to the properties and relations of the parts with respect to force, motion, and energy enable the machine to accomplish its tasks. The lever in figure 1.1 operates by virtue of the fact that the stick is rigid and is on top of the rock, which is solid. Applying force to the top of the stick makes the bottom of the stick move and lift the block, thus accomplishing the machine's task.

Ancient philosophers such as Epicurus and Lucretius realized that natural events can be explained in the same way that people explain the operations of machines. They postulated that all matter consists of atoms whose interactions determine the behavior of the objects that they constitute. According to

Lucretius (1969), even human thought is the result of the interactions of atoms. Natural phenomena are thus explained by *mechanisms*, which are like machines in that their changes result from forces and motions applied to their parts. Unlike machines, however, a natural mechanism is not constructed by humans and has no human-contrived task, although it may have a biological function. Nevertheless, the form of explanation is the same for both natural and constructed mechanisms: specify components, their properties and relations, and describe how changes in force, motion, and energy propagate through the system.

Mechanistic explanation has been fabulously successful in modern science, with triumphs such as Newton's theory of motion, the atomic theory of matter, the germ theory of disease, and the biological theories of evolution and genetics. But many philosophers, from Plato to Descartes, Leibniz, and even some modern thinkers, have resisted the extension of mechanistic explanation to mental phenomena. Plato's forms, Descartes's soul, Leibniz's monads, and twentieth-century phenomenology and hermeneutics are all attempts to understand the human mind in terms other than its material parts. Granted, early mechanistic attempts to explain mental operations were unsatisfactory, as Lucretius' atoms, Hume's associations of ideas, and modern behaviorist stimulus–response theories were much too crude to explain the richness of human thought. But I will now review a range of powerful mechanisms that have become available in the past fifty years for explaining thought in general and emotional reasoning in particular.

Kinds of Mental Mechanisms

Current cognitive science explains human thinking using a confluence of cognitive, neural, molecular, and social mechanisms. Those mechanisms most familiar are cognitive ones, which describe the mind as operating by the application of computational procedures on mental representations (for a survey, see Thagard 2005). Mental representations are cognitive structures, such as concepts, rules, and images, that are manipulated by algorithmic processes such as spreading activation of concepts, chaining of rules, and rotation of images. Connectionist explanations of mental phenomena describe them as arising from representations constructed by the activity of simple neuronlike units and processes that include spreading activation and modification of links between units.

Neural mechanisms are much closer to the operation of the brain in two key respects. First, they involve artificial neurons that are much more neurologically realistic than the highly simplified units found in connectionist

Table 1.1
Constituents of mental mechanisms

Mechanisms	Components	Relations	Interactions	Changes
Social	Persons and social groups	Association, membership	Communication	Influence, group decisions
Cognitive	Mental representations such as concepts	Constituents, associations, implication	Computational processes	Inferences
Neural	Neurons, neural groups	Synaptic connections	Excitation, inhibition	Brain activity
Molecular	Molecules such as neurotransmitters and proteins	Constituents, physical connection	Biochemical reactions	Transformation of molecules

explanations. For example, real neurons have temporal properties such as firing in coordination with each other that are crucial to their ability to support complex mental activity. Second, whereas connectionist models usually employ small numbers of interconnected units, brain mechanisms involve billions of neurons organized into functional areas such as the hippocampus and various parts of the cortex. Neural mechanisms depend on molecular mechanisms, such as the movement of ions within neurons, the flow of neurotransmitters in the synaptic connections between them, and the circulation of hormones through the brain's blood supply.

Finally, because human thought often involves interaction with other people, we need to attend to the social mechanisms that allow one person's thinking to influence another's. Social mechanisms involve verbal and other kinds of communication, including ones that make possible the transfer of emotions as well as other kinds of information. Table 1.1 summarizes some of the ingredients of the four kinds of mechanisms useful for different levels of mental explanation. Chapters 2 through 7 provide much more detailed examples of the mechanisms at each level that are relevant for understanding emotional thought.

The Nature of Complex Mechanisms

My approach to emotions is in keeping with the mechanism-based view of explanation espoused by such philosophers of science as Salmon (1984b), Bechtel and Richardson (1993), and Bechtel and Abrahamsen (2005). Machamer, Darden, and Craver (2000, p. 3) characterize mechanisms as

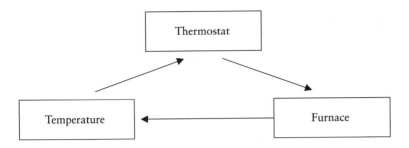

Figure 1.2
Feedback mechanism that regulates temperature.

"entities and activities organized such that they are productive of regular changes from start or set-up to finish or termination conditions." I prefer the term "component" to "entity" because it indicates that the objects in a mechanism are part of a larger system; and I prefer "interaction" and "change" to "activity" because they sound less anthropomorphic. More important, I find the reference to start and finish conditions misleading, because the mechanisms needed to explain emotional thinking involve ongoing feedback processes rather than unidirectional changes.

For a simple example of feedback, consider the system shown in figure 1.2. A thermostat is a device that detects when the temperature drops below a given threshold; it then signals a furnace to start up and heat the air. Taken separately, the thermostat and the furnace are unidirectional machines describable by simple rules: if the temperature is less than X, then signal the furnace to start; if a signal to start is received, then start the furnace. Taken together, however, they constitute a feedback mechanism that functions to maintain the temperature within a stable range. There are no start and finish conditions, but rather an ongoing process of temperature regulation. The human body contains many such feedback mechanisms, for example, ones that maintain blood pressure and cholesterol levels. As we will see in the next four chapters, those mechanisms most relevant to explaining emotions— cognitive, neural, molecular, and social—are feedback mechanisms rather than unidirectional ones with start and finish conditions.

Machamer, Darden, and Craver (2000) observe that mechanisms occur as nested hierarchies and that their description is frequently multilevel. They argue that higher-level entities and activities are essential to the intelligibility of those at lower levels and vice versa, and that mental phenomena are best explained by the integration of different levels. I fully agree, and will describe in detail how an understanding of emotional thinking needs to integrate the cognitive, neural, molecular, and social levels. This integration is much more complex than simply reducing the social to the cognitive, the cognitive to the neural, and the neural to the molecular. Some emotional events require an explanation that involves all levels simultaneously, for example, when a social interaction between two people generates fear that increases cortisol (stress hormone) levels that then change the social interaction. An insult leads to cognitive and physiological changes that incite a fight. Thus causality runs down as well as up the nested hierarchy of social–cognitive–neural–molecular mechanisms.

The nested hierarchy of mechanisms is a hierarchy of components as well as interactive changes. A social group consists of people who have brains that contain neurons made up of molecules; changes in the social group produce and are produced by changes in individual brains that arise from neural and molecular changes. Hence I reject single-level explanatory strategies, both reductive ones that privilege the lowest-level strategies, and intermediate ones that insist that only one level such as the cognitive one are appropriate for psychological explanation. Like McCauley and Bechtel (2001), I favor *explanatory pluralism*, which rejects both extreme reductionism and antireductionism. I hope to show that pluralistic, multilevel explanations based on multiple mechanisms are the best way to understand emotional thinking. It is impossible to argue for this position a priori, but the chapters to follow will provide ample experimental and theoretical support for a multilevel approach to explaining emotional thinking. (See chap. 16 for further discussion.)

At each level of the hierarchy, explanation of aspects of emotional thought will specify mechanisms consisting of components and their interactive changes. These aspects can include both positive cases of emotional thinking such as the scientist guided by excitement toward the Nobel prize, and negative cases such as the voter swayed by charisma rather than political substance. Just as knowing how machines work enables us both to understand and to fix them, so multilevel mechanisms will suggest a hierarchy of ways to explain and to improve emotional thinking.

Many of the chapters in this book employ computational models of various levels of thinking. A model is a description of a mechanism, that is, a specification of the components, relations, interactions, and changes that can be used to explain phenomena. Cognitive science routinely uses computational models for two reasons. The first reason, as seen in areas as diverse as physics and economics, is that computers provide a powerful way of describing complex interactions and discovering their consequences. The second reason, more specific to cognitive science, is that thinking itself is hypothesized to be a computational process, and that the brain is a special kind of computer. For a defense of this perspective, see Thagard 2005.

My main purpose in discussing computational mechanisms such as those described in part I is to provide explanations of important aspects of human thinking. Mechanisms do not provide explanations by describing what always happens or even what probably happens. Rather, they explain by describing the systematic interactions of the key factors that cause something to happen. In computational mechanisms, these factors include mental representations at the cognitive level and neurons at the neural level.

Guide to the Book

The rest of part I of this book describes mechanisms at different levels of analysis that are responsible for the various ways in which emotions affect thought. Chapters 2 through 4 describe the cognitive level and use a connectionist model of emotional coherence to illuminate the nature of decision making and other kinds of emotional reasoning. Chapter 2 provides a gentle introduction to decision making from the perspective of emotional coherence, and chapter 3 applies this perspective to the role of emotions in analogical thinking. Chapter 4 considers emotional thinking in terms of dynamic systems.

Chapter 5 discusses social mechanisms of emotional communication that contribute to the achievement of consensus in group decision making. Like individual decisions, group decisions are often highly emotional, and the extended HOTCO model provides computer simulations of how consensus can arise even in groups that initially diverge in their emotional reactions to different options. This chapter shows how a social model of consensus can be built on top of a cognitive model of emotional decisions.

The HOTCO models described in chapters 2 through 5 are not neurologically realistic: they employ artificial neurons that represent whole concepts and propositions; and these neurons are not organized into functional brain areas. That is why I have categorized them as employing cognitive rather than neural mechanisms. In contrast, the GAGE model presented in chapter 5 is much more neurologically realistic in that it uses spiking neurons, distributed representations, and distinct brain areas. This realism enables the model to account for the behavior of people with a particular kind of brain damage, as well as for how emotion and cognition can affect each other generally via neural mechanisms.

Chapter 6 moves down another notch to the molecular level, arguing that a full theory of thinking, particularly emotional thinking, will need to take into account mental computations accomplished by molecular mechanisms such as chemical reactions that operate within and between neurons and other cells.

The rest of the book is concerned with applying knowledge of emotional mechanisms to illuminate thinking in the domains of law, science, and religion. Chapter 8 provides an explanation of why the jury in the O. J. Simpson trial did not convict him, arguing that their decision was based on a combination of explanatory and emotional coherence. More generally, chapter 9 discusses the nature of doubt and reasonable doubt in legal and other contexts. Chapters 10 through 12 are concerned with both the positive and negative roles of emotions in scientific thinking. Chapter 10 provides a general overview of the ways in which emotions affect the pursuit, discovery, and evaluation of scientific ideas, and chapter 11 looks at how they contributed to the development of research in a particular case. Chapter 12 provides a distillation of advice on how to be a successful scientist, including valuable emotional habits. Chapters 13 and 14 discuss the application of emotional coherence to religious thinking, the former by looking at a particular case of the self-deception of a minister, the latter considering more generally the emotional content of religious beliefs.

Implicit in all these discussions of the applications of emotional reason is a set of judgments about appropriate standards for when the incursion of emotional elements into cognitive deliberation is legitimate. Chapter 15 begins the discussion of this normative question, which is continued in the concluding chapter 16. I reject the traditional assumption that emotion is inimical to good reason, but also argue against the romantic view that emotion always contributes to good thinking. Chapter 16 also sketches a number of other areas of ongoing investigation of hot thought, including its relevance to conflicts of interest, generation of explanatory hypotheses, and neuroeconomics.

We shall see that many aspects of human thinking and reasoning are influenced by emotions. An understanding of how emotions affect thought both positively and negatively requires the specification of cognitive, social, neural, and molecular mechanisms. Such mechanisms consist of components that undergo interactive changes that may involve feedback processes. Our best strategy for explaining emotional thinking is to look at multiple integrated levels of causal mechanisms.

Students face many important decisions: What college or university should I attend? What should I study? What kind of job should I try to get? Which people should I hang out with? Should I continue or break off a relationship? Should I get married? Should I have a baby? What kind of medical treatment should I use? A theory of practical reasoning should have something to say about how students and other people can improve their decision making.

I have often taught a first-year course on critical thinking intended to help students improve their reasoning about what to believe and about what to do. After spending about two-thirds of the course on ways of improving judgments about the truth and falsity of controversial claims in areas such as medicine and pseudoscience, I devote the last third to practical reasoning, with the focus on how people can make better decisions. I discuss both the kinds of erroneous reasoning that decision makers commonly fall into, and some systematic models that have been proposed by psychologists, economists, and philosophers to specify how people *should* make decisions.

Many students in the course dislike these models, and resist the claim that using them is preferable to making decisions simply by intuition. They trust their "gut feelings" more than they trust the analytical methods that require a systematic and mathematical comparative assessment of competing actions that satisfy multiple criteria. The textbooks I use (including Gilovich 1991; Russo and Schoemaker 1989; Schick and Vaughn 1999) encourage people to avoid the use of intuition and instead to base their judgments and decisions on reasoning strategies that are less likely to lead to common errors in reasoning. From this perspective, decision making should be a matter of calculation, not intuition.

While I agree that intuition-based decision making can lead to many problems, I also think that calculation-based decision making of the sort recommended by psychologists and economists has some serious pitfalls. In this chapter, I will try to offer a synthesis and partial reconciliation of intuition and calculation models of decision, using a recently developed theory of emotional coherence (Thagard 2000). This theory builds on a previous coherence-based theory of decision making developed in collaboration with Elijah Millgram. Understanding decision making in terms of emotional coherence enables us to appreciate the merits of both intuition and calculation as contributors to effective practical reasoning.

Decision as Intuition

Suppose you are a student trying to decide whether to study (1) an arts subject such as philosophy or art history in which you have a strong interest or (2) a subject such as economics or computer science which may lead to a more lucrative career. To make this decision intuitively is just to go with the option that is supported by your emotional reactions to the two alternatives. You may have a strongly positive gut feeling toward the more interesting subject along with a strongly negative feeling about the more career-oriented one, or your feelings may be just the opposite. More likely is that you feel positive feelings toward both alternatives, along with accompanying anxiety caused by your inability to see a clearly preferable option. In the end, intuitive decision makers choose an option based on what their emotional reactions tell them is preferable.

There is much to be said for intuitive decision making. One obvious advantage is speed: an emotional reaction can be immediate and lead directly to a decision. If your choice is between chocolate and vanilla ice cream, it would be pointless to spend a lot of time and effort deliberating about the relative advantages and disadvantages of the two flavors. Instead, an emotional reaction such as "chocolate—yum!" can make for a quick and appropriate decision. Another advantage is that basing your decisions on emotions helps to ensure that the decisions take into account what you really care about. If you are pleased and excited about a possible action, that is a good sign that the action promises to accomplish the goals that are genuinely important to you. Finally, decisions based on emotional intuitions lead directly to action: the positive feeling toward an option will motivate you to carry it out.

But emotion-based intuitive decision making can also have some serious disadvantages. An option may seem emotionally appealing because of failure to consider other available options. Intuition may suggest buying chocolate ice cream only because you have failed to consider a lower-fat alternative that would be a healthier choice. Intuition is also subject to the intense craving that drug addicts call "jonesing." If you are jonesing for cocaine, or for a pizza, or for a Mercedes-Benz convertible, your intuition will tell you to choose what you crave, but only because the craving has emotionally swamped other desires that you will be more aware of when the craving is less intense.

Another problem with intuition is that it may be based on inaccurate or irrelevant information. Suppose you need to decide whom to hire for a job. If you are prejudiced against people of a particular sex, race, or ethnicity, then your intuition will tell you not to hire them, even if they have better qualifications for doing the job well. It is difficult to determine introspectively whether your intuitions derive from reliable and relevant information.

Finally, intuitive reasoning is problematic in group situations where decisions need to be made collectively. If other people disagree with your choices, you cannot simply contend that your intuitions are stronger or better than the intuitions of others. Defending your emotional reactions and attempting to reach a consensus with other people requires a more analytical approach than simply expressing your gut feelings.

Decision as Calculation

Experts on decision making recommend a more systematic and calculating approach. For example, Bazerman (1994, p. 4) says that rational decision making should include the following six steps:

1. Define the problem, characterizing the general purpose of your decision.
2. Identify the criteria, specifying the goals or objectives that you want to be able to accomplish.
3. Weight the criteria, deciding the relative importance of the goals.
4. Generate alternatives, identifying possible courses of action that might accomplish your various goals.
5. Rate each alternative on each criterion, assessing the extent to which each action would accomplish each goal.
6. Compute the optimal decision, evaluating each alternative by multiplying the expected effectiveness of each alternative with respect to a criterion times the weight of the criterion, then adding up the expected value of the alternative with respect to all criteria.

We can then pick the alternative with the highest expected value and make a decision based on calculation, not on subjective emotional reactions. Using slightly different terminology, Russo and Schoemaker (1989, chap. 6) recommend essentially the same kind of decision making process based on multiple weighted factors.

Some students dismiss this kind of process as robot-like, and find it offensive that important decisions in their lives might be made mathematically. A cartoon in the *New Yorker* (Jan. 10, 2000, p. 74) shows a man sitting at a computer and saying to a woman: "I've done the numbers, and I will marry you." Some decisions, at least, seem inappropriately based on doing the numbers. But is the emotional dismissal of Bazerman's six-step calculation method justified? We can certainly see some notable advantages of the calculation method over the intuition method. First, it is set up to avoid neglecting relevant alternatives and goals. Second, it makes explicit the consideration of how the various alternatives contribute to the various goals. Third, it puts the decision making process out in the open, enabling it to be carefully reviewed by a particular decision maker and also by others involved in a group decision process.

However, the calculation method of decision making may be more difficult and less effective than decision experts claim. Suppose you are trying to decide between two courses of study, say philosophy versus computer science, and you systematically list all the relevant criteria such as how interesting you find the subjects and how well they fit with your career plans. You then weight the criteria and estimate the extent to which each option satisfies them, and proceed to a calculation of the expected value of the competing choices. Having done this, you find that the expected value of one option, say philosophy, exceeds that of the other. But what if you then have the reaction—"I don't want to do that!" Your emotional reaction need not be crazy, because it may be that the numerical weights that you put on your criteria do not reflect what you really care about. Moreover, your estimates about the extent to which different actions accomplish your goals may be very subjective and fluid, so that your unconscious estimation is at least as good as your conscious one. I once knew someone who told me that she made decisions by first flipping a coin, with heads for one option and tails for another. When the coin came up heads, she would note her emotional reaction, which gave her a better idea of whether she really wanted the option associated with heads. She then used this emotional information to help her make a choice between the two options.

There is empirical evidence that calculation may sometimes be inferior to intuition in making good judgments. Damasio (1994) describes people with injuries that have disconnected the parts of their brains that perform verbal reasoning and numerical calculation from emotional centers such as the amygdala. With their abstract reasoning abilities intact, you might think that the patients become paragons of rationality, like Spock or Data in *Star Trek*. On the contrary, these patients tend to make poor interpersonal decisions. Damasio conjectures that the deficiencies arise because the brain damage prevents the patients from making emotional evaluations that involve *somatic markers*, bodily states that indicate the positive or negative emotional value of different possibilities. The problem is that the patients just do not know what they care about. Wilson and Schooler (1991) report research that shows that there are domains where people's intuitive judgments may be more effective than their more systematic, deliberative ones. They studied college students' preferences for brands of strawberry jams and for college courses, and found that students who were asked to analyze the reasons for their preferences ended up with choices that corresponded less with expert opinion than did the choices of less analytical students. Wilson and Schooler conjecture that this happens because analyzing reasons can focus people's attention on relatively unimportant criteria. Lieberman (2000) argues that intuitions are often based on unconscious learning processes that can be interfered with by attempts at explicit learning.

It seems, therefore, that we need a model of decision making that is both more psychologically natural and more normatively effective than the calculation model. I will now argue that we can get better accounts both of how decisions are made and of how they should be made by understanding practical inference in terms of emotional coherence.

Decision as Coherence

Decision making is a kind of inference, but what is inference? Many philosophers have taken deductive logic as the model for inference. Here is a sort of deductive practical inference:

Whenever you want ice cream, you should order chocolate.
You want ice cream.
Therefore, you should order chocolate.

Unfortunately, we rarely have general rules that tell us exactly what to do, so deduction is not a good model for practical inference. A second familiar model of inference is calculation, useful for example in solving arithmetical problems and working with probability theory. But there is a third general model of inference that advocates the following rule: Accept a representation if and only if it coheres maximally with the rest of your representations. Many philosophers have advocated coherence theories of inference but have left rather vague how to maximize coherence (e.g., Harman 1986; Brink

1989; and Hurley 1989). A precise and general model of coherence-based inference can be constructed in terms of constraint satisfaction (Thagard and Verbeurgt 1998; Thagard 2000).

When we make sense of a text, a picture, a person, or an event, we need to construct an interpretation that fits with the available information better than alternative interpretations. The best interpretation is one that provides the most coherent account of what we want to understand, considering both pieces of information that fit with each other and pieces of information that do not fit with each other. For example, when we meet unusual people, we may consider different combinations of concepts and hypotheses that fit together to make sense of their behavior.

Coherence can be understood in terms of maximal satisfaction of multiple constraints, in a manner informally summarized as follows:

1. Elements are representations such as concepts, propositions, parts of images, goals, actions, and so on.
2. Elements can cohere (fit together) or incohere (resist fitting together). Coherence relations include explanation, deduction, facilitation, association, and so on. Incoherence relations include inconsistency, incompatibility, and negative association.
3. If two elements cohere, there is a positive constraint between them. If two elements incohere, there is a negative constraint between them.
4. Elements are to be divided into ones that are accepted and ones that are rejected.
5. A positive constraint between two elements can be satisfied either by accepting both of the elements or by rejecting both of the elements.
6. A negative constraint between two elements can be satisfied only by accepting one element and rejecting the other.
7. The coherence problem consists of dividing a set of elements into accepted and rejected sets in a way that satisfies the most constraints.

Computing coherence is a matter of maximizing constraint satisfaction, and can be accomplished approximately by several different algorithms. The most psychologically appealing models of coherence optimization are provided by connectionist algorithms. These use neuron-like units to represent elements and excitatory and inhibitory links to represent positive and negative constraints. Settling a connectionist network by spreading activation results in the activation (acceptance) of some units and the deactivation (rejection) of others. Coherence can be measured in terms of the degree of constraint satisfaction accomplished by the various algorithms. In general, the computational problem of exactly maximizing coherence is very difficult, but there are effective algorithms for approximating the maximization of coherence construed as constraint satisfaction (Thagard and Verbeurgt 1998).

I will now make this account of coherence more concrete by showing how it applies to inference about what to do. Elijah Millgram and I have argued that practical inference involves coherence judgments about how to fit together various possible actions and goals (Millgram and Thagard 1996; Thagard and Millgram 1995). On our account, the elements are actions and goals, the positive constraints are based on facilitation relations (the action of going to Paris facilitates my goal of having fun), and the negative constraints are based on incompatibility relations (you cannot go to Paris and London at the same time). Deciding what to do is based on inference to the most coherent plan, where coherence involves evaluating goals as well as deciding what to do.

More exactly, deliberative coherence can be specified by the following principles:

Principle 1: Symmetry   Coherence and incoherence are symmetrical relations: If a factor (action or goal) F_1 coheres with a factor F_2, then F_2 coheres with F_1.

Principle 2: Facilitation   Consider actions $A_1 \ldots A_n$ that together facilitate the accomplishment of goal G. Then

(a) each A_i coheres with G,
(b) each A_i coheres with each other A_j, and
(c) the greater the number of actions required, the less the coherence among actions and goals.

Principle 3: Incompatibility

(a) If two factors cannot both be performed or achieved, then they are strongly incoherent.
(b) If two factors are difficult to perform or achieve together, then they are weakly incoherent.

Principle 4: Goal priority   Some goals are desirable for intrinsic or other noncoherence reasons.

Principle 5: Judgment   Facilitation and competition relations can depend on coherence with judgments about the acceptability of factual beliefs.

Principle 6: Decision   Decisions are made on the basis of an assessment of the overall coherence of a set of actions and goals.

In order to assess overall coherence, we can use the computer program DECO (short for "deliberative coherence"). DECO represents each element (goal or action) by a neuron-like unit in an artificial neural network and then spreads activation through the network in a way that activates some units and deactivates others. At the end of the spread of activation, the active units represent elements that are accepted, while the deactivated ones represent elements that are rejected. DECO provides an efficient and usable way to compute the most coherent set of actions and goals.

At first glance, deliberative coherence might seem like a variant of the calculation model of decision making. Figuring out which action best coheres with your goals sounds like Bazerman's calculation of the expected value of alternatives based on the extent to which they satisfy weighted criteria. But there are some crucial differences. Unlike Bazerman's proposal, the deliberative coherence model of decision does not take the weights of the goals as fixed. In DECO, units representing some of the goals get initial activation in accord with principle 4, goal priority, but their impact depends on their relation to other goals: even a basic goal can be deactivated, at least partially, by other goals. The impact of goals on decision making depends on their activation, which depends on their relation to other goals and to various actions. For example, students trying to decide what to do on the weekend might start off thinking that what they most want to do is to have fun, but realize that having fun is not so important because it conflicts with other goals such as studying for an important exam or saving money to pay next term's tuition.

Psychologically, decision as coherence is very different from decision as calculation. Calculations are conscious and explicit, displayable to everyone on pencil and paper. In contrast, if coherence maximization in human brains is similar to what happens in the artificial neural networks used in DECO, then assessment of coherence is a process not accessible to consciousness. What comes to consciousness is only the result of the process of coherence maximization: the realization that a particular action is the one I want to perform. Thus, as an account of how decisions are made by people, deliberative coherence is closer to the intuition model of decision than to the calculation model. Coherence is not maximized by an explicit, consciously accessible calculation, but by an unconscious process whose output is the intuition that one action is preferable to others. There is, however, a major difference between the deliberative coherence account of decision making and the intuition account: intuitions about what to do are usually emotional, involving feelings that one action is a good thing to do and that alternatives are bad things to do. Fortunately, coherence theory can naturally be extended to encompass emotional judgments.

Emotional Coherence

In the theory of coherence stated above, elements have the epistemic status of being accepted or rejected. We can also speak of degree of acceptability, which in artificial neural network models of coherence is interpreted as the degree of activation of the unit that represents the element. I propose that elements in coherence systems have, in addition to acceptability, an emotional *valence*, which can be positive or negative. Depending on the nature of what the element represents, the valence of an element can indicate likability, desirability, or other positive or negative attitudes. For example, the valence of Mother Theresa for most people is highly positive, while the valence of Adolf Hitler is highly negative. Many other researchers have previously proposed introducing emotion into cognitive models by adding valences or affective tags (Bower 1981, 1991; Fiske and Pavelchak 1986; Lodge and Stroh 1993; Ortony, Clore, and Collins 1988; Sears, Huddy, and Schaffer 1986). Kahneman (1999) reviews experimental evidence that evaluation on the good/bad dimension is a ubiquitous component of human thinking.

Just as elements are related to each other by the positive and negative deliberative constraints described in the last section, they also can be related by positive and negative valence constraints. Some elements have intrinsic positive and negative valences, for example *pleasure* and *pain*. Other elements can acquire valences by virtue of their connections with elements that have intrinsic valences. These connections can be special valence constraints, or they can be any of the constraints posited by the theory of deliberative coherence. For example, if someone has a positive association between the concepts of *dentist* and *pain*, where *pain* has an intrinsic negative valence, then *dentist* can acquire a negative valence. However, just as the acceptability of an element depends on the acceptability of all the elements that constrain it, so the valence of an element depends on the valences of all the elements that constrain it.

The basic theory of emotional coherence can be summarized in three principles analogous to the qualitative principles of coherence above:

1. Elements have positive or negative valences.
2. Elements can have positive or negative emotional connections to other elements.

3. The valence of an element is determined by the valences and acceptability of all the elements to which it is connected.

As already mentioned, coherence can be computed by a variety of algorithms, but the most psychologically appealing model, and the model that first inspired the theory of coherence as constraint satisfaction, employs artificial neural networks. In this connectionist model, elements are represented by units, which are roughly analogous to neurons or neuronal groups. Positive constraints between elements are represented by symmetric excitatory links between units, and negative constraints between elements are represented by symmetric inhibitory links between units. The degree of acceptability of an element is represented by the activation of a unit, which is determined by the activation of all the units linked to it, taking into account the strength of the various excitatory and inhibitory links.

It is straightforward to expand this kind of model into one that incorporates emotional coherence. In the expanded model, called "HOTCO" for "hot coherence," units have valences as well as activations, and units can have input valences to represent their intrinsic valences. Moreover, valences can spread through the system in a way very similar to the spread of activation, except that valence spread depends in part on activation spread. An emotional decision emerges from the spread of activation and valences through the system because nodes representing some actions receive positive valence while nodes representing other actions receive negative valence. The gut feeling that comes to consciousness is the end result of a complex process of cognitive and emotional constraint satisfaction. Emotional reactions such as happiness, anger, and fear are much more complex than positive and negative valences, so HOTCO is by no means a general model of emotional cognition. But it does capture the general production by emotional inference of positive and negative attitudes toward objects, situations, and choices.

It might seem that we can now abandon the cognitive theory of deliberative coherence for the psychologically richer theory of emotional coherence, but that would be a mistake for two reasons. First, emotional coherence must interconnect with other kinds of coherence that involve inferences about what is acceptable as well as about what is emotionally desirable. The valence of an element does not depend just on the valences of the elements that constrain it, but also on their acceptability. Attaching a negative valence to the concept *dentist*, if it does not already have a negative valence from previous experience, depends both on the negative valence for *causes-pain* and the acceptability (confidence) of *causes-pain* in the current context. The inferential situation here is analogous to expected utility theory, in which the expected utility of an action is calculated by summing, for various outcomes, the result of multiplying the probability of the outcome times the utility of the outcome. The calculated valence of an element is like the expected utility of an action, with degrees of acceptability analogous to probabilities and valences analogous to utilities. There is no reason, however, to expect degrees of acceptability and valences to have the mathematical properties that define probabilities and utilities. Because the valence calculation depends on the acceptability of all the relevant elements, it can be affected by other kinds of coherence. For example, the inference concerning whether to trust someone depends largely on the valence attached to them based on all the information you have about them, where this information derives in part from inferences based on explanatory, analogical, and conceptual coherence (Thagard 2000).

The second reason for not completely replacing the cold (nonemotional) theory of deliberative coherence with the hot theory of emotional coherence is that people can sometimes come up with incompatible hot and cold judgments about what to do. Unconsciously using deliberative coherence may produce the judgment that you should not do something, while emotional coherence leads you in a different direction. For example, students seeing the first nice spring day at the end of a long Canadian winter might decide emotionally to go outside and enjoy it, while at the same time reasoning that the alternative of finishing up overdue end-of-term projects is more coherent with their central goals such as graduating from university. I am not the only person capable of thinking: "The best thing for me to do is X, but I'm going to do Y." Jonesing in reaction to vivid stimuli can make emotional coherence swamp deliberative coherence.

The theory of emotional coherence provides a psychologically realistic way of understanding the role of intuition in decisions. My gut feeling that I should go to Paris is the result of an unconscious mental process in which various actions and goals are balanced against each other. The coherence process involves both inferences about what I think is true (e.g., I'll have fun in Paris) and inferences about the extent to which my goals will be accomplished. But the coherence computation determines not only what elements will be accepted and rejected, but also an emotional reaction to the element. It is not just "go to Paris—yes" or "go to Paris—no," but "go to Paris—yeah!" or "go to Paris—yuck!"

As we just saw, however, emotional coherence may be better as a descriptive theory of how people make decisions than as a normative theory of how people should make decisions. Judgments based on emotional coherence may be subject to the same criticisms that I made against intuitive decisions:

susceptibility to jonesing and to failure to consider the appropriate range of actions and goals. I doubt, however, that people are capable of making decisions without recourse to emotional coherence—that is just how our brains are constituted. For normative purposes, therefore, the best course is to adopt procedures that interact with emotional coherence to produce intuitions that are informed and effective.

Using Intuition and Emotion to Make Good Decisions

The theory of emotional coherence shows how people's gut feelings about what to do may sometimes emerge from integrative unconscious judgments about the actions that might best accomplish their goals. But it also applies to cases where people's intuitions are too quick and uninformed. How can students and other people be helped to ensure that their decisions are based on *informed* intuition?

For important decisions, I recommend that, rather than leaping to an immediate intuitive choice, people should follow a procedure something like the following:

Informed Intuition
1. Set up the decision problem carefully. This requires identifying the goals to be accomplished by your decision and specifying the broad range of possible actions that might accomplish those goals.
2. Reflect on the importance of the different goals. Such reflection will be more emotional and intuitive than just putting a numerical weight on them, but should help you to be more aware of what you care about in the current decision situation. Identify goals whose importance may be exaggerated because of jonesing or other emotional distortions.
3. Examine beliefs about the extent to which various actions would facilitate the different goals. Are these beliefs based on good evidence? If not, revise them.
4. Make your intuitive judgment about the best action to perform, monitoring your emotional reaction to different options. Run your decision past other people to see if it seems reasonable to them.

This procedure combines the strengths and avoids the weaknesses of the intuition and calculation models of decision making. Like the intuition model, it recognizes that decision making is an unconscious process that involves emotions. Like the calculation model, it aims to avoid decision errors caused by unsystematic and unexamined intuitions. One drawback of the Informed Intuition procedure is that it is not so intersubjective as the calculation model, in which the numerical weights and calculations can be laid out on the table for all to see. It would certainly be a useful exercise in many cases for people to go through the steps of producing a calculation in order to provide some information about how different people are seeing the situation. Ultimately, however, the individual decision makers will have to make decisions based on their own intuitive judgments about what is the right thing to do. The members of the group may be poor at specifying the emotional weights they put on different goals, and they may be unaware of their assumptions about the extent to which different actions facilitate different goals. Achieving consensus among a group of decision makers may require extensive discussion that reveals the goals and beliefs of decision makers to themselves as well as to others. It is much easier to identify jonesing and other emotional distortions in others than in yourself. The discussion, including the exercise of working through a calculation together, may help the members of the group converge on evaluations of goal importance and belief plausibility that produce a shared reaction of emotional coherence. Scientific consensus concerning competing scientific theories can emerge from a process of individual coherence and interpersonal communication (Thagard 1999, chap. 7), but conflict resolution concerning what to do requires a more complex process of comparing and communicating the diverse goals driving the various decision makers. A crucial part of this process is becoming aware of the emotional states of others, which may benefit as much from face-to-face interactions involving perception of people's physical appearance as from purely verbal communication.

Informed Intuition is a much more complicated process of decision making than the practical syllogism commonly discussed by philosophers. Millgram (1997, p. 41) gives the following example:

1. Delicious things should be eaten. (Major premise)
2. This cake is delicious. (Minor premise)
3. Eat the cake. (Conclusion)

The practical syllogism gives an inadequate picture of decision making, both descriptively and normatively. Descriptively it fails to notice that the decision to eat cake is crucially influenced by the emotional value of the action of eating cake. Normatively it fails to see that deciding is a matter of deliberative coherence which has to balance competing goals (e.g., eat something delicious, be slim, be healthy) and to evaluate competing actions (e.g., eat the cake, eat an apple, drink Perrier). On the coherence model of inference, reasoning and inference are very different. Reasoning is verbal and linear, like the practical syllogism and proofs in formal logic. But inference is an unconscious mental process in which many factors are balanced against each other until a judgment is reached that accepts some beliefs and rejects others in a way that approximately maximizes coherence.

This does not mean that practical and theoretical reasoning should be sneered at. Reasoning is a verbal, conscious process that is easily communicated to other people. People are rarely convinced by an argument directly, but the fact that reasoning does not immediately translate into inference does not make it pointless. Making reasoning explicit in decisions helps to communicate to all the people involved what the relevant goals, actions, and facilitation relations might be. If communication is effective, then the desired result will be that each decision maker will make a better informed intuitive decision about what to do.

Improving inference is both a matter of recognizing good inference procedures such as Informed Intuition and watching out for errors that people commonly make. Such errors are usually called fallacies by philosophers and biases by psychologists. Psychologists, economists, and philosophers have identified a variety of error tendencies in decision making, such as considering sunk costs, using bad analogies, and being overconfident in judgments. Noticing the role of emotional coherence in decision making enables us to expand this list to include emotional determinants of bad decision making such as jonesing and failing to perceive the emotional attitudes of other people. In this paper I have emphasized the positive strategy of making decisions using a recommended procedure, Informed Intuition, but a fuller account would also develop the negative strategy of avoiding various tendencies that are natural to human thinking and that often lead to poor decisions.

The coherence model of decision making allows goals to be adjusted in importance while evaluating a decision, but it does not address the question of how we adopt new goals. Millgram's (1997) account of practical induction is useful for describing how people in novel situations can develop new interests that provide them with new goals. A full theory of decision making would have to include an account of where human goals come from and how they can be evaluated. People who base their decisions only on the goals of sex, drugs, and rock and roll may achieve local coherence, but they have much to learn about the full range of pursuits that enrich human lives.

Conclusion

I have tried in this chapter to provide students and other people with a model of decision making that is both natural and effective. Practical inference is not simply produced by practical syllogisms or cost-benefit calculations, but requires assessment of the coherence of positively and negatively interconnected goals and actions. This assessment is an unconscious process based in part on emotional valences attached to the various goals to be taken into consideration, and yields a conscious judgment that is not just a belief about what is the best action to perform but also a positive emotional attitude toward that action. Reason and emotion need not be in conflict with each other, if the emotional judgment that arises from a coherence assessment takes into account the relevant actions and goals and the relations between them. The procedure I recommend, Informed Intuition, shows how decisions can be both intuitive and reasonable. (See chaps. 15 and 16 for further discussion of normative issues.)

3 | Emotional Analogies and Analogical Inference

Paul Thagard and Cameron Shelley

Introduction

Despite the growing appreciation of the relevance of affect to cognition, analogy researchers have paid remarkably little attention to emotion. This chapter discusses three general classes of analogy that involve emotions. The most straightforward are analogies and metaphors *about* emotions, for example "Love is a rose and you better not pick it." Much more interesting are analogies that involve the transfer of emotions, for example in empathy in which people understand the emotions of others by imagining their own emotional reactions in similar situations. Finally, there are analogies that generate emotions, for example analogical jokes that generate emotions such as surprise and amusement.

Understanding emotional analogies requires a more complex theory of analogical inference than has been available. The next section presents a new account that shows how analogical inference can be defeasible, holistic, multiple, and emotional, in ways to be described. Analogies about emotions can to some extent be explained using the standard models such as ACME and SME, but analogies that transfer emotions require an extended treatment that takes into account the special character of emotional states. We describe HOTCO, a new model of emotional coherence, that simulates transfer of emotions, and show how HOTCO models the generation of emotions such as reactions to humorous analogies. Finally, we supplement our anecdotal collection of emotional analogies by discussing a more comprehensive sample culled from Internet wire services.

Analogical Inference: Current Models

In logic books, analogical inference is usually presented by a schema such as the following (Salmon 1984a, p. 105):

Objects of type *X* have properties *G*, *H*, etc.
Objects of type *Y* have properties *G*, *H*, etc.
Objects of type *X* have property *F*.
Therefore: Objects of type *Y* have property *F*.

For example, when experiments determined that large quantities of the artificial sweetener saccharine caused bladder cancer in rats, scientists analogized that it might also be carcinogenic in humans. Logicians additionally point out that analogical arguments may be strong or weak depending on the extent to which the properties in the premises are relevant to the property in the conclusion.

This characterization of analogical inference, which dates back at least to John Stuart Mill's nineteenth-century *System of Logic*, is flawed in several respects. First, logicians rarely spell out what "relevant" means, so the schema provides little help in distinguishing strong analogies from weak. Second, the schema is stated in terms of objects and their properties, obscuring the fact that the strongest and most useful analogies involve relations, in particular causal relations (Gentner 1983; Holyoak and Thagard 1995). Such causal relations are usually the key to determining relevance: if, in the above schema, *G* and *H* together cause *F* in *X*, then analogically they may cause *F* in *Y*, producing a much stronger inference than just counting properties. Third, logicians typically discuss analogical arguments and tend to ignore the complexity of analogical inference, which requires a more holistic assessment of a potential conclusion with respect to other information. There is no point in inferring that objects of type *Y* have property *F* if you already know of many such objects that lack *F*, or if a different analogy suggests that they do not have *F*. Analogical inference must be defeasible, in that the potential conclusion can be overturned by other information, and it must be holistic in that everything the inference maker knows is potentially relevant to overturning or enhancing the inference.

Compared to the logician's schema, much richer accounts of the structure of analogies have been provided by computational models of analogical mapping such as SME (Falkenhainer, Forbus, and Gentner 1989) and ACME (Holyoak and Thagard 1989). SME uses relational structure to generate candidate inferences, and ACME transfers information from a source analog to a target analog using a process that Holyoak, Novick, and Melz (1994) called copying with substitution and generation (CWSG). Similar processes are used in case-based reasoning (Kolodner 1993), and in many other computational models of analogy.

But all of these computational models are inadequate for understanding analogical inference in general and emotional analogies in particular. They do not show how analogical inference can be defeasible and holistic, or how it can make use of multiple source analogs to support or defeat a conclusion. Moreover, the prevalent models of analogy encode information symbolically and assume that what is inferred is verbal information that can be represented in propositional form by predicate calculus or some similar representational system. (One of the few attempts to deal with nonverbal analogies is the VAMP system for visual analogical mapping [Thagard, Gochfeld, and Hardy 1992].) As a later section documents, analogical inference often serves to transfer an emotion, not just the verbal representation of an emotion. We will now describe how a new model of emotional coherence, HOTCO, can perform analogical inferences that are defeasible, holistic, multiple, and emotional.

Analogical Inference in HOTCO

Thagard (2000) proposed a theory of emotional coherence that has applications to numerous important psychological phenomena such as trust. This theory makes the following assumptions about inference and emotions:

1. All inference is coherence based. So-called rules of inference such as *modus ponens* do not by themselves license inferences, because their conclusions may contradict other accepted information. The only rule of inference is: Accept a conclusion if its acceptance maximizes coherence.
2. Coherence is a matter of constraint satisfaction, and can be computed by connectionist and other algorithms (Thagard and Verbeurgt 1998).
3. There are six kinds of coherence: analogical, conceptual, explanatory, deductive, perceptual, and deliberative (Thagard 2000).
4. Coherence is not just a matter of accepting or rejecting a conclusion, but can also involve attaching a positive or negative emotional assessment to a proposition, object, concept, or other representation.

From this coherentist perspective, *all* inference is defeasible and holistic and differs markedly from logical deduction in formal systems. Philosophers who have advocated coherentist accounts of inference include Bosanquet (1920) and Harman (1986).

The computational model HOTCO (for "hot coherence") implements these theoretical assumptions. It amalgamates the following previous models of coherence:

- Explanatory coherence: ECHO (Thagard 1989, 1992);
- Conceptual coherence: IMP (Kunda and Thagard 1996);
- Analogical coherence: ACME (Holyoak and Thagard 1989);
- Deliberative coherence: DECO (Thagard and Millgram 1995).

Amalgamation is natural, because all of these models use a similar connectionist algorithm for maximizing constraint satisfaction, although they employ different constraints operating on different kinds of representation. What is novel about HOTCO is that representational elements possess not only activations that represent their acceptance and rejection, but also valences that represent a judgment of their positive or negative emotional appeal. In HOTCO, as in its component models, inferences about what to accept are made by a holistic process in which activation spreads through a network of units with excitatory and inhibitory links, representing elements with positive and negative constraints. But HOTCO spreads valences as well as activations in a similar holistic fashion, using the same system of excitatory and inhibitory links. For example, HOTCO models the decision of whether to hire a particular person as a babysitter as in part a matter of "cold" deliberative, explanatory, conceptual, and analogical coherence, but also as a matter of generating an emotional reaction to the candidate. The emotional reaction derives from a combination of the cold inferences made about the person and the valences attached to what is inferred. If you infer that a babysitting candidate is responsible, intelligent, and likes children, the positive valence of these attributes will spread to him or her; whereas if coherence leads to you infer that the candidate is lazy, dumb, and psychopathic, he or she will acquire a negative valence. In HOTCO, valences spread through the constraint network in much the same way that activation does (see the appendix to this chapter for technical details). The result is an emotional Gestalt that provides an overall "gut reaction" to the potential babysitter.

Now we can describe how HOTCO performs analogical inference in a way that is defeasible, holistic, and multiple. HOTCO uses ACME to perform analogical mapping between a source and a target, and uses copying with substitution and generation to produce new propositions to be inferred. It can operate either in a *broad* mode in which everything about the source is transferred to the target, or in a more *specific* mode in which a query is used to enhance the target using a particular proposition in the source. Here, in predicate calculus formalization where each proposition has the structure (predicate (objects) proposition-name), is an example of a scientific analogy concerning the coelacanth, a rare fish that is hard to study directly (Shelley 1999).

Source 1: centroscymnus
(have (centroscymnus rod-pigment-1) have-1)
(absorb (rod-pigment-1 472nm-light) absorb-1)
(penetrate (472nm-light deep-ocean-water) penetrate-1)

(see-in (centroscymnus deep-ocean-water) see-in-1)
(inhabit (centroscymnus deep-ocean-water) inhabit-1)
(enable (have-1 see-in-1) enable-1)
(because (absorb-1 penetrate-1) because-1)
(adapt (see-in-1 inhabit-1) adapt-1)

Target: coelacanth-3
(have (coelacanth rod-pigment-3) have-3)
(absorb (rod-pigment-3 473nm-light) absorb-3)
(penetrate (473nm-light deep-ocean-water) penetrate-3)
(see-in (coelacanth deep-ocean-water) see-in-3)
(enable (have-3 see-in-3) enable-3)
(because (absorb-3 penetrate-3) because-3)

Operating in specific mode, HOTCO is asked what depth the coelacanth inhabits, and uses the proposition INHABIT-1 in the source to construct for the target the proposition

(inhabit (coelacanth deep-ocean-water) inhabit-new)

Operating in broad mode and doing general copying with substitution and generation, HOTCO can analogically transfer everything about the source to the target, in this case generating the proposition that coelacanths inhabit deep water as a candidate to be inferred.

However, HOTCO does *not* actually infer the new proposition, because analogical inference is defeasible. Rather, it simply establishes an excitatory link between the unit representing the source proposition INHABIT-1 and the target proposition INHABIT-NEW. This link represents a positive constraint between the two propositions, so that coherence maximization will encourage them to be accepted together or rejected together. The source proposition INHABIT-1 is presumably accepted, so in the HOTCO model it will have positive activation which will spread to provide positive activation to INHABIT-NEW, unless INHABIT-NEW is incompatible with other accepted propositions that will tend to suppress its activation. Thus analogical inference is defeasible, because all HOTCO does is to create a link representing a new constraint for overall coherence judgment, and it is holistic, because the entire constraint network can potentially contribute to the final acceptance or rejection of the inferred proposition.

Within this framework, it is easy to see how analogical inference can employ multiple analogies, because more than one source can be used to create new constraints. Shelley (1999) describes how biologists do not simply use the centroscymnus analog as a source to infer that coelacanths inhabit deep water, but also use the following different source:

Source 2: ruvettus-2
(have (ruvettus rod-pigment-2) have-2)
(absorb (rod-pigment-2 474nm-light) absorb-2)
(penetrate (474nm-light deep-ocean-water) penetrate-2)
(see-in (ruvettus deep-ocean-water) see-in-2)
(inhabit (ruvettus deep-ocean-water) inhabit-2)
(enable (have-2 see-in-2) enable-2)
(because (absorb-2 penetrate-2) because-2)
(adapt (see-in-2 inhabit-2) adapt-2)

The overall inference is that coelacanths inhabit deep water because they are like the centroscysmus and the ruvettus sources in having rod pigments that adapt them to life in deep water. Notice that these are deep, systematic analogies, because the theory of natural selection suggests that the two source fishes have the rod pigments because the pigments adapt them to life in deep ocean water environments. When HOTCO maps the ruvettus source to the coelecanth target after mapping the centroscysmus source, it creates excitatory links from the inferred proposition INHABIT-NEW with both INHABIT-1 in the first source and INHABIT-2 in the second source. Hence activation can flow from both these propositions to INHABIT-NEW, so that the inference is supported by multiple analogies. If another analog or other information suggests a contradictory inference, then INHABIT-NEW will be both excited and inhibited. Thus multiple analogies can contribute to the defeasible and holistic character of analogical inference.

The new links created between the target proposition and the source proposition can also make possible emotional transfer. The coelacanth example is emotionally neutral for most people, but if an emotional valence were attached to INHABIT-1 and INHABIT-2, then the excitatory links between them and INHABIT-NEW would make possible spread of that valence as well as spread of activation representing acceptance. In complex analogies, in which multiple new excitatory links are created between aspects of one or more sources and the target, valences can spread over all the created links, contributing to the general emotional reaction to the target. The section after next provides detailed examples of this kind of emotional analogical inference.

Analogies about Emotions

The *Columbia Dictionary of Quotations* (available electronically as part of the Microsoft Bookshelf) contains many metaphors and analogies concerning love and other emotions. For example, love is compared to religion, a master, a pilgrimage, an angel/bird, gluttony, war, disease, drunkenness, insanity, market exchange, light, ghosts, and smoke. It is not surprising that writers discuss emotions nonliterally, because it is very difficult to describe the experience of emotions in words. In analogies about emotions, verbal sources help to illuminate the emotional target, which may be verbally described but which also has an elusive, nonverbal, phenomenological aspect. Analogies are also used about negative emotions: anger is like a volcano, jealousy is a green-eyed monster, and so on.

In order to handle the complexities of emotion, poets often resort to multiple analogies, as in the following examples:

(1) John Donne:
Love was as subtly catched, as a disease;
But being got it is a treasure sweet.

(2) Robert Burns:
O, my love is like a red, red rose,
That's newly sprung in June:
My love is like a melodie,
That's sweetly play'd in tune.

(3) William Shakespeare:
Love is a smoke made with the fume of sighs,
Being purged, a fire sparkling in lovers' eyes,
Being vexed, a sea nourished with lovers' tears.
What is it else? A madness most discreet,
A choking gall and a preserving sweet.

In each of these examples, the poet uses more than one analogy or metaphor to bring out different aspects of love. The use of multiple analogies is different from the scientific example described in the last section, in which the point of using two marine sources was to support the same conclusion about the depths inhabited by coelacanths. In these poetic examples, different source analogs bring out different aspects of the target emotion, love.

Analogies about emotions may be general, as in the above examples about love, or particular, used to describe the emotional state of an individual. For example, in the movie *Marvin's Room*, the character Lee played by Meryl Streep describes her reluctance to discuss her emotions by saying that her feelings are like fishhooks—you can't pick up just one. Just as it is hard to verbalize the general character of an emotion, it is often difficult to describe verbally one's own emotional state. Victims of posttraumatic stress disorder frequently use analogies and metaphors to describe their own situations (Meichenbaum 1994, pp. 112–113):

- I am a time bomb ticking, ready to explode.
- I feel like I am caught up in a tornado.
- I am a rabbit stuck in the glare of headlights who can't move.
- My life is like a rerun of a movie that won't stop.
- I feel like I'm in a cave and can't get out.
- Home is like a pressure cooker.
- I am a robot with no feelings.

In these particular emotional analogies, the target to be understood is the emotional state of an individual, and the verbal source describes roughly what the person feels like.

The purpose of analogies about emotions is often explanatory, describing the nature of a general emotion or a particular person's emotional state. But analogy can also be used to help deal with emotions, as in the following quote from Nathaniel Hawthorne: "Happiness is a butterfly, which, when pursued, is always just beyond your grasp, but which, if you will sit down quietly, may alight upon you." People are also given advice on how to deal with negative emotions, being told for example to "vent" their anger, or to "put a lid on it."

In principle, analogies about emotions could be simulated by the standard models such as ACME and SME, with a verbal representation of the source being used to generate inferences about the emotional target. However, even in some of the above examples, the point of the analogy is not just to transfer verbal information, but also to transfer an emotional attitude. When someone says "I feel like I am caught up in a tornado," he or she may be saying something like "My feelings are like the feelings you would have if you were caught in a tornado." To handle the transfer of emotions, we need to go beyond verbal analogy.

Analogies That Transfer Emotions

As already mentioned, not all analogies are verbal: some involve transfer of visual representations (Holyoak and Thagard 1995). In addition, analogies can involve transfer of emotions from a source to a target. There are at least three such kinds of emotional transfer, involved in persuasion, empathy, and reverse empathy. In persuasion, I may use an analogy to convince you to adopt an emotional attitude. In empathy, I try to understand your emotional reaction to a situation by transferring to you my emotional reaction to a similar situation. In reverse empathy, I try to get you to understand my emotion by comparing my situation and emotional response to it with situations and responses familiar to you.

The purpose of many persuasive analogies is to produce an emotional attitude, for example when an attempt is made to convince someone that abortion is abominable or that capital punishment is highly desirable. If I want to get someone to adopt positive emotions toward something, I can compare it to something else toward which he or she already has a positive attitude. Conversely, I can try to produce a negative attitude by comparison with something already viewed negatively. The structure of persuasive emotional analogies is:

You have an emotional appraisal of the source S.
The target T is like S in relevant respects.
So you should have a similar emotional appraisal of T.

Of course, the emotional appraisal could be represented verbally by terms such as "wonderful," "awful," and so on, but for persuasive purposes it is much more effective if the particular gut feeling that is attached to something can itself be transferred over to the target. For example, emotionally intense subjects such as the Holocaust or infanticide are commonly used to transfer negative emotions.

Blanchette and Dunbar (2001) thoroughly documented the use of persuasive analogies in a political context, the 1995 referendum in which the people of Quebec voted whether to separate from Canada. In three Montreal newspapers, they found a total of 234 different analogies, drawn from many diverse source domains: politics, sports, business, and so on. Many of these analogies were emotional: 66 were coded by Blanchette and Dunbar as emotionally negative, and 75 were judged to be emotionally positive. Thus more than half of the analogies used in the referendum had an identifiable emotional dimension. For example, the side opposed to Quebec separation said "It's like parents getting a divorce, and maybe the parent you don't like getting custody." Here the negative emotional connotation of divorce is transferred over to Quebec separation. In contrast, the yes side used positive emotional analogs for separation: "A win from the YES side would be like a magic wand for the economy."

HOTCO can naturally model the use of emotional persuasive analogies. The separation-divorce analogy can be represented as follows:

Source: divorce
(married (spouse-1 spouse-2) married-1)
(have (spouse-1 spouse-2 child) have-1)

(divorce (spouse-1 spouse-2) divorce-1) negative valence
(get-custody (spouse-1) get-custody-1)
(not-liked (spouse-1) not-liked-1) negative valence

Target: separation
(part-of (Quebec Canada) part-of-2)
(govern (Quebec Canada people-of-Quebec) govern-2)
(separate-from (Quebec Canada) separate-from-2)
(control (Quebec people-of-Quebec) control-2)

When HOTCO performs a broad inference on this example, it not only computes the analogical mapping from the source to the target and completes the target using copying with substitution and generation, but also transfers the negative valence attached to the proposition DIVORCE-1 to SEPARATE-FROM-2.

Persuasive analogies have been rampant in the recent debates about whether Microsoft has been engaging in monopolistic practices by including its World Wide Web browser in its operating system, Windows 98. In response to the suggestion that Microsoft also be required to include the rival browser produced by its competitor, Netscape, Microsoft's chairman Bill Gates complained that this would be "like requiring Coca-Cola to include three cans of Pepsi in every six-pack it sells," or like "ordering Ford to sell autos fitted with Chrysler engines." These analogies are in part emotional, since they are intended to transfer the emotional response to coercing Coca-Cola and Ford—assumed to be ridiculous—over to the coercion of Microsoft. On the other hand, critics of Microsoft's near-monopoly on personal computer operating systems have been comparing Gates to John D. Rockefeller, whose predatory Standard Oil monopoly on petroleum products was broken up by the U.S. government in 1911.

Persuasive analogies suggest a possible extension to the multiconstraint theory of analogical reasoning developed by Holyoak and Thagard (1995). In that theory, similarity is one of the constraints that influence how two analogs are mapped to each other, including both the semantic similarity of predicates and the visual similarity of objects. We conjecture that emotional similarity may also influence analogical mapping and predict that people will be more likely to map elements that have the same positive or negative valence. For example, if you have a positive feeling about Bill Gates and a negative feeling about John D. Rockefeller, you will be less likely to see them as analogs, impeding both retrieval and mapping. A recent advertisement for a book on cancer compared the genetically mutated cell that initiates a tumor growth to Jesus initiating Christianity. Regardless of how structurally informative this analogy might be, the correspondences between cancer cells and Jesus and between tumors and Christianity produce for many people an emotional mismatch that renders the analogy ineffective. During the Kosovo war in 1999, comparisons were frequently made between the Serbian leader Slobodan Milosovic and Adolf Hitler; these comparisons were emotionally congruent for most people, but not for Milosovic's supporters.

Another, more personal, kind of persuasive emotional analogy is identification, in which you identify with someone and then transfer positive emotional attitudes about yourself to them. According to Fenno (1978, p. 58), members of the U.S. congress try to convey a sense of identification to their constituents. The message is "You know me, and I'm like you, so you can trust me." The structure of this kind of identification is:

You have a positive emotional appraisal of yourself (source).
I (the target) am similar to you.
So you should have a positive emotional appraisal of me.

Identification is a kind of persuasive analogy, but differs from the general case in that the source and target are the people involved. A full representation of the similarity involved in identification and other analogies requires specification of the causal and other higher-order relations that capture deep, highly relevant similarities between the source and target.

Empathy also involves transfer of emotional states between people; see Barnes and Thagard (1997) for a full discussion. It differs from persuasion in that the goal of the analogy is to understand rather than to convince someone. Summarizing, the basic structure is:

You are in situation T (target).
When I was in a similar situation S, I felt emotion E (source).
So maybe you are feeling an emotion similar to E.

As with persuasion and identification, such analogizing could be done purely verbally, but it is much more effective to actually feel something like what the target person is feeling. For example, if Thagard wants to understand the emotional state of a new graduate student just arrived from a foreign country, he can recall his emotional state of anxiety and confusion when he went to study in England. Here is a more detailed example of empathy involving someone trying to understand the distress of Shakespeare's Hamlet at losing his father by comparing it to his or her own loss of a job (from Barnes and Thagard 1997):

Source: you   *Target: Hamlet*
(fire (boss, you) s1-fire)   (kill (uncle, father) t1-kill)
(lose (you, job) s2-lose)   (lose (Hamlet, father) t2-lose)
                                       (marry (uncle, mother) t2a-
                                       marry)

(cause (s1-fire, s2-lose) s3)   (cause (t1-kill, t2-lose) t3)
(angry (you) s4-angry)   (angry (Hamlet) t4-angry)
(depressed (you) s5-depressed)   (depressed (Hamlet) t5-
                                       depressed)

(cause (s2-lose, s4-angry) s6)   (cause (t2-lose, t4-angry) t6)
(cause (s2-lose, s5-depressed) s7)   (cause (t2-lose, t5-depressed) t7)
(indecisive (you) s8-indecisive)
(cause (s5-depressed, s8-indecisive) s9)

The purpose of this analogy is not simply to draw the obvious correspondences between the source and the target, but to transfer over your remembered image of depression to Hamlet.

Unlike persuasive analogies, whose main function is to transfer positive or negative valence, empathy requires transfer of the full range of emotional responses. Depending on his or her situation, I need to imagine someone being angry, fearful, disdainful, ecstatic, enraptured and so on. As currently implemented, HOTCO transfers only positive or negative valences associated with a proposition or object, but it can easily be expanded so that transfer involves an *emotional vector* which represents a pattern of activation of numerous units, each of whose activation represents different components of emotion. This expanded representation would also make possible the transfer of "mixed" emotions.

Empathy is only one kind of explanatory emotional analogy. We already saw examples of analogies whose function is to explain one's own emotional state to another, a kind of reverse empathy in that it enables others to have an empathic understanding of oneself. Here is the structure of reverse empathy:

I am in situation *T* (target).
When you were in a similar situation *S*, you felt emotion *E* (source).
So I am feeling an emotion similar to *E*.

Here is a final example of analogical transfer of emotion: "Psychologists would rather use each other's toothbrushes than each other's terminology." This analogy is complex, because at one level it is projecting the emotional reaction of disgust from use of toothbrushes to use of terminology, but it is also generating amusement. A similar dual role is also found in the following remark in *The Globe and Mail*: "Starbucks coffee shops are spreading through Toronto faster than head lice through a kindergarten class." Both these examples convey an attitude as does the remark of country music star Garth Brooks: "My job is like what people say about pizza and sex: When it's good, it's great; and even when it's bad, it's still pretty good." Note that this is a multiple analogy, for what its worth. The writer Flaubert also used an analogy to convey his attitude toward his work: "I love my work with a love that is frantic and perverted, as an ascetic loves the hairshirt that scratches his belly." Let us now consider analogies that go beyond analogical transfer of emotions and actually generate new emotions.

Analogies That Generate Emotions

A third class of emotional analogies involves ones that are not about emotions and do not transfer emotional states, but rather serve to generate new emotional states. There are at least four subclasses of emotion-generating analogies, involving humor, irony, discovery, and motivation.

One of the most enjoyable uses of analogy is to make people laugh, generating the emotional state of mirth or amusement. The University of Michigan recently ran an informational campaign to get people to guard their computer passwords more carefully. Posters warn students to treat their computer passwords like underwear: make them long and mysterious, don't leave them lying around, and change them often. The point of the analogy is not to persuade anyone based on the similarity between passwords and underwear, but rather to generate amusement that focuses attention on the problem of password security.

A major part of what makes an analogy funny is a surprising combination of congruity and incongruity. Passwords do not fit semantically with underwear, so it is surprising when a good relational fit is presented (change them often). Other emotions can also feed into making an analogy funny, for example when the analogy is directed against a person or group one dislikes:

Why do psychologists prefer lawyers to rats for their experiments?
1. There are now more lawyers than rats;
2. The psychologists found they were getting attached to the rats;
3. And there are some things that rats won't do.

This joke depends on a surprising analogical mapping between rats in psychological experiments and lawyers in their practices, and on negative emotions attached to lawyers. Further surprise comes from the addendum that psychologists have stopped using lawyers in their experiments because the results did not transfer to humans. Another humorous analogy is implicit in the joke: "How can a single woman get a cockroach out of her kitchen? Ask him for a commitment."

Some analogical jokes depend on visual representations, as in the following children's joke: "What did the 0 say to the 8? Nice belt." This joke requires a surprising visual mapping between numerals and human dress. A more risqué visual example is: "Did you hear about the man with five penises? His pants fit like a glove." Here are some more humorous analogies, all of which involve mappings that generate surprise and amusement:

(1) Safe eating is like safe sex: you may be eating whatever it was that what you're eating ate before you ate it.

(2) Changing a university has all the difficulties of moving a cemetery.

(3) Administering academics is like herding cats.

(4) An associate dean is a mouse training to be a rat.

(5) "The juvenile sea squirt wanders through the sea searching for a suitable rock or hunk of coral to cling to and make its home for life. For this task, it has a rudimentary nervous system. When it finds its spot and takes root, it doesn't need its brain anymore, so it eats it! (It's rather like getting tenure)" (Dennett 1991, p. 177).

(6) Bill James on Tim McCarver's book on baseball: "But just to read the book is nearly impossible; it's like canoeing across Lake Molasses."

(7) Red Smith: "Telling a non-fan about baseball is like telling an 8-year-old about sex. No matter what you say, the response is 'But why?'"

(8) Melissa Franklin (Harvard physicist) on quarks: "It's weird. You've got six quarks; five of them are really light, and the sixth is unbelievably heavy. It's as if you had Sleepy, Dopey, Grumpy, Happy, and Kierkegaard."

Note that Franklin only mentions four dwarfs, so the mapping is not one–one, a fact that does not undermine the analogy. Failure of one–one mapping can even be funny, as in a 1998 cartoon that showed a ship labeled "Bill Clinton" about to hit an iceberg labeled "Bill Clinton."

In the emotional coherence theory of Thagard (2000), surprise is treated as a kind of metacoherence. When HOTCO shifts from one coherent interpretation to another, with units that were previously activated being deactivated and vice versa, the units that underwent an activation shift activate a surprise node. In analogical jokes, the unusual mapping produces surprise because it connects together elements not previously mapped, but does so in a way that is still highly coherent. The combination of activation of the surprise node, the coherence node, and other emotions generates humorous amusement.

Analogies that are particularly deep and elegant can also generate an emotion similar to that produced by beauty. A beautiful analogy is one so accurate, rich, and suggestive that it has the emotional appeal of an excellent scientific theory or mathematical theorem. Holyoak and Thagard (1995, chap. 8) describe important scientific analogies such as the connection with Malthusian population growth that inspired Darwin's theory of natural selection. Thus scientific and other elegant analogies can generate positive emotions such as excitement and joy without being funny.

Not all analogies generate positive emotions, however. Ironies are sometimes based on analogy, and they are sometimes amusing, but they can also produce negative emotions such as despair:

HONG KONG (January 11, 1998 AF-P)—Staff of Hong Kong's ailing Peregrine Investments Holdings will turn up for work Monday still in the dark over the fate of the firm and their jobs.... Other Peregrine staff members at the brokerage were quoted as saying Sunday they were pessimistic over the future of the firm, saddled with an estimated 400 million dollars in debts. "I'm going to see the Titanic movie...that will be quite ironic, another big thing going down," the South China Morning Post quoted one broker as saying.

Shelley (2001) argues that irony is a matter of "bicoherence," with two situations being perceived as both coherent and incoherent with each other. The Peregrine Investments–Titanic analogy is partly a matter of transferring the emotion of despair from the Titanic situation to the company, but the irony generates an additional emotion of depressing appropriateness.

The final category of emotion-generating analogies we want to discuss is motivational ones, in which an analogy generates positive emotions involved in inspiration and self-confidence. Lockwood and Kunda (1997) have described how people use role models as analogs to themselves, in order to suggest new possibilities for what they can accomplish. For example, an athletic African American boy might see Michael Jordan as someone who used his athletic ability to achieve great success. By analogically comparing himself to Michael Jordan, the boy can feel good about his chances to accomplish his athletic goals. Adopting a role model in part involves transferring emotions, e.g., transferring the positive valence of the role model's success to one's own anticipated success, but it also generates new emotions accompanying the drive and inspiration to pursue the course of action that the analogy suggests. The general structure of the analogical inference is:

My role model accomplished the goal G by doing the action A.
I am like my role model in various respects.
So maybe I can do A to accomplish G.

The inference that I may have the ability to do A can generate great excitement about the prospect of such an accomplishment.

An Internet Survey

The examples so far discussed in this chapter were collected haphazardly, and thus amount to anecdotes rather than data. To compile analogies more systematically, Cam Shelley wrote a program to use the Internet to search for stories about analogy. Candidate news articles were collected by a key-word search for the term "analogy" and other comparative terms through Internet-based search engines, from February 1997 through September 1998. Many candidate articles were rejected due to lack of clarity. The others were classified by Shelley according to their primary practical function, including:

1. Clarification: to spell out or work through similarities between two things, often as an exercise in puzzle solving;
2. Inference: to complete some target concept with information supplied from a source concept;
3. Description: to provide lively or colorful reading.

Inferential analogies were further divided into two types: "hot" and "cold." Hot analogies serve to transfer emotional tags or attitudes from the source to target, whereas cold analogies serve simply to transfer structured information without producing any particular affect.

Hot analogies were further broken down into the three types of emotional analogies discussed above, namely empathy, reverse empathy, and persuasion. Very often the analogies conveyed in each news article were complex and appeared to serve more than one of the functions listed here. However, we counted each analogy only once on the basis of its most salient function. Figure 3.1 displays the results. Note that well over half of the analogies had emotional content and purpose. Perhaps this result is not surprising, since news reports, particularly those of the major wire services such as the Associated Press or Reuters, tend to be sensational to attract readers.

Many of the nonemotional analogies came from reports of scientific advances, such as medical research on the origin of the human immune system. For example, when Dr. Gary Litman expresses an enthusiastic interest in the analogy between human and shark immune systems, the comparison serves largely to inform his research rather than to create excitement among his colleagues (from "Scientist goes fishing," 11 February 1998, *St. Petersburg Times*).

Remarkably few of the emotional analogies seem to display the process of empathy. News reports were counted as examples of empathy where they showed people attempting to understand another person by analogies about their own emotional experiences. Given the interest that reporters have in

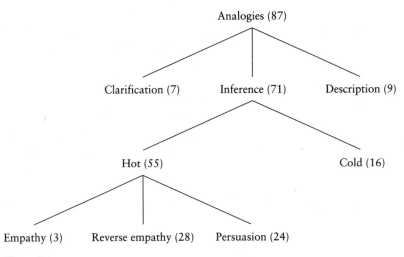

Figure 3.1
Classification of analogies found on Internet wire services.

recording people in the grip of highly emotional experiences, it appears surprising that so few examples of empathy should be present in the database. But there are at least two reasons to suppose that the lack of examples is illusory.

First, we might expect people to empathize based on their own personal experiences. But this expectation is implicitly based on the idea that our personal experiences are necessarily the most immediate or salient experiences that we might recall. This idea appears to be untrue. The examples of empathy in the database show people empathizing with others based on conventional or stereotypical experiences. For example, Dr. William Catalona expresses empathy with middle-aged men who are clamoring for the potency drug Viagra by comparing it to the demand for wrinkle cream (from "Baby Boomers fight aging in a variety of ways," by P. B. Librach, 1 June 1998, Scripps Howard News Service): "It's like the Fountain of Youth," said Catalona. "Viagra is analogous to anti-wrinkle cream. This is something that will turn back the clock and make men the way they were when they were young."

In other words, Catalona empathizes with middle-aged men by comparing their desire for Viagra with what he imagines to be the desire of middle-aged women for wrinkle cream. This source analog, although it does not represent Catalona's own experience, was selected due to (a) the surface similarity between Viagra as a drug and wrinkle cream as a cosmetic and (b) the representativeness of the wrinkle-cream situation as a stereotype of the (foolish?)

desire to feel young. Because people tend to pick out stereotyped analogs when empathizing, it is not always clear whether they are truly empathizing instead of simply persuading the reporter that two emotional situations are indeed similar. Empathy and persuasion can be difficult to tell apart as they are reported in news articles.

The second reason why empathy appears to be rare is that it may serve as a first step in the process of persuasion or reverse empathy, both of which involve someone attempting to influence someone else's judgment of emotions. But, in order to affect people's judgments on such issues to a particular end, it is necessary to have some estimate of their emotional repertoire or their opinions on emotional situations. Getting the correct emotional response out of people requires some idea of their view of emotions and emotional topics. Empathy is an important means for getting such an idea about someone. (There are other means, of course, such as using a general set of rules about people's emotional responses.) For example, consider the analogy made by Israeli Prime Minister Benjamin Netanyahu who compared the Palestinian Authority to "a regime facilitating terror" (from "U.S. raps Arafat, Netanyahu for rhetoric," 7 August 1998, Reuters):

Netanyahu equated economic pressure he exerted on the Palestinians since the bombing with economic sanctions Washington imposed on countries with alleged involvement in terrorism, like Libya. Albright said this analogy "does not work" and inflames the situation rather than lowering tensions. "The whole situation is totally different and while we respect the need for a prime minister, Prime Minister Netanyahu, to do what he can to protect the security of the people, using analogies that don't fit doesn't prove any point," she said.

Here Netanyahu compares Arafat's Palestinian Authority to Gaddafi's regime in Libya in order to project to his audience, which includes prominent Americans, his feelings about Arafat. However, Netanyahu's choice of Libya as the source analog is suggested not merely by any similarities between it and the Palestinian Authority, but also by his knowledge that Libya is particularly reviled by Americans. In other words, Netanyahu empathizes with Americans enough to know that mention of Libya and Gaddafi is likely to arouse strong, negative emotions in them. Certainly, U.S. Secretary of State Madeline Albright found his choice of source analog to be inflammatory.

Table 3.1 indicates the frequency with which emotions of positive and negative valence occur in the analogy database. Valences were assigned on a conventional basis, with emotional states suggesting fear, anger, disgust, sadness, and surprise counted as negative, whereas emotional states suggesting

Table 3.1
Frequency of positive and negative emotions in emotional analogies

	Positive emotion	Negative emotion
Empathy	1	2
Reverse empathy	15	13
Persuasion	3	21

happiness, pride, admiration, calm, and trust counted as positive. Of course, the emotional states described in the news articles were typically complex and could not be completely captured simply as instances of happiness or anger, for example. We used the so-called basic emotions (anger, fear, disgust, surprise, and happiness) to catalog each example of an emotional analogy. Where such a description was obviously impossible or inadequate, terms referring to more complex states were used, e.g., pride and admiration. Eleven emotion terms were employed for the purposes of basic categorization: fear, happiness, admiration, calm, disgust, anger, pride, trust, sadness, surprise, and discomfort. Other terms were used to supplement these terms where they failed to completely capture the emotional content of an analogy.

The low number of examples of empathy precludes drawing any conclusions about that process, but the figures for reverse empathy and persuasion are more interesting. Instances of reverse empathy were fairly evenly distributed between positive and negative valences. As we described above, reverse empathy involves using an analogy in order to get someone else to understand your own emotional state. Consider the example given by Norman Siegel, executive director of the Civil Liberties Union, who joined a 28-member task force created by New York Mayor Rudolph Giuliani to look into the problem of police brutality (from "Under fire, Guiliani forms panel on police," by Fred Kaplan, 20 August 1997, *Boston Globe*): "Although Siegel remained cautious about Guilani's committment to the task force, he emphasized that he is willing for now to take the mayor at his word, saying Giuliani is in a unique position 'to, once and for all, confront the systemic problems of police brutality.' 'The analogy is Nixon going to China,' Siegel said in a telephone interview earlier yesterday." Just as President Nixon, who long was known as a foe of communism, could recognize China without facing accusations of being soft on communism, so Giuliani—a former US prosecutor who has supported the police at nearly every turn of his political career—can mount an attack on the police force without prompting charges of being soft on crime.

This analogy suggests that Guiliani is at least in a good position to undertake a review of police misbehavior. But it also conveys Siegel's emotional attitude toward the task force. Siegel explains why he trusts Guiliani (takes him at his word) in terms of the trust that people invested in Nixon due to his long-standing anticommunist activities when he recognized communist China. In both cases, the trust signals belief in a positive outcome of the activity concerned, although the choice of "Tricky Dick" as a source analog might also signal that Siegel's belief in Giuliani's sincerity remains qualified by doubt.

An excellent example of the projection of a positive emotion in reverse empathy is given by astronaut David Wolf's description of what it felt like when he began his mission on the Mir space station (from "Astronaut describes life on Mir in wry e-mail home," by Adam Tanner, 2 December 1997, Reuters):

Named NASA's inventor of the year in 1992, Wolf also describes feeling a wide array of emotions, including the moment when the U.S. space shuttle undocked from Mir, leaving him behind for his four-month mission.

"I remember the place I last felt it. Ten years old, as my parents' station wagon pulled away from my first summer camp in southern Indiana. That satisfying thrill that something new is going to happen and we don't know what it is yet."

Here, Wolf projects his feelings about being left behind on a space station by reference to his feelings about being left behind at summer camp as a youth. Besides conveying the structure of the event, Wolf's use of a source analog shared by many Americans helpfully conveys the positive thrill of anticipation that he felt during an event very few people have ever experienced themselves.

Persuasive emotional analogies usually serve not to communicate an emotion between people of varied experience, but to have one person transfer some emotional attitude from one concept to another. For example, in order to persuade people to feel calm about an apparently dangerous situation, you might remind them of analogous situations that they regard calmly. Such a case actually occurred in response to volcanic activity in the neighborhood of Mexico City (from an untitled article, 24 April 1997, Associated Press):

The picturesque Popocatepetl volcano that overlooks Mexico City spouted plumes of gas and ash 2 to 3 miles into the air on Thursday in what experts described as the geologic equivalent of a belch. Although it was the largest volcanic activity at the snow-covered peak in the last five to six months, Robert Quass of Mexico's National Center for Disaster Prevention said the flare-up did not portend a full-scale eruption. "The explosions are simply an opening up ... of respirator tubes that have been blocked with magma since about March," Quass said. "It is better that this pressure be liberated than contained."

In this example, Quass attempts to persuade the public to feel calm regarding the volcanic activity of Popocatepetl by comparing it to a belch, an event no one presumably feels is too grave. Positive occurrences of persuasion tend to involve such humorous belittlement of some situation or concern.

Table 3.1 shows that there is a great asymmetry in the database between positive and negative valences in cases of persuasion. It appears that persuasive analogies are mostly used to condemn a person or situation. Consider the reaction of a *Boston Globe* reporter to a vegetarian burger being tested in McDonald's outlets in New York's Greenwich Village by its inventor Jim Lewis (from "Will McDonald's beef up menu with veggie burger?," by Alex Beam, 10 June 1998, *Boston Globe*):

Ah, taste. Even Lewis concedes that taste is not the long suit of his custom-made, soybean-based, Archer Daniels Midland "meat analog" patty. Although it has more fat than the ordinary burger, it is curiously tasteless. Lewis explains that the patty was engineered to duplicate the tactile sensation of eating a burger, rather than to mimic the taste. Call it the inflatable blow-up doll of the hamburger world.

Here, Beam expresses disgust, or at least distaste and derision, for the vegetarian burger patty by comparing the act of eating it with the act of having sex with an inflatable doll. Beam does not need to elaborate on his source analog; it and the emotional attitude attached to it are readily available (or imaginable) to the reading audience.

It is not clear why negative emotions should dominate persuasive analogies. One possibility is bias in story selection, i.e., it may be that news reporters are more interested in describing negative emotions. But this possibility does not gibe with the symmetry of positive and negative emotions in cases of reverse empathy. A second and more likely possibility is bias in the source itself, i.e., it may be that the use of analogies for the purpose of persuasion lends itself better to negative emotions than to positive ones. But the reason for this situation is unclear: Do people simply have more negative experiences stored up for others to remind them of? Are negative experiences more readily recalled than positive ones? Are negative experiences more readily attached to new situations than positive ones? Is it more socially acceptable to persuade people that something is blameworthy rather than praiseworthy? The database suggests no clear answer, but the nature of reverse empathy suggests that social factors could play an important role. Of the three kinds of emotional analogies discussed here, persuasion is the one by which a speaker imposes on his or her audience to the greatest degree; that is, the speaker is deliberately trying to change other people's minds. The indirection achieved by evaluating something analogous to the real topic of discourse may serve to mitigate the imposition and make the audience more likely to adopt the speaker's opinion.

Social factors such as this one also tend to obscure the distinction between reverse empathy and persuasive analogies in practice. As Grice (1989) observed, much human communication and interaction depends on people adopting a cooperative stance in dealing with each other. Thus, to return to a classic example, someone might request a salt shaker not by asking for it directly but by stating something like "this lasagna could use some salt." Similarly, someone could employ an indirect method of persuasion by using reverse empathy. Consider the following analogy stated by Microsoft's William Neukom, senior vice president for law and corporate affairs, during a court appeal concerning Microsoft's practice of forcing computer makers to bundle its Internet Explorer with every installation of the Windows 95 operating system (from "Microsoft unveils defiant strategy in appeal," by Kaitlin Quistgaard and Dan Brekke, 16 December 1997, Reuters): "The central point of our position is that when a computer manufacturer licenses Windows, it should install the entire product, just as Ford requires that all its vehicles be sold with Ford engines. This is the only way to guarantee customers a consistent Windows experience." In this case, Neukom is attempting to persuade the court judge that the suit against Microsoft is as unreasonable as a suit against Ford would be. In so doing, Neukom does not directly urge the court to adopt Microsoft's position but rather simply states what their position is. In other words, he just states Microsoft's official attitude for the court in such a way as to invite the judge to adopt it—an indirect use of persuasion. This indirect approach is only one example of how social factors such as the exhibition of cooperative behavior tends to obscure the distinctions between the use of emotional analogies in persuasion and reverse empathy.

We cannot assume that the analogies found in the Internet survey are characteristic of emotional analogies in general. Perhaps a different methodology would find more instances of empathy and positive emotions. But the survey has served to collect many interesting analogies and to illustrate further the emotional nature of much analogical inference.

Conclusion

In this chapter, we have provided numerous examples of emotional analogies including: analogies about emotions, analogies that transfer emotions in persuasion, empathy, and reverse empathy; and analogies that generate emotions in humor, irony, discovery, and motivation. In order to understand the cognitive processes involved in emotional analogies, we have proposed an account of analogical inference as defeasible, holistic, multiple, and emotional. The HOTCO model of emotional coherence provides a computational account of the interaction of cognitive and emotional aspects of analogical inference.

Appendix: Technical Details

The explanatory coherence program ECHO creates a network of units with explanatory and inhibitory links, then makes inferences by spreading activation through the network (Thagard 1992). The activation of a unit j, a_j, is updated according to the following equation:

$$a_j(t + 1) = a_j(t)(1 - d) + net_j(max - a_j(t)) \quad \text{if } net_j > 0,$$

otherwise $net_j(a_j(t) - min)$.

Here d is a decay parameter (say .05) that decrements each unit at every cycle, min is a minimum activation (-1), max is maximum activation (1). Based on the weight w_{ij} between each unit i and j, we can calculate net_j, the net input to a unit, by:

$$net_j = \sum_i w_{ij} a_i(t).$$

In HOTCO, units have valences as well as activations. The valence of a unit u_j is the sum of the results of multiplying, for all units u_i to which it is linked, the activation of u_i times the valence of u_i, times the weight of the link between u_i and u_j. The actual equation used in HOTCO to update the valence v_j of unit j is similar to the equation for updating activations:

$$v_j(t + 1) = v_j(t)(1 - d) + net_j(max - v_j(t)) \quad \text{if } net_j > 0,$$

$net_j(v_j(t) - min) \quad \text{otherwise}.$

Again d is a decay parameter (say .05) that decrements each unit at every cycle, min is a minimum valence (-1), max is maximum valence (1). Based on the weight w_{ij} between each unit i and j, we can calculate net_j, the net valence input to a unit, by:

$$net_j = \sum_i w_{ij} v_i(t) a_i(t).$$

Updating valences is just like updating activations plus the inclusion of a multiplicative factor for valences.

HOTCO 2 allows units to have their activations influenced by both input activations and input valences. The basic equation for updating activations is the same as the one given for ECHO above, but the net input is defined by a combination of activations and valences:

$$net_j = \sum_i w_{ij}a_i(t) + \sum_i w_{ij}v_i(t)a_i(t).$$

ECHO and HOTCO both proceed in two stages. First, input about explanatory and other relations generates a network of units and links. The LISP code for all my coherence programs is on the Web at http://cogsci .uwaterloo.ca/CoherenceCode/COHERE/COHERE.instructions.html/. Second, activations and (for HOTCO) valences are updated in parallel in accord with the above equations. Updating proceeds until the network has settled, i.e., when all activations have reached stable values. Running the networks discussed in this book typically takes only a few seconds and a few hundred iterations of updating.

4 Emotional Gestalts: Appraisal, Change, and the Dynamics of Affect

Paul Thagard and Josef Nerb

Introduction

One Tuesday morning, Professor Gordon Atwood strode energetically into his department office at Yukon University. It was a great day—the sun was shining, his family had been good natured at breakfast, and he was finished teaching for the semester. He cheerily greeted the department secretary and went to his mailbox, eagerly noticing the long-awaited letter from the *Journal of Cognitive Chemistry*. After opening the letter, Gordon's heart sank as he read the dreaded words: "We regret to inform you that, based on the reviewers' reports, we are unable to accept your submission." As he scanned the reviews, sadness turned to anger when Gordon realized that one of the reviewers had totally failed to understand his paper, while the other had rejected it because it did not sufficiently cite the reviewer's own work. Stomping out of the department office, Gordon chided the secretary for running out of printer paper yet again.

After an unproductive morning largely spent surfing the Web, Gordon met his wife for lunch. She reminded him that he had recently had two articles accepted for publication, and the rejected article could always be published elsewhere. They chatted about their daughter's recent triumph in a ballet school performance, and made plans to see a musical that weekend. The Thai curry was delicious, and the coffee was strong. Gordon returned to work and happily updated his article for submission to a different journal.

Everyone has had days like this, with transitions between different moods and emotions. A psychological theory of affect must explain both how different emotional states arise and how one state can be replaced by another one that is qualitatively very different. Affect is a natural subject for a dynamical theory that emphasizes the flow of thought and the complex interactions of emotion and cognition. Our aim in this paper is to develop such a theory of the emergence and alteration of emotional states.

We proceed first by interpreting emotional change as a transition in a complex dynamical system. This metaphorical interpretation, however, is limited in its explanatory power without concrete specification of the structures and mechanisms that can give rise to emotions and emotional change. We argue that the appropriate kind of dynamical system is one that extends recent work on how neural networks can perform parallel constraint satisfaction. Parallel processes that integrate both cognitive and affective constraints can give rise to states that we call *emotional gestalts*, and transitions such as those experienced by Gordon can be understood as *emotional gestalt shifts*. Finally, we describe computational models that simulate such phenomena in ways that show how dynamical and gestalt metaphors can be given a concrete realization.

Emotion as a Dynamical System

At its simplest, psychological theory postulates causal relations between mental properties and behavior, for example that there is a personality trait of extraversion that leads people who have it to talk frequently with other people. Since the rise of cognitive science in the 1950s, psychological theories have increasingly postulated representational structures and computational processes that operate on the structures to produce behavior. More recently, some psychologists and philosophers have proposed that psychological theories should be analogous to theories of complex dynamical systems that have been increasingly popular in physics, biology, and other sciences (see, for example, Port and van Gelder 1995; Thelen and Smith 1994).

Thagard (2005, chap. 12) described how dynamical systems theory can be applied to psychological phenomena by means of the following explanation schema:

Explanation Target
Why do people have **stable** but **unpredictable patterns of behavior?**

Explanatory Pattern
Human thought is describable by a set of **variables.**
These variables are governed by a set of nonlinear **equations.**
These **equations** establish a **state space** that has **attractors.**
The system described by the **equations** is **chaotic.**
The existence of the **attractors** explains **stable patterns** of behavior.
Multiple attractors explain abrupt **phase transitions.**
The **chaotic** nature of the system explains why **behavior** is **unpredictable.**

It is easy to apply this explanation schema to emotions. We want to be able to explain both why people have ongoing emotions and moods, and also how they can sometimes make dramatic transitions to different emotional states. Hypothetically, we might identify a set of variables that describe environmental, bodily, and mental factors. Equations that describe the causal relations among those variables would clearly be nonlinear, in that they would require specification of complex feedback relations between the different factors. The system described by the equations would undoubtedly be chaotic, in the sense that small changes to the value of some variables could lead to very large changes in the overall system: it only took one event to dramatically change Gordon's mood. On the other hand, the emotional dynamic system does have some stability, as people maintain a cheerful or terrible mood over long periods. This stability exists because the system has a tendency to evolve into a small number of general states called attractors, and the shift from one mood to another can be described as the shift from one attractor to another.

Compare the kinds of perceptual transitions that were identified by the gestalt psychologists. When you see a Necker cube or a duck–rabbit, you see more than just the lines that make up the figure. The cube flips back and forth as you see it in different gestalts, and the duck–rabbit appears to you as a duck or as a rabbit but not both. Attending to different aspects of the drawing produces a gestalt shift in which you move from one configuration to the other. In the language of dynamical systems theory, the perceptual system has two attractor states, and the gestalt shift involves a phase transition from one attractor to the other. Analogously, we might think of an emotional state as a gestalt that emerges from a complex of interacting environmental, bodily, and cognitive variables, and think of emotional change as a kind of gestalt shift.

So much for metaphor. If we want a scientific rather than a literary explanation of emotional and perceptual phenomena, we need to flesh out the dynamical systems explanation schema by specifying the variables and the equations that relate them. We can then use computer models to simulate the behavior of the mathematical system to determine how well it models the complex behaviors of the psychological system under investigation. In particular, we want to know whether the dynamical theory can explain both stability and change in the psychological system, for example, both gestalts and gestalt shifts. We will now describe how theories of thinking as parallel constraint satisfaction can provide the desired explanations. These theories are implemented by connectionist (artificial neural network) models with variables and equations that define the behavior of dynamical systems.

Thinking as Parallel Constraint Satisfaction

Thinking has traditionally been conceived as a serial process in which rules are applied to mental representations to generate new representations. In contrast, many kinds of thinking can be usefully understood as simultaneously involving numerous representations that constrain each other, with processes that operate in parallel to maximize constraint satisfaction. For example, Kunda and Thagard (1996) explained how people form impressions of other people from stereotypes by proposing that representations of different stereotypical features, traits, and behaviors interact to produce an overall impression or gestalt. Your overall impression of someone you encounter as a male, Canadian, irritable professor will depend on the simultaneous interaction of your representations for each of these concepts. Read, Vanman, and Miller (1997) have reviewed how recent parallel constraint satisfaction theories have illuminated the relevance of traditional gestalt principles to social psychology. Many cognitive phenomena such as analogy and categorization can be understood in terms of parallel constraint satisfaction (see, for example, Holyoak and Spellman 1993; Thagard 2000).

What takes this approach beyond the metaphorical is the availability of computational models that show how parallel constraint satisfaction can be performed by artificial neural networks. Representations such as concepts and propositions can be modeled by units, which are artificial neurons with variables that indicate the degree of activation (plausibility or degree of acceptance) of each unit. The constraints between representations can be represented by excitatory and inhibitory links between units; for example, the positive constraint between the concepts *professor* and *intelligent* can be captured by an excitatory link between the corresponding units, while the negative constraint between *professor* and *rich* can be captured by an inhibitory link. Parallel constraint satisfaction is performed by means of equations that specify how the activation of each unit is updated as a function of the activations of the units to which it is linked and the strength (positive or negative) of those links. Updating usually leads such systems into stable states in which activations of all units cease to change; this is called settling. However, the systems are chaotic in that slight changes to inputs can lead the system to settle into a different state. For example, it is easy to model the Necker cube by a neural network in which each unit stands for a hypothesis about which feature of the cube is front or back (Rumelhart and McClelland 1986, vol. 2, p. 10). Slight changes to input about a particular feature being front or back can produce a flip in the overall state of the network. Thus artificial neural networks that implement parallel constraint satisfaction can naturally model gestalts and gestalt shifts. We will now describe how parallel constraint satisfaction and connectionist modeling can be extended to emotional thinking.

Emotional Gestalts: Theory

Extending parallel constraint satisfaction to emotion requires representations and mechanisms that go beyond those required for purely cognitive coherence. In addition to representations of propositions, concepts, goals, and actions, we need representations of emotional states such as happiness, sadness, surprise, and anger. Moreover, the cognitive representations need to be associated with emotional states, most generally with positive and negative evaluations or *valences* (Bower 1981; Lewin 1951). For example, Gordon Atwood's belief that his paper has been rejected has negative valence and is associated with sadness, whereas his belief that his daughter is an excellent dancer has positive valence and is associated with pride. Like beliefs, concepts can also have positive valences, for example ones representing success and sunshine, while other concepts have negative valences, for example ones representing death and disease.

In purely cognitive coherence, representations are connected by positive and negative constraints representing the extent to which they fit with each other. Similarly, representations can be connected by affective constraints. Some of these are intrinsic to the person that has the representations: most children, for example, attach an intrinsic positive valence to *candy*. In other cases the valence is acquired by associations, as when a child acquires a positive valence for *grocery store* because grocery stores sell candy.

In purely cognitive coherence models, representations are accepted or rejected on the basis of whether doing so helps to satisfy the most constraints, where a positive constraint is satisfied if the representations it connects are both accepted or both rejected. A judgment of emotional coherence requires not only inferences about the acceptance and rejection of representations, but also about their valence. Gordon is forced to accept the conclusion that his paper will not appear in the journal, and he attaches negative valence to this proposition. Emotional coherence requires not only the holistic process of determining how to best satisfy all the cognitive constraints, but also the simultaneous assessment of valences for all relevant representations.

The result can be an emotional gestalt consisting of a cognitively and emotionally coherent group of representations with degrees of acceptance and valences that maximally satisfy the constraints that connect them. Of course, circumstances may prevent the achievement of coherence, for example when

there is support for inconsistent beliefs or when competing actions are associated with conflicting valences. But normally the process of parallel constraint satisfaction will lead a person to acquire a set of stable acceptances
of propositions and concepts that apply to the current situation, as well as a
set of valences that indicate the emotional value of those representations.
Particular emotions such as happiness and sadness can then emerge from an
assessment of the extent to which the current situation satisfies a person's ongoing goals.

Emotional gestalt shifts occur when changes in representations and their
valences generate a new array of acceptances and valences that maximize
constraint satisfaction differently from before. When Gordon reads his letter
from the journal, he has to shift the cognitive status of the proposition that
his article will be published in it from accepted to rejected. Through parallel
constraint satisfaction, this shift may alter the acceptance status of other
propositions, for example ones representing whether he will get promoted
or receive a good raise this year. In addition, there may be a shift in valences
attached to his representations of the article, the journal, or even his whole
career.

The theory of emotional coherence is highly compatible with the appraisal
theory of emotion, according to which emotions are elicited by evaluations
of events and situations (Scherer, Schorr, and Johnstone 2001). Appraisal
theorists have explained in great detail how different cognitive evaluations
produce many different emotions. But they have been vague about the specific mechanisms that generate evaluations and elicit emotions. We propose
that appraisal is a process of parallel constraint satisfaction involving representations that have valences as well as degrees of acceptance, and we will
describe in the next section neural network models that are capable of performing some kinds of appraisal. According to appraisal theory, changes in
emotion such as those that occur in psychotherapy are due to changes in
how individuals evaluate their situations; the theory of emotional coherence
gives a more specific account of how cognitive therapy works, by the therapist introducing new evidence and reforming coherence relations in ways that
change emotional appraisals (Thagard 2000, pp. 208ff.). Let us now consider
more concretely how processes of parallel constraint satisfaction can produce
emotional gestalts and affective change.

Emotional Gestalts: Models

Computational models are an indispensable tool for developing psychological theories and for evaluating their explanatory and predictive power. The

view of thinking as parallel constraint satisfaction did not precede computational modeling, but rather arose because of the development of artificial neural network (connectionist) models (Rumelhart and McClelland 1986). It is useful conceptually to distinguish among the following: (1) a psychological theory of the structures and processes that produce a kind of thinking, (2) a computational model that rigorously spells out the structures and processes in terms of data structures and algorithms, and (3) a running computer program that uses a particular programming language to implement the model and serves to test the power and empirical relevance of the model and theory. In practice, however, the development of computer programs can be a major part of the creation of new models and theories.

Computer simulations are crucial for theories of complex dynamical systems. Metaphorical use of dynamical system terminology (nonlinear systems, chaos, attractors, self-organization, emergence, etc.) can be useful for reconceptualizing complex phenomena, but a deep understanding of the phenomena requires mathematical specification of the key variables that produce them and of the relations among them. Once this specification is available, it is rarely possible to infer the behavior of the system characterized by mathematical deduction or hand simulations, so computer simulations are needed for determining the implications of the mathematical model. As Vallacher, Read, and Nowak (2002) emphasize, dynamical research in psychology needs computer modeling as a complement to empirical research.

Fortunately, implemented artificial neural network models of emotional cognition are already available. We will describe how two models, HOTCO and ITERA, provide partial realizations of emotional gestalts, and indicate some directions for future work. Computer simulation of emotional or "hot" cognition originated with the work of Abelson (1963) on rationalization, but current models use artificial neural networks to integrate cognition and emotion.

HOTCO

The model HOTCO (for "hot coherence") is described elsewhere in this book (chaps. 3 and 8). In the original version of HOTCO, activations could influence valences but not vice versa (Thagard 2000). This reflects the normatively appropriate strategy that beliefs should affect emotions but not the reverse. In real life, however, people are subject to wishful thinking and motivated inference where what they want influences what they believe to be true (Kunda 1990). Support for the influence of desires on beliefs comes from recent findings in behavioral decision theory concerning cases where

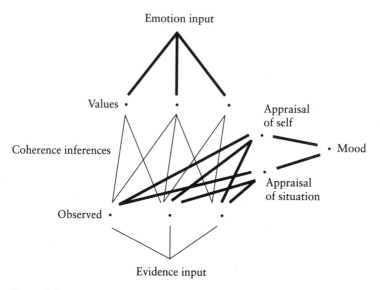

Figure 4.1
Mood changes affected by emotional coherence. Thick lines are valence links and thin lines are cognitive links. Valences spread from emotion input, while activations spreads from evidence input. Appraisals and moods are influenced by both valences and activations. Reprinted by permission from Thagard 2000, p. 209.

the outcomes of decisions or the targets of judgments are affectively rich (Finucane, Alhakami, Slovic, and Johnson 2000; Rottenstreich and Hsee 2001). These findings contradict both expected utility theory and prospect theory, which assume that probability and utilities are independent. Forgas (1995) reviews the role of affective states in social judgments, explaining motivated processing effects in his Affect Infusion Model (AIM), which specifies how and when the valence of a mood state may infuse judgments.

Accordingly, HOTCO 2 allows units to have their activations influenced by both input activations and input valences (Thagard 2003; chap. 8 below). HOTCO has been used to simulate various psychological phenomena, including trust and juror reasoning. Figure 4.1 shows an abstract network in which a combination of emotion input and evidence input generate mood by means of an overall assessment of coherence. In the case of Gordon, the new evidence that his paper has been rejected produces a temporary reappraisal of his situation and himself, dramatically altering his mood. For social psychologists, the most interesting HOTCO 2 simulation involves studies of stereotype activation reported by Sinclair and Kunda (1999; see also chap. 8).

It should be evident from the previous discussion that HOTCO models a dynamical system. The variables are activations and valences of the various units, and the equations that define a state space for the system are the equations for updating activations and valences stated above. The equations are nonlinear in the mathematical sense that the variables are related multiplicatively, and the system is also nonlinear in the metaphorical sense that there are many interactive feedback influences. The HOTCO network settles into very different states depending on changes in the input representing a positive or negative evaluation. Similarly, the experimental participants developed a very different emotional gestalt depending on whether a manager praised or criticized them (see chap. 8).

Although HOTCO can model some interesting psychological phenomena, it is far from providing a complete account of the range of emotions discussed by appraisal theory. HOTCO does not differentiate between specific positive or negative emotions such as sadness and anger directed at particular objects or situations, although it does compute a kind of global happiness and sadness based on measures of constraint satisfaction (Thagard 2000). The main specific emotion that HOTCO models is surprise, which is generated when units undergo a substantial change in degree of activation. However, another recent model allows for greater differentiation of emotions.

ITERA

Nerb and Spada (2001) present a computational account of how media information about environmental problems influences cognition and emotion. When people hear about an environmental accident, they may respond with a variety of emotions such as sadness and anger. Following the appraisal theory of emotions, Nerb and Spada hypothesized that a negative event will lead to sadness if it is caused by situational forces outside of anyone's control. But an environmental accident will lead to anger if someone is responsible for the negative event. If people see themselves as responsible for the negative event, then they feel shame; but if people see themselves as responsible for a positive event, they feel pride. Nerb and Spada (2001) show how determinants of responsibility such as agency, controllability of the cause, motive of the agent, and knowledge about possible negative consequences can be incorporated into a coherence network called ITERA (Intuitive Thinking in Environmental Risk Appraisal).

ITERA is an extension of the impression-formation model of Kunda and Thagard (1996). The main innovation in ITERA is the addition of units corresponding to emotions such as anger and sadness, as shown in figure 4.2.

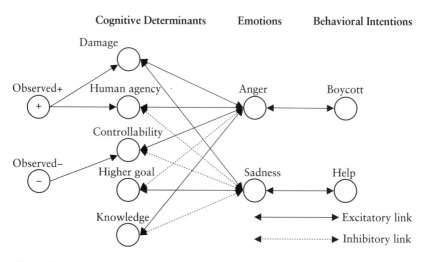

Figure 4.2
ITERA network for emotional reactions to environmental accidents. Solid lines are excitatory links, and dashed lines are inhibitory links. This example represents a situation in which a media report states that there is damage caused by human agency that could not have been controlled. Reprinted by permission from Nerb and Spada 2001, p. 528.

ITERA is given input concerning whether or not an accident was observed to involve damage, human agency, controllability, and other factors. It then predicts a reaction of sadness or anger depending on their overall coherence with the observed features of the accident. This reaction can be thought of as a kind of emotional gestalt that summarizes all the available information.

In three studies investigating the evaluation of environmental accidents, Nerb and Spada (2001) compared the performance of ITERA with people's reactions. In their empirical experiments and their simulations experiments, the authors varied the degree of responsibility for an accident by manipulating the determining factors of damage, human agency, controllability, higher goal, and knowledge (cf. Weiner 1995). In the domain of environmental problems, a higher goal may be given if the accident happened as a consequence of an action that was meant to achieve something that had a positive outcome, such as an increase in the overall benefit for society. Knowledge reflects whether agents knew in advance that there is a possible contingency between their action and threats to the environment. In the ITERA model, information that is known about the accident has a special status. Nodes representing such information have links to one of the two special nodes, OBSERVED+ or OBSERVED−; these special nodes have fixed maximal or minimal activation. A link to OBSERVED+ reflects that the corresponding determinant is given, a link to OBSERVED− means that it is not given. No link to one of the specials nodes represents that nothing is known about the determinant. By manipulating links to these nodes, different experimental settings were realized; see figure 4.2 for a concrete example of an accident scenario.

Because the determinant-emotion links are bidirectional in ITERA, there is a feedback relationship between determinants and emotions. These feedback relations allow for interactions among the activations of nodes for cognitive determinants. Hence the final activation of a node can be different across simulation experiments in which the inputs to other nodes are varied, so that the model predicts that people will construe an aspect of a situation differently depending on other aspects of the situation. Nerb and Spada called these types of model predictions *coherence effects*. For instance, ITERA predicts that manipulating the controllability node will produce coherent patterns for human agency, higher goal, and knowledge. In ITERA, a controllable cause produces high activation values for human agency and knowledge but low activation for higher goal, whereas an uncontrollable cause leads to low activation values for human agency and knowledge but high activation for higher goal. Note that there are no direct links between the cognitive determinants. The bidirectional spreading of activation within the parallel constraint satisfaction network of ITERA is sufficient for producing this coherent covariation of the cognitive determinants.

Overall, ITERA produced a good fit for the model predictions with data for anger and the intention to boycott the transgressor. In particular, the predicted coherence pattern among appraisal criteria were confirmed by empirical evidence (see Nerb, Spada, and Lay 2001 for more empirical evidence for the model). Such interaction effects among appraisal criteria are compatible with existing appraisal theories and are also supported by recent empirical findings (Lazarus 1991; Lerner and Keltner 2000, 2001). Interactions among appraisal criteria tend to be ignored by other types of computational models and by noncomputational appraisal models. For instance, rule-based appraisal models that realize the cognition-emotion relationship as a set of if-then associations do not capture the interaction effects among appraisal criteria (e.g., Scherer 1993). ITERA accounts for such affective coherence effects among appraisal criteria by using bidirectional links for the cognition-emotion relationship.

Unlike HOTCO, ITERA does not incorporate variables for valence as well as activation, and it lacks algorithms for global calculations of coherence. But it is more psychologically realistic with respect to the differentiation of particular emotions such as sadness and anger, and Nerb is now working on a synthesis of HOTCO and ITERA intended to combine the best features of both. Another connectionist model of emotional cognition has been produced by Mischel and Shoda (1995), as part of their cognitive-affective system of personality.

There are many other possibilities for future developments of computational models of the dynamics of emotion and cognition. Wagar and Thagard (2004, chap. 6 below) describe a much more neurologically realistic model of the interactions between emotion and cognition. It is more realistic than HOTCO both with respect to individual neurons and with respect to the anatomical organization of the brain. The new model uses distributed representations, which spread information over multiple artificial neurons, rather than the localist ones in HOTCO and ITERA, which use a single neuron to stand for a concept or proposition. In addition, the artificial neurons in Wagar and Thagard's model behave by spiking in the manner of real neurons, rather than simply spreading activation. Moreover, they are organized in modules corresponding to human neuroanatomy, including the hippocampus, neocortex, amygdala, and nucleus accumbens. The result is intended to be a model that captures much more of the dynamic activities of the brain than previous connectionist models of emotional cognition. Wagar and Thagard simulate some of the fascinating phenomena discussed by Damasio (1994), especially the decision-making deficits found in patients such as Phineas Gage who have brain damage that disrupts the flow of information between areas responsible for reasoning (the neocortex) and emotions (the amygdala).

Much remains to be done to understand long term emotional change. Psychotherapy can take months or even years to change the emotional tendencies of an individual by helping people to revise their cognitions and emotions. A marriage that begins with mutual love can dissolve into anger and even hatred. The terrorist leader Osama bin Laden began with a dislike for Americans that eventually turned into an intense hatred. A dynamical theory of emotion should deal with long term emotional changes as well as the sudden transitions discussed in this paper. Another direction for research on the dynamics of emotion is to expand models to capture group interactions (chap. 5).

Conclusion

Although the theoretical vocabulary and computational modeling described in this paper may seem unfamiliar to social psychologists, the basic ideas are similar to those of some of the classic theories in the field. Festinger's (1957) notion of cognitive dissonance can be accounted for in terms of parallel constraint satisfaction (Shultz and Lepper 1996); and it is possible with HOTCO to incorporate the affective dimension that later theorists found to be crucial to dissonance (Cooper and Fazio 1984). Kunda and Thagard (1996) describe how parallel constraint satisfaction can be used to understand ideas about impression formation that Solomon Asch developed from Gestalt psychology.

Emotional coherence and the kind of computational model discussed in this paper can also be applied to McGuire's (1999) dynamic model of thought systems. McGuire's theory describes thought systems as consisting of propositions with two attributes: desirability (an evaluation dimension) and likelihood of occurrence (an expectancy dimension). These dimensions express how much the content of a proposition is liked and how much it is believed. The thought system is seen as dynamic so that a change that is directly induced in one part of the system results in compensatory adjustments in remote parts of the system. Together those assumptions imply that a person's evaluative and expectancy judgments on a topic will tend to be assimilated toward one another. McGuire (1999, p. 190) postulates "that causality flows in both directions, reflecting both a 'wishful thinking' tendency such that people bring their expectations in line with their desires, and a 'rationalization' tendency such that they bring desires in line with expectations." Emotional coherence models such as HOTCO provide mechanisms for both these tendencies, as activations corresponding to likelihood interact with valences corresponding to desirability.

Some proponents of a dynamical systems approach to understanding the mind have seen it as a radical alternative to symbolic and connectionist models that have been predominant in cognitive science (van Gelder 1995). Our discussion has shown that this is a mistake: connectionist systems are one important kind of dynamical system, and they are arguably the ones best suited for explaining psychological phenomena, including ones involving emotion.

In sum, computational models based on parallel constraint satisfaction, with constraints and representations that are affective as well as cognitive, have much to contribute to a dynamical perspective on social psychology. We have shown how connectionist systems such as HOTCO and ITERA can be used to study the dynamics of emotional cognition at a concrete and not just a metaphorical level. In particular, they can model the generation and shifting of emotional gestalts.

5 Emotional Consensus in Group Decision Making

Paul Thagard and Fred Kroon

Introduction

How do you and your friends decide what movies to attend together? Do you create a chart of the movies available, each rate them numerically, and then sum the ratings to make the group decision? Or do you discuss the available movies until everyone has a good feeling about the best movie to go to? Similarly, if you are in a North American or other university department that does its own faculty hiring, how does your department proceed? Does it use either of the following procedures? Procedure A: jointly produce a rating of candidates on a scale of 1 to 10 for their potential contributions to research, teaching, and administration; jointly agree on a weighting of the importance of research, teaching, and administration; multiply the ratings times the weightings to produce a score for each candidate, and make an offer to the first one. Procedure B: argue heatedly about the strengths and weaknesses of different candidates and the value of different kinds of research and teaching; gradually reach some consensus, or at least take a vote on which candidate should be made an offer; try to mollify those who did not get the candidate they wanted. Procedure A sounds rational, but we have never heard of it being conducted, whereas something like procedure B is very common.

Movie going and academic hiring are just two examples of the pervasive phenomenon of group decision making, which abounds in organizations as diverse as families, businesses, juries, and political parties. Unless there is an autocrat empowered to make decisions for the whole group, a joint decision will often require extensive discussion and negotiation before a consensus or majority opinion is reached. In ideal cases, the discussion produces sufficient communication that all members of the group come to share the same view of what to do, for example all agreeing about which job candidate is the best.

Group decisions are often highly emotional. In academic hiring, different members of a department are usually enthusiastic about some candidates and scornful about others. These emotional attitudes partly reflect the records of the candidates, but also reflect the values of the professors doing the hiring, who often have strong opinions about the value of particular aspects of academic work, for example teaching versus research, or research on some topics rather than others. It is not coincidental that professors tend to most admire the kinds of work that they know best, so conflict arises in a department because everyone wants to hire replicates of themselves. Ideally, conflict is resolved by acquiring and exchanging enough information that the members of the department arrive at similar emotional reactions toward the different candidates.

This chapter presents a theory and computational model of group decision making understood as emotional consensus. It proposes that individual decision making is inherently emotional, and that group decision making requires communication of emotional as well as factual information. In the ideal case, sufficient communication of both facts and emotions will lead to cognitive-emotional consensus about what to do, a consensus that consists of at least partial convergence of both beliefs and emotional values. After reviewing the emotional character of individual decision making, we describe a set of mechanisms for transmitting emotional values between people. Some of these mechanisms are implemented in a computational model that simulates how emotional communication can lead to consensus in group decisions.

Emotions in Individual Decision Making

In the past decade, psychologists and neuroscientists have increasingly recognized the inherently emotional nature of decision making (e.g., Damasio 1994; Finucane et al. 2000; Lerner, Small, and Loewenstein 2004; Loewenstein et al. 2001). For most people, decisions are not the result of a cognitive calculation of the sort described in normative models such as multiattribute utility theory, but rather the result of arriving at emotional reactions to different situations. Preferences arise in favor of options associated with strong positive emotions, and against options associated with strong negative emotions.

Thagard (2000) proposed a theory of emotional coherence that we will now review, because it provides the individual basis for the theory of group decision making to be developed in the next section. On this theory, the elements in a decision include representations of competing actions and goals that they potentially accomplish. A pair of elements may cohere, as when an action and a goal fit together because the action facilitates the goal. If two elements cohere, then there is a positive constraint between them that can be satisfied either by accepting both elements or by rejecting both. On the other hand, two elements may "incohere," as when two actions resist fitting together because they are incompatible with each other. Between incoherent elements, there is a negative constraint that can be satisfied only by accepting one and rejecting the other. In a purely cognitive coherence problem, the elements are divided into ones that are accepted and rejected in such a way as to satisfy the most constraints. But in an emotional coherence problem the elements also have positive and negative *valences*, which reflect the emotional attitudes associated with the different representations. Moreover, elements can have positive or negative emotional connections to other elements, so that the valence of one element can influence the valence of the other. The valence of an element is determined by the valences and acceptability of all the elements to which it is connected.

This characterization of emotional coherence is rather abstract, but can be made clearer by means of a concrete example and a computational model. Suppose you are trying to decide whom your department should hire and you are focusing on three candidates: Chris, Jordan, and Pat. You have several main goals that you are trying to accomplish, including acquiring a colleague who will teach well, do lots of interesting research, and be reasonably easy to get along with. Then the elements of your decision are the representations: hire Chris, hire Jordan, hire Pat, good teaching, productive research, and collegiality. The positive constraints among these elements reflect the extent to which the three candidates accomplish your different goals. The negative constraints arise because you only have one position, so that hiring one candidate means not hiring the others. See the coherence theory of decision developed by Thagard and Millgram (1995; Millgram and Thagard 1996).

So far, this just sounds like standard multiattribute decision making with different jargon, but the differences will become apparent when the emotional and computational aspects of the decision come into view. It is possible that your decision about whom you want to hire is coldly cognitive, but if you are like most people you will have definite emotional reactions to the candidates, ranging from enthusiasm to disgust. How do these reactions arise?

According to the theory of emotional coherence, the reactions result from emotional valences attached to the goals that affect the decision making. If

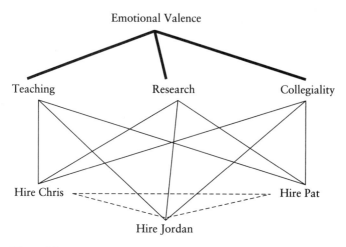

Figure 5.1
Structure of the constraint network for the hiring decision. Thick lines indicate emotional strength of various goals, and thin solid lines indicate the extent to which the different hiring options contribute to those goals. Dotted lines indicate negative constraints between pairs of options. Not shown are weights that indicate the strength of the various constraints.

you think that research is extremely important and care little about teaching and social interaction, then you will end up with a positive emotional reaction toward the candidate who is the best researcher. The positive valence of the goal thus transfers to the action, so you feel good at the prospect of hiring the candidate who excels in research. Normally, however, decisions involve a trade-off among different goals, so you may have to balance a fairly good researcher off against a superb teacher. Figure 5.1 shows the structure of the constraint network involving the actions, goals, and their emotional inputs.

Decision problems like those in figure 5.1 are naturally solved in a computationally powerful and psychologically natural way by artificial neural networks. HOTCO (for HOT COherence) is a computational model of emotional inference that has been applied to various kinds of thinking, including trust, legal reasoning, and emotional analogies.

HOTCO is not very neurologically realistic, in that it uses single artificial neurons to stand for complex representations such as "hire Chris," and it does not take into account how cognitive and emotional processing is carried out by different brain areas. However, HOTCO is compatible with a much more detailed neurocomputational model, GAGE, which models decision making using distributed representations over spiking neurons that are organized into anatomical groups, including the prefrontal cortex, hippocampus, amygdala, and nucleus accumbens (Wagar and Thagard 2004, chap. 6 below). Each HOTCO unit that stands for a high-level representation can be viewed as corresponding to groups of connected neurons in GAGE, including ones in the prefrontal cortex whose joint spiking activity corresponds to the unit's activation, and ones in the amygdala and nucleus accumbens whose joint spiking activity corresponds to the unit's valence. HOTCO uses activations and valences of units to integrate cognition and emotion, and GAGE uses firing behavior of groups of spiking neurons in different brain areas to accomplish the same task in a more neurologically realistic way. However, GAGE is much more complex to program and run simulations, so for the purpose of modeling group decisions we will use HOTCO instead, viewing it as a useful approximation to GAGE's closer approximation to brain activity.

Below we will describe HOTCO 3, which expands HOTCO 2 into a multiagent system with emotional communication. HOTCO 2 only models a single agent, operating alone by virtue of a neural network that generates emotional decisions. In contrast, HOTCO 3 models any number of agents, each one of which is an agent running a HOTCO 2 simulation. The multiple agents in HOTCO 3 communicate and shape each other's decisions by transmitting emotional information, a social process that we will now characterize.

Social Mechanisms of Emotional Transmission

Group decisions that are not based on autocratic pronouncement or simple voting require achievement of some sort of consensus. In a purely cognitive model of consensus concerning what to believe, group agreement can be reached simply by exchanging information about relevant hypotheses, evidence, and explanatory relations between them (Thagard 2000, chap. 7). However, if decision making by individuals is inherently emotional, then group decision making will require attainment of a kind of emotional consensus in which members of the group share similar positive and negative feelings about different actions and goals. Cognitive consensus can come about by verbally exchanging propositional information, but emotional communication is much more complicated. In this section we will describe what seem to be the most important mechanisms of emotional transmission leading toward consensus, and in the following describe how some of them can be implemented computationally.

What is a social mechanism? In general, a mechanism consists of "entities and activities organized such that they are productive of regular changes" (Machamer, Darden, and Craver 2000, p. 3). Familiar examples are machines such as bicycles that have parts interacting in ways that produce desired results, and biological systems such as organs that have parts such as cells interacting in ways that perform functions useful to the organism involved. In social mechanisms, the parts are human agents, the activities are communication and other interactions between agents, and the regular changes involve groups of humans.

Suppose now that we have a university department whose members need to make a joint decision about whom to hire, and that each member has made a preliminary choice based on emotional coherence. If there is no general agreement, then the people need to talk to each other in order to try to convince their colleagues to hire their preferred candidate. Communication of emotional valences can take place by very different kinds of social mechanisms, including means–ends and analogical arguments, emotional contagion, altruism, and empathy. Each of these mechanisms can be characterized by four parts: a *trigger* that initiates the mechanism by which a sender influences the emotional decision making of a receiver, *inputs* that the sender gives to the receiver, *changes* in the mental state of the receiver, and *effects* on the receiver's decision making. These mechanisms are social in that they involve interactions of 2 or more agents, but they do not require that the sender intentionally produce the communication. For example, with emotional contagion senders may not even be aware that they are communicating their enthusiasm or other reaction to receivers, and with altruism all that matters is that receivers care enough about the senders to pick up some of their values. The social mechanisms of emotional communication are processes that involve interactions between agents, and are only sometimes intentional strategies that a sender uses to convince a receiver.

The most familiar kind of communication in group decisions is verbal argument, which is triggered by the desire of one person, the sender, to influence the decision of another person, the receiver. The most straightforward kind of argument is means–ends, in which the sender tries to convince the receiver of an action by showing the receiver that the action contributes to one or more of the receiver's goals. For example, in hiring, the sender may argue that the department should hire Chris because of fine teaching, on the assumption that the receiver has the goal of having a department with good teachers. Here the input to the receiver is the verbal claim that Chris is a good teacher, and the desired change is that the receiver should acquire a stronger association between the action of hiring Chris and the goal of teaching. If this change is made, then it could have the desired effect on the receiver's decision making, producing agreement between the receiver and sender and moving the department toward consensus.

Analogical argument operates more indirectly by comparing prospective actions to ones that have worked well or badly in the past. In a hiring discussion, someone might argue for Pat as "the next Herbert Simon," drawing an analogy between the intellectual abilities and accomplishments of Pat and those of a distinguished researcher. Alternatively, if department members are familiar with a previous disastrous hire, Schmerdly, the sender may use a negative analogy and say that they should not hire Jordan who is another Schmerdly. In both these cases, the inputs are the verbal comparison that the sender gives to the receiver, and the desired changes are rearrangements of the receiver's cognitive-emotional network to make a connection between the source analog (Simon or Schmerdly) and the target analog, Pat. This connection makes possible the spread of the positive or negative valence of the source to the target, increasing or decreasing its valence, which may have the desired effect of making the target action more or less emotionally attractive. See chapter 3 above for an extended discussion of emotional analogies, and Blanchette and Dunbar (2001) for empirical evidence that analogies are often used in persuasion.

Means-ends and analogical argument are verbal means by which senders attempt to modify the emotional reactions of receivers, but non-verbal means may be more effective. Hatfield, Cacioppo, and Rapson (1994) provided an extensive discussion of emotional contagion, in which one person "catches" another's emotions. Their theory is summarized in the following propositions (pp. 10–11):

Proposition 1 In conversation, people tend automatically and continuously to mimic and synchronize their movements with the facial expressions, voices, postures, movements, and instrumental behavior of others.

Proposition 2 Subjective emotional experiences are affected, moment to moment, by the activation and/or feedback from such mimicry.

Proposition 3 Given propositions 1 and 2, people tend to "catch" others' emotions, moment to moment.

The trigger for the mechanism of emotional contagion is face-to-face meetings between individuals. The inputs that the sender provides to the receiver are nonverbal, consisting of bodily states that the receiver unconsciously imitates. Then the receiver undergoes physiological changes that change the psychological valences associated with different aspects of the situation, with the possible effect that the overall decision of the receiver shifts. Unlike means–ends and analogical arguments, contagion is a social process that is usually not an intentional strategy used by a sender to convince a receiver.

In hiring situations, emotional contagion can work with both positive and negative emotions. If there is a discussion of a candidate, and one person is displaying great enthusiasm by smiling and displaying positive body language, then there will be a tendency for others to catch some of the enthusiasm. On the other hand, if people exhibit skepticism about a candidate by scowling, sneering, or turning away, then others may pick up some of the negative attitude toward the candidate. Barsade (2002) provides an insightful discussion of the contribution of emotional contagion to group processes.

Other social mechanisms for emotional transmission—altruism, compassion, and empathy—may combine verbal and nonverbal information. Altruism is the unselfish regard for the welfare of others. If you care about a person, your altruism may lead you to acquire an emotional attitude toward something that is valued by that person. Altruistic transmission is triggered in situations where the receiver cares for the sender, and receives verbal or nonverbal input concerning what the sender's goals are. Then the altruistic receiver may change by acquiring at least a weak version of the sender's goals, changing the receiver's emotional constraint network in a way that may have the effect of generating a different decision. For example, if you have a colleague you care about who desperately wants to hire a candidate who would be a useful collaborator, then you may adopt such a goal as a way of helping out your colleague. You then come to the same decision as your colleague in part because you have adopted his or her goals as your own.

Compassion is triggered when you notice that someone is distressed, and might be viewed as a special kind of altruism. It is probably not a factor in faculty hiring, but could easily affect personal and political decisions. Whereas altruism assumes that you care enough generally for people to adopt their goals, compassion requires only that you do not want to see them suffer. The input to the compassion mechanism is verbal or nonverbal information conveyed from the sender to the receiver concerning the sender's distress. This information then augments the receiver's emotional constraint network to include the goal of relieving the sender's distress. The result may be a shift in the receiver's decision making toward an action that is at least partially in the interest of the sender.

The most complicated mechanism of emotional transfer is empathy, which we will treat as a special form of analogy (Barnes and Thagard 1997, chap. 3). Empathy involves putting yourself in other people's shoes so that you understand their emotions by virtue of having an experience that is an image of theirs. The trigger for this mechanism is information about the sender's situation that reminds the receiver of a similar situation that the receiver had personally experienced emotionally. Then the receiver can infer from the similarities between the two people and their situations that the sender is experiencing something like what the receiver did. In empathy, this inference is not verbal, but rather involves projecting the receiver's imagined experience back on to the sender. Empathy does not by itself change the emotional constraint network of the receiver, but may inspire altruistic feelings that do. For example, suppose you and I disagree about whom to hire, and you say that you feel intellectually isolated in the department. If I remember another department in which I felt distressed about being intellectually isolated, then I may come to appreciate your distress, and then through compassion and altruism come to adopt the goal of relieving your intellectual isolation. The new emotional constraint network that incorporates the goal of relieving your distress that empathy has enabled me to perceive may then lead me to prefer a decision similar to the one you prefer.

In any realistic social situation, the mechanisms of means–ends argument, analogical argument, emotional contagion, altruism, compassion, and empathy may interact with each other. For example, a means–ends argument may inspire enthusiasm in one person whose excitement spreads by emotional contagion to another. Or, as we have just suggested, empathy may generate compassion and altruism. Figure 5.2 summarizes some of the ways in which the mechanisms of emotional transmission may interact. Even though it shows that all other mechanisms may influence contagion, this should not

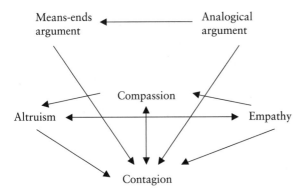

Figure 5.2
Interactions among mechanisms of emotional transmission.

be taken to mean that contagion is somehow the fundamental process of emotional communication. Each of the other mechanisms can be used to influence the emotional state of a receiver independently of whether contagion is also operating as well. How frequently the different mechanisms are used in group decisions, and how frequently they interact, are empirical questions, currently unanswered. In order to make discussion of these mechanisms more precise, we now describe a computational model of emotional group decision making.

A Computational Model of Emotional Consensus

In order to get a deeper understanding of the social mechanisms that can lead to emotional consensus, we have constructed a computational model, HOTCO 3, which builds on earlier models of emotional coherence and cognitive consensus. This section describes the data structures and algorithms of HOTCO 3, and their application to simulations of a movie decision and a hiring decision. HOTCO 3 is programmed in Common LISP.

The basic structure in HOTCO 3 is a person, whose properties include a group that the person belongs to, a list of people that the person cares for, and a set of inputs concerning actions, goals, facilitation relations, and emotional valences. For example, the facilitation relations for a moviegoer might include (FACILITATE 'ACTION-MOVIE 'EXCITEMENT) which represents the proposition that going to an action movie can contribute to this person's goal of being excited. If the person's emotional valences include EXCITEMENT, then this input will encourage the spread of positive valence to ACTION-MOVIE. For modeling each person's decision making, the basic data structures are units, which are highly artificial neurons that possess activations and valences, which are real numbers between 1 and −1. Thus there will be a unit to stand for ACTION-MOVIE, EXCITEMENT, and other actions and goals. These units are connected by links, including excitatory links created by facilitation relations such as the one between ACTION-MOVIE and EXCITEMENT, and inhibitory links created by incompatibility relations, such as the one between ACTION-MOVIE and ROMANTIC-COMEDY.

The algorithms for individual decision making are mostly those for previous versions of HOTCO. Units for the person's fundamental goals receive activations and valences from an external source, and these spread to other connected units. Parallel updating leads after a reasonable number of iterations (typically 50–100) to stability of activations and valences that represent the overall decision of the individual. Units with high activations and valences are interpreted as indicating which action or actions the individual chooses to perform, while units with low activations and valences stand for rejected choices.

What is novel about HOTCO 3 is that it simulates decision making by a group of interacting emotional agents. The main procedure works as follows:

1. Perform individual decision making for each member of the group.
2. If all members agree about what to do, then stop: consensus has been reached.
3. Otherwise, simulate a meeting to exchange factual and emotional information between two randomly selected members of the group.
4. Reevaluate individual decision based on emotional coherence for both newly informed members.
5. Repeat from step 2.

The key step in this process is the third, information exchange, which should include all of the mechanisms described above, although currently only means–ends, contagion, and altruism are implemented in HOTCO 3. Contagion works by identifying actions on which a group member meeting with another has a strong positive or negative emotional valence. A member with a strong valence becomes a sender whose emotional reactions are received in weakened form by the receiver. Obviously, HOTCO 3 lacks the physiological processes by which contagion takes place in people, but it simulates the result of having some part of the strong emotional reactions of a sender transferred to a receiver. Contagion in HOTCO 3 works by providing a unit representing the action for the receiver with an emotional input that is a reduced version of the strong valence that the sender attaches to the action. Thus emotional valence spreads by contagion from the sender to the receiver. For example, if the sender attaches strong positive valence to that unit for ACTION-MOVIE, then a new link will encourage the spread of positive valence to the receiver's unit for ACTION-MOVIE. Thus the receiver acquires by contagion a weakened version of the sender's attitudes toward various actions.

The altruism mechanism in HOTCO 3 affects goals rather than actions. A participant in a meeting who cares for the other member becomes a receiver in the altruism process. The other member becomes a sender, with the effect that part of the emotional valence attached to the sender's goals is transferred to the receiver's goals. This is accomplished by creating a new link between the unit that represents a goal of the receiver and the unit for emotional input. For example, if the sender has the valenced goal EXCITE-MENT, then the receiver will acquire some emotional input to the unit that represents this goal. Thus, because the receiver cares for the sender, the sender appreciates, at least weakly, the sender's goals. The altruism procedure also transfers from the sender to the receiver information about what actions facilitate the receiver's newly acquired goals, making it more likely that the receiver will reach the same decision as the sender. The compassion procedure is not yet implemented in HOTCO 3, but would work much like the altruism procedure except that it would be triggered by perception of a sender's distress.

HOTCO 3 models a kind of means–ends argument by having a sender notice that the receiver has a goal that can be accomplished by one of the sender's preferred actions. For example, if the receiver has the goal EXCITE-MENT, but has not noticed that ACTION-MOVIE facilitates it, then the sender can transfer to the receiver the information that ACTION-MOVIE facilitates EXCITEMENT. Then the LISP expression (FACILI-TATES 'ACTION-MOVIE 'EXCITEMENT) becomes part of the input that determines the decision made by the receiver. This is not a full-blown argu-ment, since HOTCO 3 does not do natural language processing, but it has the same effect in that the sender is trying to convince the receiver to do what the sender wants by pointing out to the receiver that the action favored by the sender actually contributes to the goals of the receiver. Means–ends argument is a different mechanism from altruism, in which the receiver adopts the sender's goals in addition to input about facilitation.

For the three mechanisms currently implemented in HOTCO 3, table 5.1 summarizes the triggering conditions, inputs that the sender transmits to

Table 5.1
Summary of mechanisms of emotional transfer

	Trigger	Inputs from sender to receiver	Changes in and effects on receiver
Contagion	Receiver perceives sender	Sender's valence of action transferred to receiver	Receiver acquires some of sender's attitude to action
Altruism	Receiver cares about sender	Sender's valence of goal transferred to receiver	Receiver acquires some of sender's attitude to goal
Means–ends	Sender tries to convince receiver	Information that an action facilitates a goal	Receiver sees greater attractiveness of goal

the receiver, and changes and effects experienced by the receiver. Only in the case of means–ends argument is emotional transmission triggered by the conscious intention of the sender to convince the receiver.

We have not yet implemented analogical argument and empathy, because of technical complications in adapting the analogical mapping program ACME (Holyoak and Thagard 1989) to use the kind of information available to HOTCO 3. But it is easy to see how they would work in principle. In analogical argument, a sender would try to convince a receiver to change decisions by communicating to the receiver a description of a situation similar to the one at issue. Then the receiver would make new analogically derived connections that would shift the emotional inputs in a way that could result in a different decision. In empathy, the receiver would end up modifying a decision because of noticing an analogical connection between the sender's situation and some previous emotional experience of the sender. In both analogical argument and empathy, the receiver would end up with a modified emotional constraint network that could increase the likelihood of consensus.

There are undoubtedly other social mechanisms of emotional transmission that we have not considered. For example, senders who want to increase the likelihood that receivers will acquire their emotional attitudes can employ social strategies such as providing compliments, gifts, or sexual favors. Such behaviors are beyond the scope of HOTCO 3, although certainly prevalent in human activity. In the conclusion, we briefly discuss coercive social processes that can also influence group consensus.

Simulations

To test the HOTCO 3 implementation of emotional contagion, altruism, and means–ends reasoning, we have used it to simulate simple cases of group decision making. The first concerns a male–female couple making a joint decision about what movie to attend. In accord with their stereotypical preferences, we will call them Mars and Venus; they need to choose between going to an action, comedy, or suspense movie. They are in conflict because Mars mostly wants excitement and so prefers an action movie, whereas Venus mostly wants laughter and so prefers a comedy. The input to HOTCO 3 gives Mars the following emotional valences for various goals: 1 for excitement, .8 for interest, and .5 for laughter. His beliefs about how to accomplish these goals are represented by the following facilitation relations:

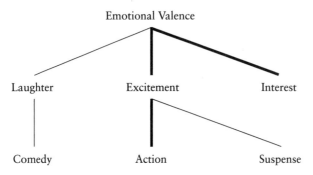

Figure 5.3
Emotional constraint network for Mars. The thickness of the lines corresponds to the strength of the connections. Not shown are inhibitory connections among the three actions.

(facilitate 'go-action 'M-excitement 1)
(facilitate 'go-suspense 'M-excitement .6)
(facilitate 'go-comedy 'M-laughter .5)

The first of these indicates that Mars believes that going to an action movie would maximally contribute to his goal of excitement. The structure of the emotional coherence network for Mars is displayed in figure 5.3.

The structure of the coherence network for Venus is similar, but she attaches different valences to the goals: 1 for laughter, .8 for interest, and .3 for excitement. Here beliefs about how different options would contribute to these goals are represented by the following facilitation relations:

(facilitate 'go-action 'V-excitement .2)
(facilitate 'go-suspense 'V-excitement .5)
(facilitate 'go-comedy 'V-laughter 1)

The inputs for the Mars and Venus decisions distinguish M-excitement, which is Mars' excitement, from V-excitement, which is Venus'; this assumes that Mars and Venus are initially concerned with their own goal satisfaction rather than the other's. It is obvious from the above inputs that Mars will initially want to go to an action movie, whereas Venus will want to go to a comedy. How can the conflict be resolved?

We have run this example using both contagion and altruism, and the results surprised us. Mars and Venus had repeated meetings to exchange emotional information. With contagion alone, Mars and Venus acquired some of the positive and negative valences that the other attached to the various options. For example, Mars attached a new positive valence to going to a comedy. But contagion did not change their decisions: Mars still preferred the action movie, and Venus the comedy. Similarly, altruism did not produce a consensus, even though Mars adopted some of Venus's goals such as V-excitement, i.e., excitement for Venus as well as himself, and Venus adopted some of Mars's goals. Curiously, however, when emotional transmission included both contagion and altruism, Mars changed his decision and agreed to go to the comedy. He was influenced both by contagion of Venus's desire to go to the comedy, and by his altruistic adoption of her goals. Figure 5.4 graphs how meetings lead to consensus when both contagion and altruism influence Mars.

An extension to the Mars–Venus example shows that the phenomenon scales to a decision with three agents. A third agent, "Neptune" (of indeterminate gender), was added to the original simulation. Neptune's valences were 1 for interest, .6 for excitement, and .4 for laughter. The facilitation relations were:

(facilitate 'go-action 'N-excitement .6)
(facilitate 'go-suspense 'N-interest 1)
(facilitate 'go-comedy 'N-laughter .5)

As a result, Neptune's first choice is to see a suspense film. As with the two agent Mars-Venus example, when contagion was the only form of emotional communication, the group fails to reach consensus. Restricting emotional communication to altruism gives similar results. However, when the two are combined the group reaches consensus in just a few meetings. The exact number varies, since, unlike a group with only two members, the order of meetings may be different in different simulation runs. This possibility adds additional complexity to larger groups, which we investigated in another example concerning hiring.

This second case is a highly simplified approximation to a university department making a faculty hiring decision. The department has only three members, Professors A, B, and C, and they are trying to choose collectively between two candidates, Pat and Chris. The professors differ in their emotional attachments to different hiring criteria: A cares most about research, B about teaching, and C about administration. They have different beliefs about how the candidates would contribute to these goals. For example, Professor A attaches a full 1.0 emotional valence to research, in contrast to .8 for teaching and .5 for administration. The comparable valences for Professor B, respectively, are .5, 1, and .5, and for Professor C, .5, .5, and .8. Here are the facilitation relations that represent their beliefs about the candidates:

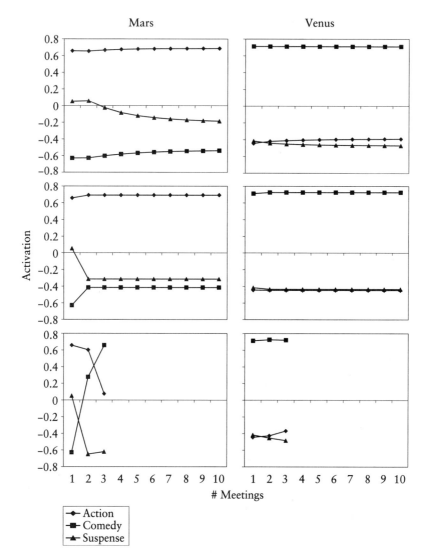

Figure 5.4

Graphs of the activation of each of the three possible decisions for Mars and Venus. The top row uses contagion as the only emotional communication, the middle only altruism, and the bottom both contagion and altruism. Note that consensus is reached almost immediately in the third case, so the simulation stops after 3 meetings.

Prof A:
(facilitate 'hire-Chris 'research .8)
(facilitate 'hire-Pat 'research .6)
(facilitate 'hire-Pat 'teaching .3)

Prof B:
(facilitate 'hire-Pat 'research .7)
(facilitate 'hire-Chris 'research .8)
(facilitate 'hire-Chris 'teaching .7)

Prof C:
(facilitate 'hire-Pat 'research .6)
(facilitate 'hire-Chris 'teaching .7)
(facilitate 'hire-Pat 'administration 1)

While it may not be immediately obvious, Professors A and C initially prefer Pat, and Professor B prefers Chris. Note that the simulation assumes that all three professors have the same three goals, but have an incomplete set of beliefs about how different candidates contribute to them. This makes room for the use of means–ends arguments to convince a decision maker of the need to augment their network with additional facilitation relations. For example, Professor C can point out to Professor B that Pat can make a good contribution to administration. The emotional constraint networks are thus not as complete as the one depicted in figure 5.1.

What happens when the professors meet to discuss the candidates and exchange emotional reactions about them? The interesting (because we did not expect it) answer is that it depends very much on the order of the meetings. HOTCO 3 randomly chooses two members of a group to meet and exchange information by the various social mechanisms. Altruism is not relevant here, since all three professors have the same goals. We had expected that Professors A and C would eventually convince B, and this usually happens.

But surprisingly, sometimes consensus is not reached, if B first meets with A and convinces A by adding new facilitation relations about the advantages of Chris. Then A switches to Chris, but this does not produce consensus, because C still prefers Pat, and if B meets with C then contagion and means–ends transfers lead B to come to prefer Pat too. The odd result then is that consensus is not reached because both Professors A and B have changed their minds in opposite directions! The next experiment to be done is to see what happens if A, B, and C have a series of joint meetings in which everyone transmits to everyone else.

Why is it that altruism has such an impact in the Mars–Venus–Neptune example, and yet, though altruism is not active in this simulation, consensus is still achieved? This is a side effect of the fact that all of the agents in this simulation have identical goals initially. As a result, altruism is never used, since no agent can adopt a new goal altruistically. This fact allows the direct use of means–ends communication to fill the gap. To further see the impact of altruism on this example, we implemented a quantitative version of altruism in which agents adopt goals as a kind of weighted sum of the goals of themselves and others. This, as expected, reduced the time needed to reach consensus, but otherwise made little difference.

Additional computational experiments with larger groups show that the number of meetings required to reach consensus increase with the size of the group. Additionally, increasing the number of possible choices also increases the average number of meetings required for consensus. Furthermore, these experiments support the observation that meeting order strongly affects the time needed to reach consensus, as well as whether consensus is reached at all. Some meeting orders produce a form of group polarization. If the first meetings are between agents with similar initial choices, this leads to a strengthening of those agents' feelings. A small group of like-minded agents meeting repeatedly may generate a contagion feedback loop, with each agent strengthening the other's feelings. If two or more such clusters form, neither has the ability to budge the other's now entrenched position, thus blocking any consensus from forming.

Obviously, both the movie and hiring simulations are highly artificial in their simplifications and choice of inputs. But they still show that even small simulated groups can exhibit interesting decision making behavior as the result of emotional transmission. Future work may implement additional mechanisms such as empathy and apply them to larger groups of more complex individuals.

Related Work

In recent years, there has been rapid growth in the computer simulation of organizations as multiagent systems (e.g., Wooldrige 2002). But little research has been done on the development of consensus in such systems, and we have not been able to find any previous work on emotional consensus.

Johnson and Feinberg (1989) describe computer simulation of consensus as it occurs in crowds. Their model differs from ours in three important ways. First, for the crowd to achieve consensus, not every member had to agree. Rather, consensus was said to be achieved when the amount of variability fell below a certain amount. Second, each agent was highly simplified, varying only in their initial predisposition to a certain plan of action. Furthermore, the agents did not have any reasoning ability whatsoever. Instead, all agents had a fixed likelihood that they would change their decision. Third, the model included information on the spatial distribution of agents. Individual communications were dependent on this distribution. Finally, two forms of communication were modeled. First, there was communication within small subgroups, and then communication between such groups.

Hutchins (1995, chap. 5) discusses communication among members of navigation teams on ships. He describes a computer simulation of a system of members, each of which is a constraint satisfaction system much like those in HOTCO 3, although their function is to interpret events rather than to make decisions. Hutchins considers four parameters that characterize communication: the pattern of interconnections among members of the community; the pattern of interconnectivity of units in the constraint networks; the strength of connections between communicating networks, that is, degree of persuasiveness; and the time course of communication. Hutchins provides a highly illuminating discussion of the advantages and disadvantages of different modes of decision making including consensus and voting, but does not discuss the role of emotion in decision making.

Ephrati and Rosenschein (1996) computationally model an economic decision process that can be used to derive multiagent consensus. Consensus is reached by a process of voting with financial bids: each agent expresses its preferences and a group choice mechanism is used to select the result. The mechanism they advocate involves a tax that charges voters based on the extent to which their bids affect final outcomes. The procedure is clever but complex, and seems more suited to automated systems than to modeling decision making in groups of humans.

Another model (Moss 2002) attempts to simulate multilateral negotiation. Like our simulation, Moss is interested in multiple agents coming to a consensus. However, the reasoning ability of his agents is limited. Agent goals are represented by two strings, one giving the desired outcomes, and one establishing the importance of each goal to the agent. In addition, each agent has a representation of other agents consisting of values on a variety of scales, and a ranking of the importance of each of these scales. Both the values and the ranking change with each negotiation. Negotiation between two agents consists of making tradeoffs, in order to achieve consensus. This model works well for situations of bilateral negotiation, but never reaches consensus in cases of multilateral negotiation, since reaching an agreement with one agent may cause a new disagreement with another. In contrast to Moss, our model did generally achieve consensus. Like the other research described in this section, Moss ignores emotional aspects of consensus formation.

Conclusion

This chapter has presented a novel theory of the contribution of emotions to group decision making. We have described social and psychological mechanisms that can encourage the emergence of emotional consensus within a group of decision makers, each of whom makes decisions based on a combination of cognitive and emotional factors. Mechanisms such as emotional contagion, altruism, means–ends argument, analogy, and empathy can transfer emotional attitudes across individuals and lead to the resolution of conflicts. Some of these are modeled computationally by HOTCO 3, a program that shows how group interactions of emotion-driven decision makers can lead to interesting developments, including consensus.

There are undoubtedly additional mechanisms of social transmission of emotions that we have not addressed. On the dark side of group decision making, there are coercive social processes that operate much less benignly than contagion, argument, and empathy. For example, intimidation can lead to group agreement because powerful members convince others to go along with them out of fear of being harmed. Propaganda uses non-argumentative rhetorical techniques such as appeals to xenophobia to manipulate people's emotional attitudes. We have chosen to concentrate on the more positive contributions of emotions to group decision making, but must acknowledge that emotion can also have less savory contributions. Additional mechanisms for emotional transmission might also include the opposite of contagion, where a history of conflicts leads one member to adopt emotional attitudes opposite to another on the assumption that the other is always wrong. Other possible sources of emotional influence are respect for authority and the desire to conform with group opinions and behavior.

Real-life decision making is much more emotionally complex than the account we have presented here. There are many different emotions that involve a much broader range of feelings than is captured by our discussion of positive and negative valences. On the negative side, anger is different from fear; on the positive side, enthusiasm is different from desperate craving. We have also not discussed complex social emotions, such as those that arise in social situations when people strive to present themselves positively to other group members, to avoid embarrassment, and to maintain group solidarity. For the individual, the relation between actions and goals is often not so narrowly verbal as our facilitation relations suggest, but could reflect visual and other non-verbalized experiences, just as the emotional inputs and outputs to decision are more a matter of experience than verbal representation.

Despite these limitations, this chapter has contributed to the theory of group decision making by highlighting the role of emotions at both the individual and group levels. It has also shown how computational modeling can help to specify the kinds of psychological and social mechanisms that underlie group conflict and movement toward agreement. Simulations with HOTCO 3 also reveal some surprising results of those mechanisms, even in simple examples.

The focus in this chapter has primarily been descriptive, aiming to describe how emotions operate in group decisions. But future work should also address normative issues, assessing how group decision making can be improved by taking into account the ineliminable role of emotions in important choices. We can ask not only the empirical question of which mechanisms of emotional transmission are most effective in bringing a receiver around to a sender's point of view, but also the normative question of which mechanisms are most effective in securing a consensus that best reflects the interests of the whole group. Presumably coercive mechanisms such as threats and propaganda are inferior in this regard to logical and ethical mechanisms such as means–ends argument and altruism. Perhaps future computer simulations will provide a tool for evaluating the desirability of different ways in which transmission of emotional information can lead members of a group toward consensus.

Spiking Phineas Gage: A Neurocomputational Theory of
Cognitive-Affective Integration in Decision Making

Brandon Wagar and Paul Thagard

Introduction

Some people like to make decisions by flipping a coin, after assigning one choice to heads and another to tails. The point is not to make the decision indicated by the flip, but rather to see how they feel about the choice that the coin flip tells them to do. Flipping the coin is an effective way to find out their emotional reactions to various alternatives, indicating the emotional weight they attach to them. From the perspective of mathematical theories of decision making such as those that say that people do or should maximize expected utility, the coin-flip exercise is bizarre. But there is increasing appreciation in cognitive science that emotions are an integral part of decision making (e.g., Churchland 1996; Damasio 1994; Finucane, Alhakami, Slovic, and Johnson 2000; Lerner and Keltner 2000, 2001; Loewenstein, Weber, Hsee, and Welch 2001; Rottenstreich and Hsee 2001). In this paper, we present a neurocomputational theory of how the brain produces these covert emotional reactions.

Current artificial neural network models of cognitive-affective processing use simplified neurons and neglect neuroanatomical information about how different parts of the brain contribute to decision making (Mischel and Shoda 1995; Nerb and Spada 2001; Thagard 2000; chaps. 2–5 above). Here we present a new computational model, GAGE, which is much more neurologically realistic than previous models. It organizes neurons into anatomically recognized groups corresponding to crucial brain areas, including the ventromedial prefrontal cortex (VMPFC), the hippocampus, and the amygdala. Our model shows how another area, the nucleus accumbens (NAcc), can serve to integrate cognitive information from VMPFC and the hippocampus with emotional information from the amygdala. Consistent with Damasio's somatic-marker hypothesis, our model indicates that the VMPFC and the amygdala interact to produce emotional signals (i.e.,

somatic markers) indicating expected outcomes, and that these expected outcomes compete with immediate outcomes for amygdala output. However,
our model moves beyond Damasio's claim, highlighting the importance of
the NAcc gateway. In order for the somatic markers from the VMPFC and
amygdala to access those brain areas responsible for higher-order reasoning,
context information from the hippocampus must unlock the NAcc gate,
allowing this information to pass through. Also, the individual neurons in
our model are more realistic than those used in most artificial neural network
models in cognitive science, in that they exhibit the spiking behavior found in
real neurons. This level of representation highlights another important aspect
of cognitive-affective integration in the brain: time. GAGE shows that temporal coordination between the VMPFC and the amygdala is a key component when eliciting covert emotional reactions to stimuli.

Our model is implemented in a computer program that successfully simulates two kinds of cognitive-affective integration: people's performance on
the Iowa Gambling Task (Bechera, Damasio, Damasio and Anderson 1994),
and the integration of physiological arousal and cognition in determining
emotional states (Schachter and Singer 1962). In the Iowa Gambling Task,
people with intact brains are able to use covert emotional reactions to guide
their behavior when choosing cards, whereas people with damage to the
VMPFC are unable to use such reactions in order to play the game successfully. According to Bechara et al. (1994), this deficit is the result of their inability to integrate cognitive and emotional information in order to discern
the future consequences of their actions. In normal people, it is the emotional
reactions to good and bad cards that signals predicted outcomes and guides
people's behavior (cf. the coin-flip exercise). Our computational model shows
both how normal people perform cognitive-affective integration to succeed in
the Iowa Gambling Task, and why this integration breaks down in people
with damage to the ventromedial prefrontal cortex.

In addition to modeling performance on the Iowa Gambling Task, GAGE
also models the integration of physiological arousal and cognition in determining emotional states (Schachter and Singer 1962). Schachter and Singer
showed that, given a state of emotional arousal for which no immediately
appropriate explanation is available (i.e., ambiguous emotional arousal),
participants could be manipulated into states of euphoria or anger by manipulating the context. All participants were injected with epinephrine leading
to the same state of physiological arousal, yet this arousal led to different
appraisals of emotional reaction as determined by the current context.
Though we are not concerned with the high-level mechanism(s) underlying
the cognitive appraisal of one's emotional state, we are interested in the

mechanism whereby context exerts a moderating effect on the emotional re-action to different stimuli. Our computational model shows how context is capable of exerting such an effect.

The most famous person with damage to the ventromedial prefrontal cortex was a nineteenth-century patient, Phineas Gage. Our model, called GAGE in his honor, explains why his ability to make decisions declined drastically after he received brain damage presumed to have occurred in the ventromedial prefrontal cortex (Damasio et al. 1994). We therefore begin by reviewing his case and the somatic-marker hypothesis that Damasio developed to account for it. Our model is compatible with Damasio's explanation of the decision-making deficits of VMPFC damage, but goes beyond it in providing a much more detailed and computationally implemented account of the role the NAcc plays in effective and defective decision making.

Phineas Gage was the foreman of a railway construction gang working for the contractors preparing the bed for the Rutland and Burlington Rail Road near Cavendish, Vermont. On September 13, 1848, an accidental explosion of a charge he had set blew his tamping iron through his head. Most of the front part of the left side of his brain was destroyed.

Some months after the accident Phineas felt strong enough to resume work. But because his personality had changed so much, the contractors who had employed him were reluctant to reinstate him. Before the accident he had been their most capable and efficient foreman, one with a well-balanced mind, and who was looked on as a shrewd, smart businessman. He was now fitful, irreverent, and grossly profane, showing little respect for his fellow coworkers. He was also unable to settle on any of the plans he devised for future action. His friends said he was "No longer Gage" (Macmillan 2000).

It should be noted that the claim that Phineas Gage's brain damage included the VMPFC has recently been drawn into question (Macmillan 2000). Given indeterminacy about where the tamping iron entered and left the skull, individual differences in the position of the brain inside the skull, and the fact that historical accounts are questionable, we might never know the true nature of Gage's lesions. However, the fact remains that, regardless of these concerns, the folklore surrounding his story still makes Gage the most famous person with apparent damage to the ventromedial prefrontal cortex.

Damasio's Somatic-Marker Hypothesis

Phineas Gage represents the first reported case of an individual who has suffered damage to the ventromedial prefrontal cortex. What is of particular interest is the nature of the deficits resulting from damage to this brain region. Although basic cognitive, intellectual, and language skills remain intact, the ability to reason—particularly within a social context—is seriously impaired. Concretely, Gage could think and speak, yet he lost all of his friends and was unable to hold down a job. Importantly, Phineas Gage is not the only instance of this fascinating constellation of subtle deficits; there have been several other documented cases of lesions localized to the VMPFC (see Damasio 1994). In general, VMPFC damage is characterized by insensitivity to future consequences. Although the impairment is usually discussed in the context of real-life decision making (i.e., as an impairment in the ability to predict the consequences of one's actions within a complex social environment), the impairment extends to other decision-making tasks that involve distinctions between long-term and short-term consequences in an environment containing punishment and reward. Evidently, damage to the VMPFC injures the ability to predict the future consequences of one's actions and behave accordingly.

According to Antonio Damasio (1994), the VMPFC is critically involved in the production of somatic markers. Somatic markers are the feelings, or emotional reactions, that have become associated through experience with the predicted long-term outcomes of certain responses to a given situation. According to the somatic-marker hypothesis, sensory representations of a given response to the current situation activate knowledge tied in with previous emotional experience. The resulting covert emotional signals (i.e., somatic markers) act as biases influencing the mechanisms responsible for higher-level cognitive processes and/or the motor effector sites. Somatic markers assist us during the decision making process by rapidly highlighting those options that have positive predicted outcomes, and eliminating those options that have negative predicted outcomes from further consideration. Somatic markers make the decision process more efficient by narrowing the number of feasible behavioral alternatives, while allowing the organism to reason according to the long-term predicted outcomes of its actions.

Cognitive-Affective Integration in the Nucleus Accumbens

We now present a neurological theory of how cognitive information and emotional information are integrated in the NAcc during effective decision making. Damasio's proposed somatic-marker mechanism suggests that interconnections between the VMPFC and the amygdala are responsible for the formation of memory traces that allow the organism to predict the future outcome of a given response. We expand on this mechanism (see figure 6.1),

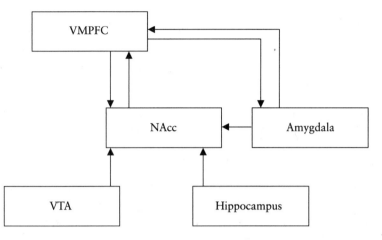

Figure 6.1
Schematic of the neuronal mechanism implemented in GAGE. VMPFC (ventromedial prefrontal cortex); NAcc (nucleus accumbens); VTA (ventral tegmental area).

discussing how somatic markers are passed on to the nucleus accumbens (NAcc), which acts as a gateway allowing only context-consistent behavior (as determined by hippocampal inputs to the NAcc), to pass through. In addition, GAGE shows that temporal coordination between the VMPFC and the amygdala is a key component to eliciting emotional reactions to stimuli. Information that passes through the NAcc is redirected back to the VMPFC and other prefrontal and neocortical sites, providing the covert emotional reaction that feeds into higher-level cognitive processes and/or the motor effector sites.

In the following sections we describe the processes of establishing predicted outcomes and gating of NAcc throughput, in more detail. We then move to a description of the predicted large-scale dynamics of the mechanism using a test of VMPFC damage as an example.

Establishing Predicted Outcomes
Emotional signals in decision making bias the organism to avoid decisions that will lead to negative future outcomes, and promote decisions that will lead to positive future outcomes. In this manner the neural basis for the production of emotional signals impels the organism to behave in ways that promote achievement and long-term survival within a given environment. To this end, the mechanism must recruit brain regions involved in the processing and storage of bodily states (in order to avoid unpleasant states and promote

homeostatic ones). It must also recruit regions responsible for cognitive processes (in order to process sensory representations), so as to be able to link the latter to the former.

Damasio (1994) highlights two key structures as primarily responsible for the production of somatic markers: the VMPFC and the amygdala. The ventromedial prefrontal cortex receives input from sensory cortices, representing the behavioral options, and from limbic structures, most notably the amygdala, which processes somatic states. Through these interconnections between cognitive and emotional processes, the VMPFC records the signals that define a given response by encoding the representations of certain stimuli and the behavioral significance of the somatic states that have been previously associated with the given response. It thereby lays down a memory trace (somatic marker) that represents a given action and the expected consequences of the action. Once the memory trace is encoded, the VMPFC houses the critical output for somatic markers to influence decision making. When a set of inputs to the VMPFC elicit a response, the VMPFC, through its reciprocal connections with the amygdala, elicits a reenactment of the bodily state consistent with the predicted future outcome of the given behavior. Then, this covert emotional reaction is passed on to overt decision making processes and/or motor effector sites. If the predicted outcome is positive, the response remains active for further consideration or is chosen for action. If the predicted outcome is negative, the option is eliminated from the set of possible alternatives.

Gating of Nucleus Accumbens Throughput

The mechanism responsible for the production of emotional signals in decision making pretunes the organism to behave in ways that promote achievement and long term survival within a given environment. To this end, Damasio's somatic-marker mechanism elicits emotional reactions signaling the predicted outcome of a given event. We now build on this mechanism, demonstrating hippocampal gating of prefrontal cortex throughput in NAcc neurons (see figure 6.2 for a schematic depiction). Our extended mechanism describes how the nucleus accumbens narrows down the alternative choices by allowing only those behaviors that are consistent with the current context to access higher-level cognitive processes and/or the motor effector sites responsible for action.

Hippocampal input limits NAcc gateway throughput to those behaviors that are consistent with the current context (figure 6.3; O'Donnell and Grace 1995). The nucleus accumbens is responsible for mediating basic locomotor and appetitive behaviors that are driven by the affective state of the organism

(Mogenson, Jones, and Yim 1980). Thus, it provides the ideal location for cognitive-affective integration during covert decision-making tasks. To this end, recent studies have shown that the NAcc is involved in reward learning (Breiter et al. 2001; Berns et al. 2001; Knutson et al. 2001), drug addiction (Hitchcott and Phillips 1997; Calabresi, De Murtas, and Bernardi 1997; Mogenson, Jones, and Yim 1980), and affective processes (Calabresi et al. 1997; Mogenson et al. 1980).

The nucleus accumbens receives afferent connections from the VMPFC, the amygdala, and the hippocampus, and massive dopamine input from the ventral tegmental area (see figure 6.1; O'Donnell and Grace 1995). The ventromedial prefrontal cortex and the amygdala produce brief, small amplitude membrane depolarizations in the NAcc, which themselves cannot cause NAcc neurons to fire (Grace and Moore 1998; O'Donnell 1999; O'Donnell and Grace 1995). This is because NAcc neurons are typically in a hyperpolarized state as a result of the massive inhibitory dopamine input from the ventral tegmental area (Grace and Moore 1998; O'Donnell, 1999; O'Donnell and Grace 1995). So, NAcc neurons are being constantly bombarded with VMPFC- and amygdala-driven excitatory post-synaptic potentials, yet none of the information is getting through. Hippocampal input, on the other hand, produces large-amplitude, long-duration, plateau-like depolarizations (Grace and Moore 1998; O'Donnell 1999; O'Donnell and Grace 1995). For the subset of NAcc neurons receiving hippocampal input, their typical hyperpolarized state is disrupted by temporary depolarization plateaus that bring NAcc neurons' activity levels close to firing threshold, thereby allowing any coincidental VMPFC and amygdala activity to elicit spike activity in NAcc neurons and pass through the NAcc gateway (see figure 6.3).

Thus, the hippocampus controls VMPFC and amygdala throughput in the NAcc by allowing only those patterns active in NAcc neurons that are consistent with the current context to elicit spike activity in NAcc neurons. The combined VMPFC and amygdala input to NAcc neurons represents the multitude of potentially effective responses (and their associated emotional reactions) to a given situation. The hippocampus influences the selection of a given response by facilitating within NAcc only those responses that are congruent with the current context.

The amygdala provides a facilitatory influence on VMPFC activity in the NAcc, but only if the amygdala activity precedes VMPFC stimulation within a brief, 40 ms period (Grace and Moore 1998; O'Donnell and Grace 1995). This event-related facilitation provides the means by which an emotional valence representing the predicted outcome of a given response can be passed through the NAcc to higher-level cognitive processes, thereby creating the

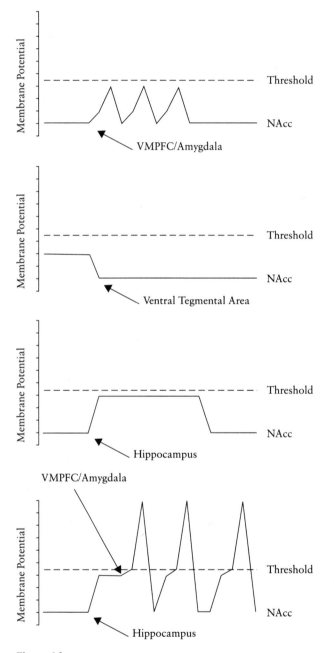

Figure 6.2
The nucleus accumbens (NAcc) gateway. A: The ventromedial prefrontal cortex (VMPFC) and the amygdala produce brief, small-amplitude membrane depolariza-

covert emotional reaction predicting the future outcome of a given response. The strict time constraint here also highlights the importance of a coincidental increase in the firing rate between the VMPFC and the amygdala in cognitive-affective integration. Because the VMPFC is constantly bombarding the NAcc with multiple patterns, the amygdala activity must be in close temporal proximity to the appropriate VMPFC response. If the amygdala input to NAcc neurons were to exert a long-lasting influence, emotional valences could become inappropriately associated with alternative responses.

Because the VMPFC elicits a predicted outcome through reciprocal connections with the amygdala, the VMPFC signal representing a given response and the amygdala signal representing the emotionally laden predicted outcome of that response are generated together and will arrive at NAcc neurons together. This allows them to fulfill the strict time constraints of the event-related facilitation previously mentioned. Also, because the amygdala produces rapid, small amplitude excitatory postsynaptic potentials, the representation of a given response and its associated emotional valence will degrade rapidly, preventing the occurrence of any possible confusion between response and predicted outcome.

To summarize, the NAcc and the hippocampus are key contributors to the covert production of emotional reactions, which can direct decision-making processes. The NAcc forms a gateway for somatic markers, and the hippocampus determines what passes through this gateway by limiting throughput to those responses that are consistent with the current environment.

Network Dynamics

To summarize information representing current context, bodily states associated with the current situation, and potential responses to or appraisals of the current situation are represented in the hippocampus, amygdala, and VMPFC, respectively (see figure 6.4 for a schematic depiction). Through memories stored in its reciprocal connections with the amygdala, the

tions in NAcc, which themselves cannot cause the NAcc neurons to fire. B: This is because NAcc neurons are typically in a hyperpolarized state as a result of the massive inhibitory dopamine input from the ventral tegmental area. C: Hippocampal input, conversely, produces large-amplitude, long-duration, plateaulike depolarizations. D: For the subset of NAcc neurons receiving hippocampal input, their typical hyperpolarized state is disrupted by temporary depolarization plateaus that bring NAcc neurons' activity levels close to firing threshold, thereby allowing any coincidental VMPFC and amygdala activity to elicit spike activity in NAcc neurons and pass through the NAcc gateway.

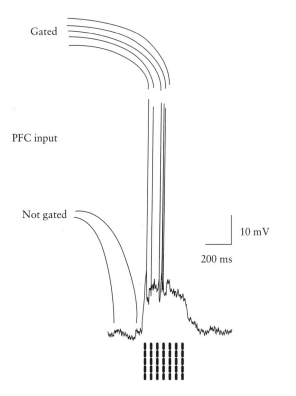

Figure 6.3
Hippocampal gating of the prefrontal cortex (PFC) throughput in nucleus accumbens (NAcc) neurons. During the down state, excitatory postsynaptic potentials (EPSPs) from the PFC afferent activation (indicated by the lines labeled *not gated*) do not result in NAcc firing. The up state is dependent on hippocampal inputs (indicated by the broken upward lines beneath the tracing). Because the up state elicited by hippocampal inputs brings the NAcc membrane potential close to firing threshold, EPSPs from the PFC afferent activation (indicated by the lines labeled *gated*) easily elicit NAcc firing. Adapted from "Ensemble Coding in the Nucleus Accumbens," by P. O'Donnell, 1999, *Psychobiology* 27, p. 188. Copyright 1999 by the Psychonomic Society. Adapted with permission.

VMPFC elicits an emotional signal representing the predicted future outcome of a given response, and this information is fed into the NAcc. Because NAcc neurons are typically in a hyperpolarized state as a result of dopamine inhibition from the ventral tegmental area, VMPFC and amygdala inputs alone are insufficient to elicit spike activity in NAcc neurons. However, a subset of NAcc neurons will become depolarized by hippocampal input representing the current context. Those responses in the VMPFC that are consistent with the current context, i.e., make synapses on NAcc neurons that are experiencing hippocampal depolarization, will then be able to elicit spike activity in NAcc neurons, thereby passing the given response and its emotionally laden predicted outcome on to higher-level cognitive processes and/or motor effector sites.

We have tested the proposed mechanism using a computer simulation that implements it in a network of spiking artificial neurons, GAGE. A critical component of the model is that input from the hippocampus is required to elicit NAcc firing. To ensure that this constraint was met, we compared in vivo electrophysiological recordings from rats (Grace and Moore 1998), and GAGE (see figure 6.5). In the intact system, the upstate elicited by hippocampal inputs depolarizes the NAcc membrane potential enabling it to elicit NAcc firing. When hippocampal input is inactivated (either by a local anaesthetic or lesioning GAGE), the NAcc membrane potential remains hyperpolarized, thereby preventing NAcc firing.

We have applied GAGE to simulations of two kinds of cognitive-affective integration: people's performance on the Iowa Gambling Task, and the integration of physiological arousal and cognition in determining emotional states. In Experiment 1, we hypothesized that the network will elicit emotional reactions (signifying which card to choose from a deck) based on the predicted outcome of a given response, even though the immediate outcome contradicts the future outcome. We specifically found that—consistent with the performance of human patients—when presented with a given response, an intact network will function in this way, whereas a network in which the VMPFC has been lesioned will make decisions based on immediate outcomes rather than future outcomes.

In Experiment 2, we hypothesized that in the presence of ambiguous emotional input, the network will elicit different emotional reactions depending on the current context. We specifically found that—consistent with the performance of human patients—when presented with an emotional input for which no immediately appropriate explanation is available, NAcc throughput is determined by the context information from the hippocampus.

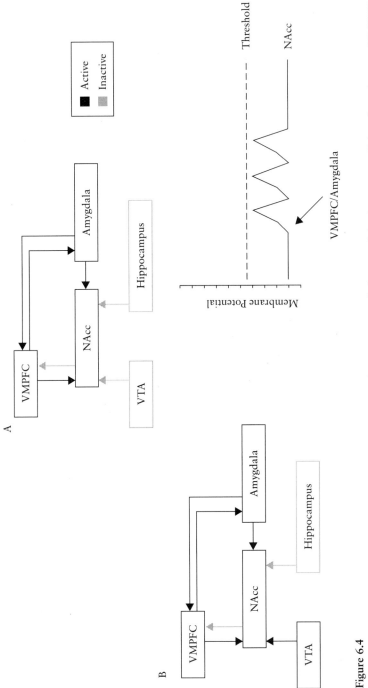

Figure 6.4
Network dynamics. A: Through memories stored in its reciprocal connections with the amygdala, the ventromedial prefrontal cortex (VMPFC) elicits an emotional signal representing the predicted future outcome of a given response, and this information is fed into the nucleus accumbens (NAcc). B: Because NAcc neurons are typically in a hyperpolarized state as a result of dopamine inhibition from the ventral tegmental area (VTA), the VMPFC and amygdala inputs alone are insufficient to elicit spike activity in NAcc neurons.

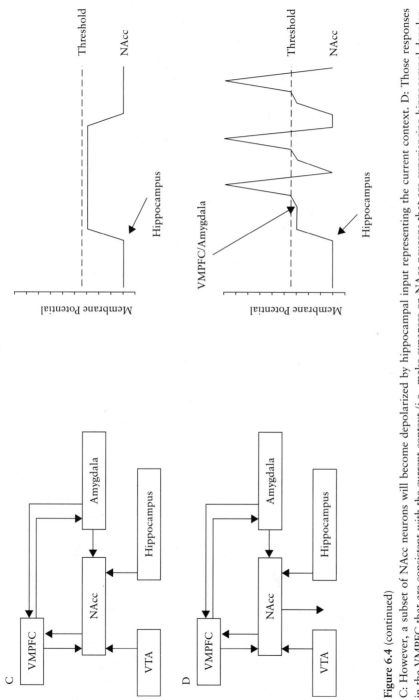

Figure 6.4 (continued)

C: However, a subset of NAcc neurons will become depolarized by hippocampal input representing the current context. D: Those responses in the VMPFC that are consistent with the current context (i.e., make synapses on NAcc neurons that are experiencing hippocampal depolarization) will then be able to elicit spike activity in NAcc neurons, thereby passing the given response and its emotionally laden predicted outcome on to higher-level cognitive processes and/or motor effector sites.

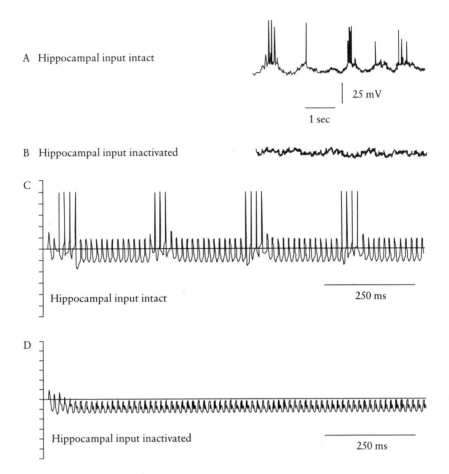

A Hippocampal input intact

25 mV

1 sec

B Hippocampal input inactivated

C

Hippocampal input intact

250 ms

D

Hippocampal input inactivated

250 ms

Figure 6.5
Input from the hippocampus is required to elicit nucleus accumbens (NAcc) firing:
Comparison of in vivo electrophysiological recording from rats (A and B) and GAGE
(C and D). A: In the intact system, the up state elicited by hippocampal inputs
depolarizes the NAcc membrane potential, enabling it to elicit NAcc firing. B: When
hippocampal input is inactivated by a local anesthetic, the NAcc membrane potential
remains hyperpolarized, thereby preventing NAcc firing. C: In the intact network, the
up state elicited by hippocampal inputs depolarizes the NAcc membrane potential,
enabling it to elicit NAcc firing. D: When hippocampal input is removed, the NAcc
membrane potential remains hyperpolarized, thereby preventing NAcc firing. A and
B are adapted from "Regulation of Information Flow in the Nucleus Accumbens: A
Model for the Pathophysiology of Schizophrenia," by A. Grace and H. Moore, in
*Origins and Development of Schizophrenia: Advances in Experimental Psychopathol-
ogy* (p. 134), 1998. Copyright 1998 by the American Psychological Association.
Adapted with permission of the author.

That is, hippocampal input elicited different emotional reactions to a given physiological state, based on the current context.

GAGE

In this section, we describe a network of spiking neurons, GAGE, based on the neural mechanism for cognitive-affective integration in the NAcc described above (see also Wagar and Thagard 2003). Figure 6.1 shows the overall architecture of the model. The model has 700 spiking neurons with 670 connections. The modeled regions consist of the VMPFC, the amygdala, the NAcc, the hippocampus, and the ventral tegmental area. Each region contains 100 neurons that receive input from other regions and/or external input, and pass information on to other regions as well as 40 inhibitory interneurons.

The pattern of afferent, efferent, and internal connectivity follows that of the proposed neural mechanism. The model includes intraregional connections and interregional connections. Individual neurons are modeled as single-compartment integrate-and-fire units, and synaptic interactions followed a Hebbian-based learning rule.

In the following section we describe the layout of the various connection pathways. The equations for the neuronal and synaptic learning properties are summarized in the appendix of Wagar and Thagard (2004; see also Wagar and Thagard 2003).

Connectivity

In constructing the model, emphasis was put on the incorporation of realistic network properties for the relative proportions of the various sets of connections composing the inter- and intraregional circuitry. Specific patterns of connectivity were classified as either sparse or dense on the basis of anatomical data. The sparse connection pattern resulted in each presynaptic neuron forming synapses with 30 percent of the neurons in the postsynaptic population. The dense connection pattern resulted in each presynaptic neuron forming synapses with 60 percent of the neurons in the postsynaptic population. Synaptic connections were distributed evenly over the postsynaptic population, with the pattern of connectivity determined in a random fashion. All connection strengths were initialized to a random value.

Interregional connectivity As can be seen from figure 6.1, the NAcc receives afferent connections from all four of the remaining regions, each of which form a dense connectivity pattern with NAcc transmission neurons

(Calabresi et al. 1997; Mogenson et al. 1980). The ventromedial prefrontal cortex receives afferent connections from the NAcc and the amygdala, with the former establishing a dense connectivity pattern (Calabresi et al. 1997; Mogenson et al. 1980), while the latter establishes a sparse connectivity pattern (Aggleton 2000). The amygdala receives afferent connections from the VMPFC, which is also sparse (Aggleton 2000).

Intraregional connections   Each of the modeled brain regions in the network contains inhibitory interneurons modeling the presence of basket cells in these neuronal populations. Basket cells project predominantly to the same layer where their soma are located, and execute fast-acting inhibitory postsynaptic potentials. In the model, basket-like inhibitory interneurons receive and project dense connections within each region.

Also modeled in our network are the NAcc gap junctions responsible for the lateral transfer of information among NAcc transmission neurons (O'Donnell 1999). These gap junctions were modeled as having very sparse (5%) connectivity between each of the transmission neurons in the NAcc population.

Simulations

All simulations were run using a program written in Java. Numerical integration of the differential equations for the membrane potentials and synaptic weight were performed with a time step of approximately 0.5 ms. The generation of noise and statistical distribution of model parameters was based on Java's random number generator routines. The simulations were performed on a PC equipped with 640 Mbytes of memory and a 750 MHz processor.

Experiment 1

The goal of Experiment 1 was to test GAGE's ability to simulate experimental results concerning the Iowa Gambling Task (Bechera et al. 1994). In this task, individuals are given a $2,000 loan of play money, four decks of cards, and instructed to make a series of card selections from any of the four decks, until they are told to stop. Participants are instructed to play so that they maximize profit on the loan. Turning each card carries an immediate reward (which is large in decks A and B, and small in decks C and D). Additionally, after turning some cards, the participants receive both a reward and a punishment (which is large in decks A and B, and small in decks C and D). Playing mostly from the bad decks (A and B) results in an overall loss. Playing from the good decks (C and D) results in an overall profit. Decks A and B are equivalent in terms of overall net loss, but in deck A the punishment is more frequent and of smaller magnitude than in deck B. Decks C and D are equivalent in terms of overall net gain, but in deck C the punishment is more frequent and of smaller magnitude than in deck D. Participants are told that they are free to switch from any deck to another, at any time, and as often as they wish. However, participants are not told how many card selections must be made, and are blind to the punishment schedules.

Typically, after encountering a few losses normal participants adopt the strategy of picking predominantly from the good decks and avoiding the bad decks. This has been interpreted as indicating that normal participants are generating predicted outcomes in the form of covert emotional reactions (Bechera et al. 1994, 1997). However, patients with VMPFC damage are oblivious to the future consequences of their actions, and pick predominantly from the bad decks. This is because such patients appear to be guided by immediate rewards (the high initial reward from the bad decks) rather than future outcomes (the overall profit from the good decks). The goal of Experiment 1 was to simulate the above described experimental results concerning the Iowa Gambling Task using GAGE.

Stimuli To simplify the experiment we limited the stimuli to two decks rather than four. Because the punishment schedule (for example, the difference between decks A and B), was not a predictive factor in the original experiments (see Bechera et al. 1994), we collapsed across decks A and B to form a single bad deck, and decks C and D to form a single good deck. On each trial in the experiment, GAGE was presented with a set of stimulus patterns consisting of activation vectors feeding into the VMPFC, the ventral tegmental area, the hippocampus, and the amygdala. Each pattern consisted of 50 active units (thereby exciting 50% of the neurons in the receiving region). The ventromedial prefrontal cortex received either an activation pattern representing the good deck, or an activation pattern representing the bad deck. The amygdala received an activation pattern representing a positive body state, or an activation pattern representing a negative body state. To simplify the task, each set of patterns (good deck/bad deck, positive/negative body state) forms a complementary pair.

Stimulation was achieved by applying constant synaptic excitation independently to each neuron corresponding to nodes active in the stimulus pattern.

Procedure Initially, GAGE was trained on two combinations of stimuli: good deck with positive body state, and bad deck with negative body state.

This produced the requisite somatic markers between the VMPFC and the amygdala. Training occurred in an interleaved fashion over 4,000 time steps, alternating stimulus combinations (positive body state/good deck and negative body state/bad deck) every 400 time steps.

Hebbian learning was then turned off, and the model was presented for epochs of 2,000 time steps each with the positive body state/good deck and negative body state/bad deck stimuli in order to establish baseline ensemble activity in the NAcc for the expected representations.

Finally, the model was presented for epochs of 2,000 time steps with each of the test stimulus combinations. Test stimuli consisted of a given choice (for example, good deck) and its immediate body state (for example, negative body state). This allowed us to test whether the network would elicit emotional reactions based on future outcomes (for example, pick the good deck even though the immediate outcome is negative) or immediate rewards (for example, pick the bad deck even though the overall outcome is negative).

Hippocampal and ventral tegmental area inputs were constant throughout training, baseline, and test. The above experiments were performed with an intact network (simulating normal participants), and with a network in which the VMPFC had been removed after training (simulating patients with VMPFC damage). GAGE was lesioned by deleting all VMPFC connections.

Data collection and analysis   The spike trains (step-by-step record of whether a neuron was firing or not) for each neuron in the network were recorded for the entire run of the experiment. In order to characterize the ensemble activation pattern of the NAcc population (i.e., the subgroup of NAcc neurons that responded to each stimulus), spike trains were converted into rate graphs. This was accomplished by placing a 20-time-step window over the spike train at each time step, and taking the average number of spikes (i.e., the firing rate) within the window.

Once the rate graphs were acquired, cluster analysis was used in order to separate the entire NAcc population into those neurons that were active in response to the stimulus and those that were not responsive (see Everitt, Landau, and Leese 2001). In cluster analysis, a cluster is defined as a subset of elements that are cohesive among themselves but relatively isolated from the remaining elements. Cluster analysis sorts cases (for example, neurons) into groups, or clusters, so that the degree of association is strong between members of the same cluster (for example, neurons that are active) and weak between members of different clusters (for example, neurons that are inactive). This was done for the baseline representations and the test representations.

The test representations were then compared to the baseline representations to determine the emotional reactions that GAGE passed through the NAcc in response to each of the decks. In order to determine GAGE's ability to elicit appropriate emotional reactions in response to test stimuli, signal detection theory was used. In this analysis, A' was calculated (Snodgrass, Levy-Berger, and Haydon 1985). A' is a nonparametric analog to d', the signal detection measure of sensitivity. To analyze the data we calculate a hit rate, which is the proportion of active neurons in the baseline representation that were also active in the test representation, and a false alarm rate, which is the proportion of inactive neurons in the baseline representation that were also inactive in the test representation. This information was used to determine A' for each test representation. A' varies from 0 to 1 with 0.5 indicating chance performance. The larger the A', the closer the test representation is to the baseline representation. The closer the test representation is to the baseline representation, the better is GAGE's ability to elicit appropriate emotional reactions in response to test stimuli.

Results and discussion   To obtain a measure of GAGE's overall performance, all results were averaged over 50 replications of the experiment (with activation patterns and weights generated randomly for each replication). The results are presented in figure 6.6.

The task of the network was to elicit a positive or negative emotional reaction given a choice (for example, good deck) and an inconsistent body state (for example, negative). That is, after having been trained on the predicted affective outcomes of each deck, the network was tested by presenting the VMPFC and the amygdala with activation patterns that simulated a condition in which future outcome and immediate outcome were in opposition. The goal was to determine whether an intact GAGE would elicit NAcc activation representing emotional reactions. based on predicted future outcomes, whereas a VMPFC-lesioned GAGE would elicit NAcc activation representing emotional reactions based on immediate outcomes.

As expected, the predicted affective outcome of a given response drives GAGE's behavior when the VMPFC is intact. Stored associations between the VMPFC and the amygdala are able to elicit a representation of the predicted future outcome of a given response. This information is then fed forward into the NAcc, and if it is consistent with the current context it is passed on to higher-level cognitive processes and/or the motor effector sites in the form of an emotional reaction.

Figure 6.6A shows the pattern of activity in NAcc neurons representing GAGE's ability to elicit appropriate emotional reactions in response to test

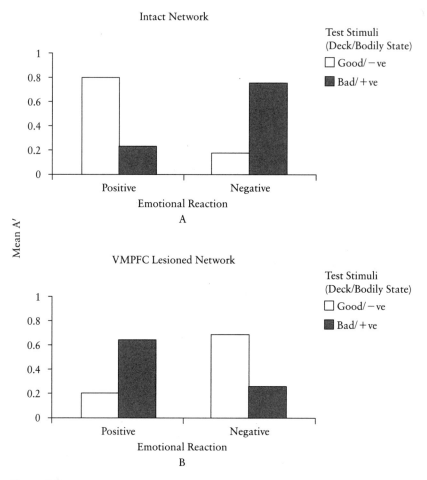

Figure 6.6

Mean A (representing similarity to baseline) for test stimuli as a function of emotional reaction when GAGE is intact (A) and when the ventromedial prefrontal cortex (VMPFC) is lesioned in GAGE (B).

stimuli. As can be seen, even in the presence of a conflicting emotional signal representing the immediate affective outcome of the response, GAGE elicits emotional reactions based on the predicted future outcome of the response. Assuming that the valence of these emotional reactions indicates which deck GAGE will choose from, the results show that when the VMPFC is intact, GAGE will predominantly choose from the good deck rather than the bad deck. It should be noted, however, that GAGE's performance was not all or none; there were a small percentage of occasions when GAGE produced the complementary patterns of activity (eliciting a negative emotional reaction when presented with the good deck, 8%; eliciting a positive emotional reaction when presented with the bad deck, 6%). This is consistent with the performance of normal participants on the Iowa Gambling Task described above. Choosing from the good deck is the most efficient decision, as it ensures that an organism will behave in ways that promote long-term survival, rather than short-term satisfaction. However, even normal participants take a risk sometimes and pick from the bad decks (Bechara et al. 1994).

On the other hand, results from individuals suffering from VMPFC damage suggest that the mechanism no longer functions effectively. In these patients immediate affective outcomes drive behavior rather than long-term benefits. Damage to the VMPFC prevents stored associations from eliciting a representation of the predicted future outcome of a given response. Thus, the only information fed into the NAcc is that which is initiated by the amygdala's response to current body states. Because the response promoted by this information is consistent with the current context (for example, picking from the bad deck), the amygdala-driven decision is passed on to higher cognitive processes and/or the motor effector sites.

Figure 6.4B shows the pattern of activity in NAcc neurons representing GAGE's ability to elicit appropriate emotional reactions in response to test stimuli when the VMPFC has been lesioned. As can be seen, the immediate affective reward of a given response now drives behavior. GAGE now elicits emotional reactions based on the immediate outcome of the response. Again, assuming that the valence of these emotional reactions indicates which deck GAGE will choose from, the results show that when VMPFC is damaged, GAGE will choose from the bad deck rather than the good deck. This is consistent with the performance of VMPFC-damaged patients on the Iowa Gambling Task described above. Rather than behaving in an efficient manner and promoting decisions based on long-term survival, the organism will behave in ways that appear impulsive and even irrational, as did Phineas Gage.

Experiment 2

The goal of Experiment 2 was to test GAGE's ability to simulate experimental results concerning the integration of physiological arousal and cognition in determining emotional states (Schachter and Singer 1962). Schachter and Singer injected participants with epinephrine and then had participants fill out questionnaires in the presence of a confederate. In the euphoria condition the cohort was pleasant, whereas in the anger condition the cohort was unpleasant. Results showed that the same dose of epinephrine led to different emotional experiences depending on the context: participants showed pleasant emotional experiences in the euphoric condition, and unpleasant emotional experiences in the anger condition. Given a constant state of sympathetic activation, for which no immediately appropriate explanation is available (i.e., amygdala input is ambiguous), participants can be manipulated into states of euphoria or anger depending on the current context. It is important to note that the claims made by the Schachter theory of emotion have been drawn into question (for example, Reisenzein 1983). However, the goal of Experiment 2 was to simulate the role of context in cognitive-affective integration using GAGE. We are not concerned with the high-level mechanisms underlying the cognitive appraisal of one's emotional state. Instead, we are only interested in the mechanism whereby context exerts a moderating effect on the emotional reaction to different stimuli.

Stimuli   On each trial in the experiment, GAGE was presented with a set of stimulus patterns consisting of activation vectors feeding into the VMPFC, the ventral tegmental area, the hippocampus and the amygdala. Each pattern consisted of 35 active units (thereby exciting 35% of the neurons in the receiving region). In order to perform the tests, the VMPFC and the hippocampus required two separate activation patterns each. Note that in Experiment 1, context (i.e., hippocampal input) was held constant while body signal (i.e., amygdala input) was manipulated; whereas in Experiment 2 context was manipulated and bodily input was held constant. The ventromedial prefrontal cortex received either an activation pattern representing the euphoria appraisal, or an activation pattern representing the anger appraisal. The hippocampus received an activation pattern representing a pleasant context, or an activation pattern representing an unpleasant context. Again, to simplify the task, each set of patterns (euphoria/anger appraisal, pleasant/unpleasant context) forms a complementary pair.

Procedure   Initially, GAGE was trained on two combinations of stimuli: euphoria appraisal with pleasant context, and anger appraisal with unpleasant context. This produced the requisite associations between VMPFC and hippocampal synapses in NAcc dendrites. Training occurred in an interleaved fashion over 4,000 time steps, alternating stimulus combinations every 400 time steps.

Hebbian learning was then turned off, and the model was then presented for epochs of 2,000 time steps each with the euphoria/pleasant and anger/unpleasant stimuli in order to establish baseline ensemble activity in the NAcc for the expected representations.

Finally, the model was presented for epochs of 2,000 time steps with each of the test-stimulus combinations. Test stimuli consisted of both appraisals (euphoria and anger) presented simultaneously with a given context (pleasant or unpleasant). This allowed us to test whether the network would elicit emotional reactions based on the current context. Amygdala and ventral tegmental area inputs were constant throughout training, baseline, and test.

Data collection and analysis Data collection and analyses were as described in Experiment 1.

Results and discussion To obtain a measure of GAGE's overall performance, we averaged all results over 50 replications of the experiment (with activation patterns and weights generated randomly for each replication). The results are presented in figure 6.7.

The task of the network was to elicit a euphoric or anger appraisal given a context (for example, pleasant). The network was tested by presenting the VMPFC and the hippocampus with activation patterns that simulated a

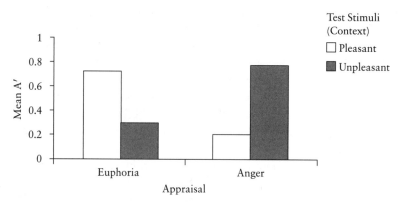

Figure 6.7
Mean A for test stimuli as a function of appraisal with constant amygdala input.

condition in which both euphoric and anger appraisals were active in the VMPFC. The goal was to determine whether GAGE would elicit emotional reactions based on the current context.

As expected, hippocampal-determined context drove GAGE's behavior when the NAcc was presented with two different VMPFC representations simultaneously. Stored associations between the VMPFC and the hippocampus in NAcc dendrites are able to elicit a representation consistent with the current context.

General Discussion

Experiment 1 shows both how normal people perform cognitive-affective integration to succeed in the Iowa Gambling Task, and why this integration breaks down in people with damage to the ventromedial prefrontal cortex. Consistent with Damasio's somatic-marker hypothesis, we show that the VMPFC and the amygdala interact to produce emotional signals indicating expected outcomes, and that these expected outcomes compete with immediate outcomes for amygdala output. In addition, GAGE shows that temporal coordination between the VMPFC and the amygdala is a key component to eliciting emotional reactions to stimuli.

Experiment 2 shows how context is capable of exerting an effect on cognitive-affective integration. It does so by highlighting the importance of hippocampal input to the NAcc gateway. In order for the signals from the VMPFC and amygdala to access brain areas responsible for higher-order reasoning, context information from the hippocampus must unlock the NAcc gate, allowing this information to pass through.

In this paper we presented a new computational model of decision making that is much more neurologically realistic than previous models. GAGE organizes neurons into populations related to brain areas, including the VMPFC, the hippocampus, and the amygdala. GAGE shows how the NAcc integrates cognitive information from the VMPFC and the hippocampus with emotional information from the amygdala. Consistent with Damasio's somatic-marker hypothesis, we showed that the VMPFC and the amygdala interact to produce emotional signals indicating expected outcomes, and that these expected outcomes compete with immediate outcomes for amygdala output. GAGE then moves beyond this claim, highlighting the importance of the NAcc gateway. In order for the signals from the VMPFC and the amygdala to pass through NAcc to access brain areas responsible for higher-order reasoning, the hippocampus must unlock the NAcc gate. Furthermore, the individual neurons in our model are more realistic than those used in most artificial neural network models, in that they exhibit the spiking behavior found in real neurons. This level of representation highlights another important aspect of cognitive-affective integration in the brain: time. GAGE shows that temporal coordination between the VMPFC and the amygdala is a key component to eliciting emotional reactions to stimuli.

GAGE is capable of producing effective decision-making strategies similar to those observed in normal humans, as well as the defective decision-making exhibited by modern-day equivalents of Phineas Gage. It does so by exhibiting a phenomenon like cognitive-affective integration during covert decision making. The central idea is that the VMPFC establishes predicted outcomes of responses through its connections with the amygdala, and that this information is passed through the context-moderated gateway in the NAcc in order to promote behaviors that are most beneficial to the long-term survival of the organism within the current environment.

The Iowa Gambling Task is a clinical test of VMPFC damage, and GAGE is capable of simulating successful performance by people with normal cognitive-affective integration, and unsuccessful performance by people with damage to the VMPFC. Also, by implementing the proposed neurological theory of how cognitive information and emotional information are integrated in effective decision making, GAGE has the capacity to move beyond this particular situation. In the Iowa Gambling Task, poor choices (picking the bad deck) are consistent with the current context. However, GAGE is more robust in its ability to model the neural basis for the production of emotional signals in decision making so as to promote achievement and long-term survival within a given environment. As was mentioned above, VMPFC damage causes the ability to reason—particularly within a social context—to become seriously impaired. Although the Iowa Gambling Task is an effective test of VMPFC damage, it fails to factor in the role of context. Thus, GAGE is capable of incorporating the role of context via its implementation of NAcc, ventral tegmental area, and hippocampal interrelations.

Experiment 2 provides a test of this capacity. Hippocampally determined context drives GAGE's behavior when the NAcc is presented with two different VMPFC representations simultaneously. Stored associations between the VMPFC and the hippocampus in NAcc dendrites are able to elicit a representation consistent with the current context.

The ability to replicate human performance in the Iowa Gambling Task, and the capacity to incorporate the role of context, demonstrate that GAGE, and the underlying neurological theory, contribute to current understanding of decision making. According to the affect-as-information hypothesis, feelings influence decision making when experienced as reactions to the imminent decision, but not if attributed to an irrelevant source (Clore, Schwarz, and Conway 1994). The constraints imposed by our neurological theory demand that in order for emotional information from the amygdala to be tied in with VMPFC activity as it passes through the NAcc gateway, the two must occur in close temporal proximity. That is, in order to bind cognition and emotion in the NAcc, VMPFC and amygdala activity must exhibit a coincidental increase in firing rate. Given this constraint, it does not seem surprising that researchers have found that feelings affect judgments when experienced as reactions to the imminent decision, but not if attributed to an irrelevant source (Clore et al. 1994). If a given event (choosing a card) is associated with a given emotion, the two will co-occur in the brain—i.e., they will exhibit a coincidental increase in firing rate. If this is the case, then they will impact the NAcc in close temporal proximity and be associated with one another. If, however, they are not associated with one another, they will fire out of phase with one another. As a result, they will not be bound in the NAcc and the emotion will not be attributed to the event.

According to the risk-as-feelings hypothesis, feelings of fear in the face of a decision have an all-or-none characteristic (Loewenstein et al. 2001). Concretely, participants are sensitive to the possibility rather than the probability of negative outcomes. Here too, GAGE can shed some light on how the neural underpinnings of cognitive-affective integration produce this phenomenon. The basic idea is that feelings of fear, or any emotional reaction in a decision-making task, are insensitive to probability variations. Recall that NAcc neurons are being constantly bombarded with VMPFC- and amygdala-driven excitatory postsynaptic potentials. That is, the VMPFC elicits several possible reactions to/appraisals of the current situation, and the hippocampus sorts through these options to find those that are context-consistent. Implicit in this statement is the idea that VMPFC signals do not carry more or less weight relative to one another (i.e., they do not carry probability information). The emotional reactions elicited by the NAcc are immediate affective responses, providing fast but crude assessments of the current situation (Damasio 1994; see also LeDoux 1996). As such, the emotional reactions described here simply signal affective significance of a given reaction/appraisal. The role of probability might be factored into the decision process later, once the emotional reactions elicited here have been passed on to brain areas responsible for higher-order decision-making processes. But by then the emotion has already been elicited, hence the all-or-none characteristic of emotional reactions in decision making.

Limitations of GAGE

Although GAGE and the underlying neurological theory increase our understanding of how cognitive information and emotional information are integrated in the NAcc during effective decision making, it is important to note that it does not answer every question. There are several levels on which GAGE is too simple or underspecified to address important questions.

Given the discussion presented thus far, one would have to conclude that if the NAcc were lesioned, the entire network would fall apart. However, given the plasticity of the brain there are alternate brain areas (for example, the cingulate or the supplementary motor area), which may compensate in the event of striate lesions. Given the limited number of brain areas currently implemented, GAGE is unable to address this issue. Also, the current implementations of GAGE focus on VMPFC lesions and the role of the hippocampus under uncertainty. Further simulations will be needed to clarify what happens when either the amygdala or the hippocampus are lesioned. Finally, it is important to note that GAGE only models how the brain produces covert emotional reactions—it is not concerned with the high-level mechanisms underlying overt decisions or the cognitive appraisal of one's emotional state.

Conclusion

There is increasing appreciation in cognitive science that emotions are an integral part of decision making. GAGE and the underlying neurological theory increase our understanding of the neural cause of the covert emotional reactions that are an essential part of effective decision making. In addition, GAGE's ability to incorporate the role of context in determining emotional signals endorses the ability to model other appraisal processes, and other kinds of cognitive-affective integration in general.

While there are limitations to the model, with time and closer implementation of neuroanatomical mechanisms, GAGE may be improved so as to simulate the process of human decision making to an even greater extent. As such, GAGE represents a first step in using computational neuroscience to aid in our understanding of human decision making and what goes wrong in the brain when these skills become impaired, and may even help us to formulate better hypotheses concerning how to compensate for or correct the problems.

Introduction

The functioning of brains in humans and other animals involves dozens of chemical messengers, including neurotransmitters, hormones, and other molecules. Yet almost all computational models of the mind and brain ignore molecular details. Symbolic models such as those based on production rules abstract entirely from neurological details (e.g., Anderson 1993; Newell 1990). Neural-network computational models typically treat neuronal processing as an electrical phenomenon in which the firing of one neuron affects the firing of all neurons connected to it by excitatory and inhibitory links (e.g., Churchland and Sejnowski 1992; Eliasmith and Anderson 2003; Levine 2000; Parks, Levine, and Long 1998; Rumelhart and McClelland 1986; see also such journals as *Cognitive Science*, *Neural Computing*, *Neural Networks*, and *Neurocomputing*). The role of neurotransmitters and other molecules in determining this electrical activity is rarely discussed.

The neglect of neurochemistry in cognitive science would be appropriate if the computational properties of brains relevant to explaining mental functioning were in fact electrical rather than chemical. But there is considerable evidence that chemical complexity really does matter to brain computation. I will review that evidence by discussing the role of proteins in intracellular computation, the operations of synapses and neurotransmitters, and the effects of neuromodulators such as hormones. Attending to the ways in which the brain is a chemical as well as an electrical computer provides a qualitatively different view of mental computation than is found in traditional symbolic and connectionist models. I conclude with a discussion of the implications of neurochemical computation for issues involving emotions, cognition, and artificial intelligence. First some general remarks are needed concerning the explanatory functions of computational models of mind.

Modeling the Mind

During the 1930s, Alan Turing and others produced rigorous mathematical accounts of computation, and in the 1940s the first general digital computers were built. The development of the theory and practice of computation had a huge impact on psychology and the philosophy of mind, because it showed how thought could plausibly be construed as mechanical. Psychologists such as George Miller and philosophers such as Hilary Putnam recognized the computational construal of mind as a powerful alternative to behaviorist ideas that had tried to make the mind go away. Allan Newell and Herbert Simon and other researchers began to produce computer programs that model intelligent behavior.

Abstract models of computation include the Turing machine, which is an imaginary device consisting of a tape with squares that contain a 0 or 1 and a head that can move from square to square. A table of very simple instructions completely determines the movements and reading and writing behavior of the head. The Turing machine, and mathematically equivalent abstractions such as recursive function theory, are very useful for clarifying what computation is. But they play no direct role in explaining particular mental functions. In order to explain particular kinds of mental abilities such as problem solving and language use, researchers develop specific kinds of computational models that posit mental representations such as rules and computational procedures such as forward chaining that operate on those rules. Rule-based systems are much better cognitive models than Turing machines because they concretely describe mechanisms that can replicate mental behavior. As far as abstract computational power goes, rule-based systems are no more powerful than a Turing machine, but they are much closer to capturing the mechanisms that underlie cognitive functions.

Besides rules, many cognitive scientists espouse alternative or complementary ways of modeling the mind, involving such representations as concepts, mental models, analogies, visual imagery, and artificial neural networks (Thagard 2005). In particular, artificial neural networks have the same abstract computational power as Turing machines and rule-based systems, but they are advocated by many researchers because they implement structures and procedures that seem to capture more closely the operations of the brain. For example, the brain uses distributed representations in which symbolic information is represented collectively by numerous simple neuronal elements, and uses massively parallel computations to draw inferences. Neural networks can be used to implement rule-based systems, but they also can support modes of computing qualitatively different from those in rule-based systems.

Most cognitive models using artificial neural networks describe the behavior of neurons by a parameter called *activation*, which represents the firing rate of the neuron, i.e., the rate at which it sends an electrical signal to other neurons. Recent models have more sophisticated dynamics, describing not only the rate of firing but the pattern of firing. Consider, for example, a neuron that fires 5 times, with the firing state represented by a 1 and the resting state represented by a 0. The firing pattern 10101 and the pattern 11100 both show the same rate of activation (firing 3 times out of 5), but they can represent very different neuronal behaviors. Neural networks that take into account such firing patterns are called *spiking* or *pulse* networks, and they have computational advantages over networks that only use rate codes. For example, there are functions that can be computed by a single spiking neuron whose computation would require many traditional rate-coding neurons (Maass and Bishop 1999, p. 79). Moreover, spiking neurons have psychologically important qualitative properties such as becoming synchronized with each other, and neural synchrony has been proposed as a crucial ingredient in inference, analogy, and consciousness (Engel et al. 1999; Hummel and Holyoak 1998; Shastri and Ajjanagadde 1993). Thus spiking neural networks provide a promising new approach to computational modeling of the brain.

I have gone into this brief review of cognitive modeling to indicate the form of argument that I want to develop. Just as rule-based models capture aspects of cognition that Turing machines do not address, and just as neural networks capture aspects of cognition that rule-based systems do not address, and just as spiking neural networks capture aspects of cognition that rate-coded neural networks do not address; so chemical neural networks have the potential to illuminate aspects of thinking that purely electrical neural networks do not adequately address. In order to provide a useful supplement to existing computational accounts of mind, a new account must show that it has quantitative and qualitative advantages over old models, suggesting mechanisms of mental computing that are more powerful and more biologically and psychologically natural than in previous models. My task is to show that such advantages are to be found in chemical neural networks that explicitly recognize molecular mechanisms.

I do not mean to suggest that molecular models should supersede existing ones. Models are like maps, intended to correspond to reality but varying greatly in the level of detail that is useful for different purposes. To determine that Italy is south of Switzerland, a large scale map of the world is appropriate, whereas a much more detailed map is better for hiking in the Alps. Similarly, there are aspects of mental computing that are conveniently and accurately describable by rule-based systems and traditional electrical neural networks, but there are also aspects for which it is explanatorily useful to move down to the molecular level.

Proteins and Cells

How neurons and neural networks can perform computations is well understood. Each neuron receives and integrates electrical signals from other neurons, then passes its own signal on to other neurons to excite or inhibit their signaling. Neural networks are Turing complete, in that they can compute any function that a Turing machine can, and more importantly they can behave in ways that account for human cognitive functions. Only recently, however, have the computational capabilities of nonneuronal cells been appreciated.

The human body contains trillions of cells, and a typical cell contains around a billion protein molecules, with about 10,000 different kinds of protein in each cell (Lodish et al. 2000). The outer membranes of cells have *receptors*, which are proteins that bind signaling molecules circulating outside the cells. The receipt of a signaling molecule by a receptor activates *signal-transduction* proteins within the cell that initiate chemical reactions affected by *enzymes*, which are proteins that accelerate reactions involving small molecules. The chemical pathways within a cell can lead to diverse results, including cell division producing new cells, cell death, and the production of new signaling molecules that are expelled from the cell and then circulate to be bound by the receptors of other cells. For example, when the hormone epinephrine (also known as adrenaline) is produced by the adrenal gland in response to fright or heavy exercise, it circulates through the blood stream and binds to cells with appropriate receptors. These include liver cells that are stimulated to emit glucose into the blood stream, and heart muscle cells that increase the heart's contraction rate and the supply of blood to the tissues. The result is an increase in available energy for major motor muscles.

We can think of individual cells, whether neurons or not, as computers that have inputs in the form of molecules that bind to receptor proteins, outputs in the form of molecules emitted from the cells, and internal processes carried out by chemical reactions involving proteins (Gross 1998). Proteins can function as on-off switches, for example by the process of *phosphorylation* in which proteins are modified by adding groups of atoms including phosphorus. Signals within a cell can be rapidly amplified by enzymes that can each activate hundreds of molecules in the next stage of processing. Molecular computing within the cell is massively parallel, in that many receptors can simultaneously initiate many chemical reactions that proceed concurrently in the billion or so proteins in the cell.

Multicellular computing also exhibits massive parallelism as cells independently receive and send signals to each other. There are three types of signaling by secreted molecules (Lodish et al. 2000, chap. 20). In *autocrine* signaling, a cell signals itself by secreting molecules that bind to its own receptors. For example, cells often secrete growth factors that stimulate their own proliferation. In *paracrine* signaling, a secretory cell signals an adjacent cell that has receptors for the secreted molecules. Neuronal signaling is paracrine, with neurotransmitters as the molecular signals, but there are also other kinds of paracrine signaling involved in cellular communication. Adjacent cells can also communicate with each other more directly than via secretions, by means of the attachment proteins that enable cells to adhere to each other and form tissues. The third type of signaling by secreted molecules is *endocrine*, in which a cell secretes a molecule, called a *hormone*, that travels through blood vessels to be received by distant target cells that may be several meters away. The computational functions of hormones are discussed below.

Is describing proteins and cells as performing computations a stretched metaphor that violates the mathematically precise notion of computation developed by Turing and others? Not at all, for there are several recent mathematical and experimental results that show that molecular processing is computational in the most rigorous sense. Magnasco (1997) proved that chemical kinetics is Turing universal in that the operations of a Turing machine can be carried out by chemical reactions. Bray (1995) showed how protein molecules can function as computational elements in living cells and can even be trained like a neural network. Adleman (1994) demonstrated that a hard combinatorial problem in computer science could be solved by molecular computation involving strands of DNA. DNA can provide cells with a kind of permanent memory, whereas protein operations serve to process information. Thus the description of cells and proteins as carrying out computations is more than metaphorical, and therefore is potentially relevant to understanding mental computation. Whether it is actually relevant requires looking more closely at the behavior of neurons.

Neurotransmitters

Properties of Neurotransmitters
The last section discussed the signaling capabilities of cells in general, but was not meant to suggest that organs such as the liver have mental properties.

Human minds depend on a particular kind of organ, the brain, which has billions of cells capable of interacting with each other in special ways. A typical neuron takes input from more than a thousand neurons, and provides output to thousands of others, via special connections called synapses. Some synapses are electrical, passing ions directly from one cell to another, but most are chemical, enabling neurons to excite or inhibit each other by means of neurotransmitters that pass from the presynaptic cell to the postsynaptic cell. Neurotransmitters are not the only chemicals that allow one neuron to influence another; the next section will discuss hormones and other molecules that modulate the effects of neurotransmitters. Human brain chemistry is fundamentally the same as that found in other vertebrates.

The most important neurotransmitters include: aspartic acid and glutamic acid (excitatory), gamma-aminobutyric acid and glycine (inhibitory), epinephrine (also a hormone), acetylcholine, dopamine, norepinephrine, serotonin, histamine, neurotensin, and endorphins. Does the abundance of different neurotransmitters used by the brain matter to mental computation? One might argue that the only computational significance is in the excitatory and inhibitory behavior of synaptic connections, and that the particular chemicals involved in excitation and inhibition are largely irrelevant to how the brain computes. I propose, however, that the array of neurotransmitters makes both qualitative and quantitative differences to mental processing, affecting both its style and speed.

The computational operation of a neural network depends on three kinds of properties of the network. The first is the internal processing capability of the neurons in the network, which may vary depending on how much the neuron can do with the various inputs coming to it and how complex its outputs can be. Most models of artificial neural networks used in cognitive science have very simple processing power, enabling them to translate input activation into output activation. Spiking neural networks have greater internal processing power in that they can respond differently to different patterns of spikes coming into them, and they produce different output patterns of spiking behavior, not just a rate of activation. The earlier discussion of the computational power of proteins showed that chemical neurons have still greater internal processing power than those found in artificial spiking networks, because the chemical reactions that occur within cells are qualitatively and quantitatively different from the electrical integration and firing performed by spiking neurons.

The second key property is the topography of the network, which is the pattern of connectivity that enables one neuron to affect the firing of another. In typical artificial neural networks, topography is determined by the excitatory and inhibitory links that connect neurons, but we shall see that chemical brains have a greatly enhanced topography. The third key kind of property is temporal. A neural network is a dynamic system that evolves over time, and how it evolves is very much affected by the order and rate of different occurrences in it. For example, artificial neural networks are sometimes synchronous, with all neurons having their activations updated at the same time, but it is more biologically natural when they are asynchronous. Real neurons are asynchronous and depend on temporal history in the form of the spike patterns that are input to them. Spiking neural networks thus have temporal properties that are different from rate-activation networks, although they are no different topographically from rate-activation networks. Chemical networks differ in all of these kinds of properties—internal processing, topographical, and temporal—from purely electrical networks. I will now discuss the topographic and temporal effects of neurotransmitters and neuromodulators.

Topographic Effects of Neurotransmitter Pathways

Neurotransmitters occur in specific nerve pathways in the brain (Brown 1994, p. 70). A pathway consists of connected neurons whose synapses all involve the transmission of the same chemical. For example, there are specific pathways for acetylcholine, dopamine, norepinephrine, and serotonin. Different pathways have different functions, for example the integration of movement by dopamine and the regulation of emotion by serotonin. Disruptions in these pathways can cause various mental illnesses, for example Parkinson's disease resulting from lack of dopamine, and depression resulting from lack of serotonin. Drugs can be used to treat illnesses by increasing or decreasing the amounts of neurotransmitters, as when MAO inhibitors are used to treat depression by increasing the availability of dopamine and serotonin.

The computational significance of neurotransmitter pathways is that they provide the brain with a kind of organization that is useful for accomplishing different functions. If a neuron could be connected to any other neuron, it would be difficult to orchestrate particular patterns of neuronal behavior. The brain requires cascades of activity, for example, when perception of a dangerous object such as a snake leads to the activation of fear centers in the amygdala and the release of stress hormones. Neurotransmitters provide a coarse kind of wiring diagram, organizing general connections between areas of the brain that need to work together to produce appropriate reactions to different situations. Of course, the brain might have evolved with purely electrical pathways, but the fact is that the different kinds of neurotransmitters have served to establish patterns of connectivity that are important for its operation. Neurotransmitters serve to restrict connectivity within the brain, but different kinds of chemical communication that enhance connectivity are discussed below.

Temporal Effects of Neurotransmitters

There are two types of synapse, the relatively rare electric synapse and the more common chemical synapse in which neurotransmitters are emitted from the vesicles of the presynaptic cell and bind to the receptors of the postsynaptic cell. The effects of chemical synapses are electrical, allowing ions to cross the membrane of the postsynaptic cell. But these effects are much slower than in an electric synapse, in which ions move directly from one neuron to another (Lodish et al. 2000, p. 943). Heart cells, for example, are electrically coupled, allowing groups of muscle cells to contract in synchrony. Signals are transmitted across electric synapses in a few microseconds, without the delay of .5 milliseconds found in chemical synapses.

Given the greater speed and reliability of electric synapses, it might seem puzzling why most synapses are chemical. According to Lodish et al. (2000, p. 942), chemical synapses have two important transmission advantages over electric ones. The first is *signal amplification*, for example when a single presynaptic neuron causes contraction of multiple muscle cells. The second is *signal computation*, in which a single neuron is affected by signals received at multiple excitatory and inhibitory synapses. "Each neuron is a tiny computer that averages all the receptor activations and electric disturbances on its membrane and makes a decision whether to trigger an action potential" (Lodish et al. 2000, p. 943). Thus chemical synapses, even though slower, allow for more flexible kinds of computation.

In chemical synapses, there are two classes of neurotransmitter that operate at vastly different speeds (Lodish et al. 2000, p. 939). Fast synapses, using receptors to which neurotransmitters bind and cause an immediate opening of ion channels, enable ions to cross the postsynaptic cell membrane in less than two milliseconds. In contrast, slow synapses are more indirect, requiring binding of a neurotransmitter to a receptor that initiates a chemical reaction that eventually affects ion conductance. Such postsynaptic responses are slower and longer lasting than those involving fast synapses, working on a scale of seconds rather than milliseconds.

Particular neurotransmitters can have special temporal properties. One kind of glutamate receptor, the NMDA receptor, functions as a coincidence detector (Lodish et al. 2000, p. 947). These receptors open a channel only if two conditions are met: glutamate must be bound and the membrane must be partly polarized by a previous transmission. Thus the NMDA receptor makes possible a simple kind of learning. Galarreta and Hestrin (2001) found that networks of neurons that release gamma-aminobutyric acid (GABA) spike fast enough to be able to detect synchrony in input neurons. It used to be thought that each neuron could release only one kind of neurotransmitter, but there is evidence that a neuron can release different transmitters and different amounts and combinations of transmitters at different times (Black 1991, p. 79). This complexity makes possible a degree of electrochemical encoding that has more variables than the activations and spike trains in purely electrical networks.

In sum, the different temporal properties of neurotransmitters enable them to operate on very different time scales, ranging from microseconds (electric synapses) to milliseconds (fast chemical synapses) to seconds (slow chemical synapses). We will see in the next section that even longer time effects are possible with hormones.

Neuromodulators

Brown (1994, p. 14) provides a useful taxonomy of *neuroregulators*, the chemicals that affect neuronal activity, dividing them into neurotransmitters and neuromodulators. As just described, neurotransmitters are released by neurons and act on other neurons via synapses. Neuromodulators, in contrast, can be released by nonneuronal cells as well as neuronal cells, and they act nonsynaptically on both the presynaptic and postsynaptic cell to alter synthesis, storage, release, and uptake of neurotransmitters. Neuromodulators include hormones, which travel through the bloodstream, and nonhormone molecules that pass more directly between cells. The point of this section is to argue that the variety of neuromodulators used by the brain expands its computational abilities in ways that help to explain aspects of human thinking. Contrary to most computational models of neural networks, whether a neuron fires is not simply a function of its synaptic input. The influence of neuromodulators affects both the topographical and temporal properties of neural networks.

Topographical Effects of Neuromodulators

Neuromodulators dramatically change the causal structure of a neural network. Instead of having a kind of local causality, in which whether a neuron fires is determined only by the neurons that provide synaptic inputs to it, it becomes possible for neurons and other cells that are even meters away to affect firing. A neuron in one part of the brain such as the hypothalamus may fire and release a hormone that travels to a part of the body such as the adrenal glands, which stimulates the release of other hormones that then travel back to the brain and influence the firing of different neurons. Complex feedback loops can result, involving interactions between the neurotransmitter control of hormone release and the hormonal regulation of neurotransmitter release. These feedback loops can also involve the immune system, because brain cells also have receptors for cytokines, which are protein messengers produced by immune system cells such as macrophages.

How do hormones affect neuronal firing? The internal processing of a neuron depends on a host of inputs, including neurotransmitters, hormones, and growth factors (Brown 1994, p. 200). All of these are *first messengers* that activate proteins to produce intracellular signals via second messengers such as the molecule cAMP, which then activate specific protein kinases (enzymes) that function as third messengers. The kinases phosphorylate proteins that act as fourth messengers to stimulate changes in membrane permeability and protein synthesis in the cell. Such changes influence the ability of the neuron to spike, and hence affect the rate and pattern with which it fires. The key point here is that whether a neuron fires and hence contributes to the computation performed by the neural network is not simply a function of neurons that provide synaptic inputs, but can also be affected by a host of other cells that produce hormones. Hence the topography of the brain is far more complex than recognized by purely electrical models in which the inputs to artificial neurons are just activations and spike trains.

Hormonal chemical effects operate over long distances, but there are also nonsynaptic connections between adjacent neurons. Cell adhesion molecules not only bind cells together to form tissues, they also carry signals between cells that can affect their development (Crossin and Krushel 2000). Song et al. (1999) discovered neuroligin, a synaptic cell adhesion molecule that not only enables neurons to establish synaptic connections with each other, but also allows for direct signaling from the postsynaptic neuron back to the presynaptic one. Such retrograde signaling is thought to be important for learning. Other molecular mechanisms for retrograde signaling have been identified. The postsynaptic neuron can also send chemical signals back to the presynaptic neuron by means of gases such as nitric oxide and carbon monoxide, or by peptide hormones (Lodish et al. 2000, p. 915). Nitric oxide is a small molecule that can easily diffuse to affect many neurons, greatly expanding the computational topography of neural networks beyond synaptic connections. Koch (1999, p. 462) conjectures that, because of the spread of nitric oxide: "the unit of synaptic plasticity might not be individual synapses, as assumed by neural network learning algorithms, but groups of adjacent synapses, making for a more robust, albeit less specific learning rule."

Neuronal firing is also affected by glial cells, which were formally thought to function only to hold neurons together. There are 10 to 50 times more glial cells in the brain than neurons, and glial cells affect both the formation of connections by nerve cells and their firing. A factor released by glial cells makes transmitting neurons release their chemical messengers more readily in response to an electrical signal (Pfrieger and Barres 1997). Stimulated glial cells release calcium that triggers surrounding glia to release calcium too, producing a spreading signal (Newman and Zahs 1998). The calcium wave releases glutamate from the glial cells, which has a direct impact on the firing of the neurons in the vicinity.

In sum, there is evidence from the behavior of hormones, nitric oxide, and glial cells that the topography of brain networks is far more complex than is captured by electrical models based only on synaptic connections. Not surprisingly, the operation of nonsynaptic chemical messengers also affects the temporal patterns of neurons.

Temporal Effects of Neuromodulators

Hormones can affect the firing rate of neurons (Brown 1994, pp. 166–167). Gonadal hormones increase the electrical activity of some neurons and inhibit the activity of other neurons. For example, estrogen can modulate the release of dopamine and serotonin. Thus hormones can slow down or speed up neuronal firing.

Many neurons secrete neuropeptides such as endorphins and oxytocin. Unlike classical neurotransmitters, these molecules are released outside the synaptic zone, and can have effects that last for hours or days (Lodish et al. 2000, p. 936). Thus the temporal effects of neuropeptides operate on a very different scale from the much briefer effects of the neurotransmitter emissions described above.

Thus a computational system that involves neuromodulators can be expected to have different temporal behaviors than one with neurotransmitters only, and we already saw that different neurotransmitters give rise to different temporal properties. Hence molecules matter for the temporal behavior of neural networks.

Emotional Cognition

My general argument to this point has been that there are reasons to expect that neurochemistry should matter to mental computation, but I have not shown any particular kinds of mental computation that are affected. There is little direct evidence that the highest-level mental computations involved in problem solving are tied to the influences of specific neurotransmitters and neuromodulators. However, there is substantial evidence that these neuroregulators are important for emotions, and there is also evidence that emotions greatly affect problem solving and learning. I will review these two bodies of evidence and conclude that even the most cognitive of mental functions are subject to neurochemical understanding. Chemistry has both positive and negative effects on emotions and problem solving.

Emotions and Neurochemistry

Panksepp (1993) provides a concise review of the neurochemical control of moods and emotions, including examples of how neurotransmitters are linked to particular emotions. Adminstration of glutamate, the most common excitatory neurotransmitter in the brain, can precipitate aggressive rage and fear responses. NMDA receptor blockage in the amygdala can modulate the extinction of fear behaviors. The inhibitory neurotransmitter GABA figures in the control of anxiety. Norepinephrine influences sensory arousal and becomes prominent in high-affect situations such as threat. Dopamine is associated with positive emotionality, and adenosine is a natural soporific that is blocked by weak mood enhancers such as caffeine.

Neuroregulators also play prominent roles in specific emotions. Corticotropin-releasing factor instigates a stress response that has a major impact on fear and anxiety. Oxytocin enhances maternal behavior as well as feelings of acceptance and social bonding, and contributes to sexual gratification. Arginine vasopressin is under testosterone control and can provoke male aggression. Estrogen receptors in the brain are involved in female sexual behavior, aggression, and emotionality (Brown 1994, p. 154). Many other peptides also affect emotional behavior.

Additional evidence concerning neurochemical influences on mood and emotion comes from the medical effectiveness of drugs that target particular neurotransmitters (Panksepp 1998, p. 117). Depression can be treated both by drugs like Prozac that prolong the synaptic availability of neurotransmitters such as serotonin and dopamine and by drugs that inhibit the enzyme monoamine oxidase (MAO) that normally helps degrade neurotransmitters following release. Antipsychotic drugs used to treat schizophrenia generally dampen dopamine activity. Most antianxiety agents interact with a specific receptor that can facilitate GABA activity, whereas newer drugs reduce anxiety by interacting with serotonin receptors. A new generation of psychiatric medicines is being developed to deal with problems such as bulimia that may arise from imbalances in particular neuropeptides.

There is thus abundant reason to believe that understanding of human emotions will require attention to the effects of neuroregulators on thinking.

It follows immediately that neurochemistry is relevant to understanding the nature of emotional consciousness. Feelings of happiness, sadness, fear, anger, disgust and so on emerge from brain activity by mechanisms not yet understood, but the diverse ways in which neurochemicals influence emotion suggest that it is unlikely that emotional consciousness emerges only from the electrical activities of the brain. I return to this topic in the discussion of artificial intelligence below.

Cognition

It might be argued that, even though chemical explanations are relevant to emotion, they have no bearing on central cognitive processes such as problem solving, learning, and decision making. However, there is increasing evidence in psychology and neuroscience that cognition and emotion are not separate systems and that emotion is an intrinsic part of human cognition (Dalgleish and Power 1999). Reviewing this evidence would take a book in itself, but here I will only report a few salient examples of the cognitive impact of emotions.

Isen (1993) reviews an extensive literature on the impact of positive affect on decision making. The presence of positive feelings can cue positive materials in memory, making access to such thoughts easier. Positive but not negative emotion provides retrieval cues for situations relevant to a current problem. Positive affect also promotes creativity in problem solving and negotiation, and efficiency and thoroughness in decision making. People in whom positive affect have been induced are able to categorize material more flexibly and to see more similarities among items. Kunda (1999, p. 248) reports that mood manipulations by small gifts or pleasant music have been shown to influence a host of judgments, including assessment of one's own competence, one's general satisfaction of life, and evaluations of the quality of political leaders. Affect may also influence our cognitive strategies: people in a bad mood are more likely to use elaborate, systematic processing strategies. Happiness has been found to increase our reliance on social stereotypes, whereas sad people have reduced reliance on negative stereotypes. Thus basic cognitive functions such as categorization, problem solving, and decision making are under emotional influence.

Ashby, Isen, and Turken (1999) have developed a neuropsychological theory of how positive affect influences cognition. They propose that positive affect is associated with increased brain dopamine levels that improve cognitive flexibility. Many readers of this chapter are familiar with the enhancement in problem solving ability brought about by caffeine, which blocks the inhibitory neurotransmitter adenosine (Brown 1996). In contrast, alcohol can disrupt mental functioning by inhibiting receptors for the excitatory neurotransmitter glutamate, including NMDA receptors important for learning. (More pleasantly, alcohol reduces anxiety by binding to GABA receptors and increasing their inhibitory function, while inducing euphoria through increased dopamine levels in the brain's reward centers and released endorphins.)

It might be thought that decision making would improve if emotions were removed from decisions, but the neurophysiological research of Damasio (1994) and his colleagues suggests that this is emphatically not the case. People who have brain damage that severs links between the most cognitive areas of the brain in the neocortex and the most emotionally important areas in the amygdala are very ineffective decision makers, even though their verbal and mathematical abilities are unaffected. Their problem is that they have lost the emotion-driven ability to make decisions on the basis of what really matters to them. Bechara et al. (1997) found that this disability also made it difficult for patients to learn a card playing task in which normal subjects unconsciously learned strategies that enabled them to avoid bad outcomes.

This neurological research on the role of emotions in decision making fits well with recent psychological theories that find deficiencies in purely cognitive accounts of decision. Loewenstein, Weber, Hsee, and Welch (2001) show that many psychological phenomena involving judgment and decision making under uncertainty can be accounted for by understanding people's estimates of risk as inherently emotional. Similarly, Finucane et al. (2000) propose that human decisions are heavily affected by what they call the "affect heuristic." Legal and scientific thinking are also inherently emotional (see chaps. 8, 10).

I have mentioned only a small part of the evidence that challenges the traditional psychological division between cognition and emotion and the ancient philosophical distinction between reason and passion. But it suffices for the purpose at hand, to show that the demonstrable relevance of neurochemistry to emotions carries over to cognition in general. If human cognition is mental computation, it is a kind of computation determined by the chemical as well as the electrical aspects of the brain. This conclusion has important implications for the prospects of developing intelligence in nonhuman computers.

Artificial Intelligence

Kurzweil (1999) and Moravec (1998) have predicted that artificial intelligence will be able to match human intelligence within a few decades. Their prediction is based on the exponential increase in processing speed of computer chips, which continues to double every 12 to 18 months as it has for decades. Kurzweil estimates the computing speed of the human brain at around 20 million billion calculations per second, based on 100 billion neurons each with a thousand connections and the slow firing rate of 200 calculations per second. Assuming continued exponential increase in chip speed, digital computers will reach the 20 million billion calculations (on the magnitude of 10^{15}) per second mark around 2020.

However, the molecular chemistry of the brain suggests that this estimate of its computational power may be very misleading, both quantitatively and qualitatively. If we count the number of processors in the brain as not just the number of neurons in the brain, but the number of *proteins* in the brain, we get a figure of around a billion times 100 billion, or 10^{17}. Even if it is not legitimate to count each protein as a processor all by itself, it is still evident from the discussion above that the number of computational elements in the brain is more than the 10^{11} or 10^{12} neurons. Moreover, the discussion of hormones and other neuroregulators showed that the number of computationally relevant causal connections is far greater than the thousand or so synaptic connections per neuron. I do not know how to estimate the number of neurons with hormonal receptors that can be influenced by a single neuron that secretes hormones or that activates glands which secrete hormones, but the number must be huge. If it is a million, and if every brain protein is viewed as a miniprocessor, then the computational speed of the brain is on the order of 10^{23} calculations per second, far larger than the 10^{15} calculations per second that Kurzweil expects to be available by 2020, although less than where he expects computers to be by 2060. Thus quantitatively it appears that digital computers are much farther away than Kurzweil and Moravec estimate from reaching the raw computational power of the human brain.

Moreover, intelligence is not merely a matter of raw computational power, but requires that the computer have a sufficiently powerful program to produce the desired task. My Macintosh G4 laptop computer can calculate $2^{100,000}$ in a couple of seconds, the same amount of time in which I can only calculate 2^5, but the computer lacks the programming to be able to understand language and solve complex problems. Kurzweil and Moravec are aware that it is a daunting task to write the billions or trillions of lines of software that would be needed to enable the superfast computers of the future to approach human cognitive capabilities, but they blithely assume that evolutionary algorithms will allow computers to develop their own intelligent software. Evolutionary computation, which uses algorithms modeled in part on human genetics, is indeed a powerful means of developing new software (Koza 1992), but it is currently limited by the need for humans to provide the evolving programs with a criterion of fitness that the genetic algorithms serve to maximize. In humans, the evaluation of different states is provided by emotions, which direct us to what matters for our learning and problem solving. Computers currently lack such intrinsic, biologically provided motivation, and so can be expected to have difficulties directing their problem solving in nonroutine directions.

Perhaps software will be developed that does for computers what emotions do for us, but current computational research on emotions is very limited compared to the complexity of the human emotional system based on numerous neurotransmitters and neuromodulators. There is a current resurgence in AI of interest in emotions, which is however treated by researchers as a symbolic or electrical rather than a chemical phenomenon. The complexity of human emotions, based on looping interactions among neural, hormonal, and immune systems, may be too complex for people to figure out how to program and also too complex for a program created by humans to evolve.

This does not mean that computers of great intelligence in special areas will not be developed. It may be quantitatively and qualitatively difficult for AI to duplicate the human brain, but intelligent computers may be developed by other means, just as IBM managed to build the world's best chess player by combining clever software with extraordinarily fast computer chips. But we should not expect a computer developed in this way to have all the mental capacities of humans, and we certainly should not expect it to have anything like human consciousness, which I suggested is intrinsically tied to human emotions and hence to our peculiar brain chemistry.

Conclusion

My arguments that neurochemistry matters to mental computation are not meant to show that computational models of the mind have to be at the molecular level. As I stated earlier, models are like maps in that various levels of detail are useful for different purposes. Symbolic models of high-level inference and neural network models with and without spiking neurons have proven very useful in explaining many facets of cognition, and I have no doubt that they will continue to be useful. Cognitive science benefits from a combination of many different fields and methodologies, with different researchers attacking the problem of understanding mind and intelligence at different levels.

Without recommending abandonment of the techniques of computational modeling that have served cognitive science well, it is nevertheless evident that there are new possibilities for enhancing the understanding of mind by working more at the molecular level. Consider, for example, the computational study of emergent properties of chemical pathways conducted by Bhalla and Iyengar (1999), including integration of signals across multiple time scales and self-sustaining feedback loops. It is possible that computational modeling of brain activity at the molecular level will discover additional emergent properties that are important for understanding some of the most currently intractable problems in cognitive science, such as the origins of emotional consciousness. Hence without abandoning traditional concerns and methods, it may be time for psychology and the philosophy of mind to become, like current biology and medicine, molecular.

II | Applications

Introduction

In 1995, O. J. Simpson was tried for the murder of his ex-wife, Nicole Brown Simpson, and her friend, Ron Goldman, both of whom had been found with multiple knife wounds. To the surprise of many, the jury found Simpson not guilty of the crime, and many explanations have been given for the verdict, ranging from emotional bias on the part of the jury to incompetence on the part of the prosecution. Of course, there is also the possibility that, given the evidence presented to them, the jury rationally made the decision that Simpson was not guilty beyond a reasonable doubt.

This chapter evaluates four competing psychological explanations for why the jury reached the verdict they did:

1. *Explanatory coherence* The jury found O. J. Simpson not guilty because they did not find it plausible that he had committed the crime, where plausibility is determined by explanatory coherence.
2. *Probability theory* The jury found O. J. Simpson not guilty because they thought that it was not sufficiently probable that he had committed the crime, where probability is calculated by means of Bayes's theorem.
3. *Wishful thinking* The jury found O. J. Simpson not guilty because they were emotionally biased toward him and wanted to find him not guilty.
4. *Emotional coherence* The jury found O. J. Simpson not guilty because of an interaction between emotional bias and explanatory coherence.

I will describe computational models that provide detailed simulations of juror reasoning for explanatory and emotional coherence, and argue that the latter account is the most plausible. Application to the Simpson case requires an expansion of my previous theory of emotional coherence to introduce emotional biasing of judgments of explanatory coherence.

Social psychologists distinguish between "hot" and "cold" cognition, which differ in that the former involves motivations and emotions (Abelson 1963; Kunda 1999). The first two explanations above involve cold cognition, the third based on wishful thinking involves only hot cognition, but my preferred emotional-coherence explanation shows how hot and cold cognition can be tightly integrated.

Explanatory Coherence

At first glance, the evidence that O. J. Simpson was the murderer of his ex-wife was overwhelming. Shortly after the time that the murder took place, he caught a plane to Chicago carrying a bag that disappeared, perhaps because it contained the murder weapon and bloody clothes. Police who came to Simpson's house found drops of blood in his car that matched his own blood and that of Ron Goldman. In Simpson's back yard, police found a bloody glove that was of a pair with one found at the scene of the crime, and they found a bloody sock in his bedroom. Simpson had a cut on his hand that might have been caused by a struggle with the victims who tried to defend themselves. Simpson's blood was found on a gate near the crime scene. Moreover, there was a plausible motive for the murder, in that Simpson had been physically abusive to his wife while they were married and was reported to have been jealous of other men who saw Nicole after their divorce.

Based on all this evidence, many people judged that Simpson was guilty. One way of understanding this judgment is in terms of the theory of explanatory coherence, which I developed to explain how scientists evaluate competing theories but which has also been applied to legal and other kinds of reasoning (Thagard 1989, 1992, 1999, 2000). On this theory, a hypothesis such as the claim that Simpson killed Nicole is accepted if doing so maximizes the overall coherence among pieces of evidence and the conflicting hypotheses that compete to explain the evidence. The theory of explanatory coherence can be summarized in the following principles, discussed at length elsewhere (Thagard 1992, 2000).

Principle E1: Symmetry Explanatory coherence is a symmetric relation, unlike, say, conditional probability. That is, two propositions p and q cohere with each other equally.

Principle E2: Explanation (a) A hypothesis coheres with what it explains, which can either be evidence or another hypothesis; (b) hypotheses that together explain some other proposition cohere with each other; and (c) the more hypotheses it takes to explain something, the lower the degree of coherence.

Principle E3: Analogy   Similar hypotheses that explain similar pieces of evidence cohere.

Principle E4: Data priority   Propositions that describe the results of observations have a degree of acceptability on their own.

Principle E5: Contradiction   Contradictory propositions are incoherent with each other.

Principle E6: Competition   If *P* and *Q* both explain a proposition, and if *P* and *Q* are not explanatorily connected, then *P* and *Q* are incoherent with each other. (*P* and *Q* are explanatorily connected if one explains the other or if together they explain something.)

Principle E7: Acceptance   The acceptability of a proposition in a system of propositions depends on its coherence with them.

The theory of explanatory coherence is implemented in a computational model, ECHO, that shows precisely how coherence can be calculated. Hypotheses and evidence are represented by units, which are highly simplified artificial neurons that can have excitatory and inhibitory links with each other. When two propositions cohere, as when a hypothesis explains a piece of evidence, then there is an excitatory link between the two units that represent them. When two propositions are incoherent with each other, either because they are contradictory or because they compete to explain some of the evidence, then there is an inhibitory link between them. Standard algorithms are available for spreading activation among the units until they reach a stable state in which some units have positive activation, representing the acceptance of the propositions they represent, and other units have negative activation, representing the rejection of the propositions they represent. Thus algorithms for artificial neural networks can be used to maximize explanatory coherence, as can other kinds of algorithms (Thagard and Verbeurgt 1998; Thagard 2000).

Figure 8.1 shows the structure of an explanatory-coherence account of why O. J. Simpson might be judged guilty. The hypothesis that he was the killer explains why Nicole Simpson and Ron Goldman are dead, why Simpson's blood was found on a gate at the crime scene, why there was blood in his car, why a bloody glove was found in his yard, and why his sock had blood on it. Moreover, there is an explanation of why Simpson killed Nicole based on his past history of abuse and jealousy. In the computational model ECHO, the principle of data priority, E4, is implemented by spreading activation directly to units representing evidence, from which activation spreads to the unit representing the hypothesis that Simpson was the murderer. Given the inputs shown in figure 8.1, ECHO activates this unit and finds the accused guilty.

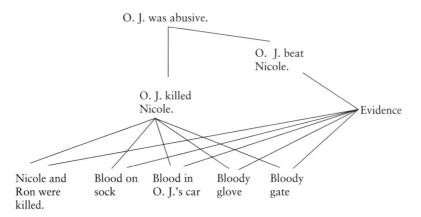

Figure 8.1
Part of the evidence supporting the hypothesis that O. J. Simpson killed his ex-wife.
Solid lines indicate coherence relations.

In the criminal trial, Simpson was represented by a stellar team of fourteen
lawyers, who needed to convince the jury that there was reasonable doubt
whether Simpson was guilty. They realized that they needed to provide alternative explanations of the apparently damning evidence that implicated
Simpson as the murderer. According to Schiller and Willwerth (1997,
p. 417), the defense lawyers were familiar with the story model of juror decision making (Pennington and Hastie 1992, 1993). On this model jurors
reach their decisions based on whether the prosecution or the defense
presents a more compelling story about the events of the case. One of Simpson's main attorneys, Johnnie Cochran wrote (1997, pp. 236–237):

Whatever the commentators may say, a trial is not really a struggle between opposing
lawyers but between opposing stories.... What juries require is a story into whose
outline they can plug the testimony and evidence with which they are relentlessly
bombarded.

As Byrne (1995) has argued, the story model of juror reasoning can be
viewed as an instantiation of the theory of explanatory coherence, which
provides a fuller and more rigorous account of what it is for one story to be
more plausible than another. In accord with the theory of explanatory coherence, the defense lawyers set out to generate and support hypotheses that
explained the deaths and other evidence using hypotheses that would compete with the hypothesis of Simpson's guilt.

The first task of the defense lawyers was to generate an alternative explanation of who killed Nicole Simpson and Ron Goldman. Based on Nicole's

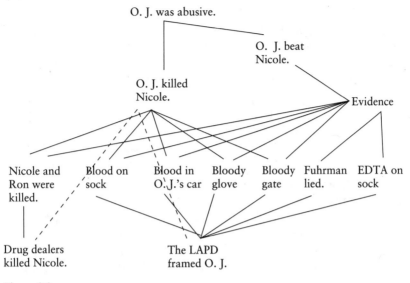

Figure 8.2
Expanded explanatory coherence analysis of the competing stories in the Simpson trial. Solid lines indicate coherence relations, while dotted lines indicated incoherence relations between competing hypotheses.

known history of cocaine use, they hypothesized that she was killed by drug dealers, and argued that a more thorough police investigation right after the murders would have turned up evidence that supported this explanation. In order to explain the circumstantial evidence linking O. J. Simpson to the crime scene, including the bloody car, glove, and sock, the defense contended that the items had been planted by Los Angeles Police Department officers determined to frame Simpson for the crime. With the help of a strong team of forensic experts, the lawyers were able to identify irregularities in the conduct of the investigation by LAPD detectives and forensic specialists. For example, one of the detectives, Philip Vannatter, had carried a sample of Simpson's around with him for hours; and some of the blood taken from Simpson was unaccounted for. After much digging, the defense team found evidence that Mark Fuhrman, the detective who had allegedly found the bloody glove in Simpson's yard, was a raving racist who, contrary to his claim on the stand, frequently used the word "nigger" and had bragged in the past about framing blacks, especially ones involved with white women.

Figure 8.2 shows part of an explanatory-coherence analysis of the case made by the defense. The hypothesis that Nicole and Goldman were killed by drug dealers competes with the hypothesis that O. J. Simpson was the killer. Unfortunately for the defense, they were unsuccessful in finding any substantial evidence for this hypothesis. But they were very effective in offering alternative explanations of the blood evidence using the hypothesis that the LAPD had planted evidence. The glove that Simpson had supposedly used in the murder did not appear to fit his hand when he tried to put it on in court. Blood had not been noticed on the sock until weeks after it had been held by the police. The blood on the glove and sock showed traces of EDTA, a chemical used as an anti-coagulant in samples taken from O. J. Simpson and Ron Goldman. Fuhrman and other detectives had ample opportunity to plant the evidence that implicated Simpson, and Fuhrman had a racist motivation to do so.

The complex of hypotheses and evidence shown in figure 8.2 provides a possible cold-cognitive explanation of why the jurors found Simpson not guilty. Perhaps, given the evidence and all the competing hypotheses, they found greater explanatory coherence in the story that Simpson had not been the killer. However, when the program ECHO is given input that corresponds to the evidence, hypotheses, and explanations in figure 8.2, it accepts the proposition that Simpson was the killer and rejects the alternative hypothesis that the murder was committed by drug dealers. Interestingly, ECHO also accepts the hypothesis urged by the defense that the LAPD tried to frame Simpson. Frankly, the conclusion that Simpson was guilty *and* he was framed strikes me as quite reasonable.

The jury did not see additional evidence that is best explained by the hypothesis that Simpson was the murderer. For procedural reasons, evidence was not admitted concerning the finding of unusual fibers from Simpson's car at the crime scene. Months after the trial, photographs were found that showed that Simpson had owned a pair of size 12 Bruno Magli loafers of the sort that had left bloody foot prints at the scene of the crime. But even without this additional evidence, ECHO's assessment of explanatory coherence accepts the hypothesis that Simpson was the killer. ECHO, unlike the jury, finds Simpson guilty. Hence given the evidence and explanations shown in figure 8.2, explanatory coherence fails to account for why the jury did not convict him.

It is of course possible that the jurors were mentally working with a different explanatory network, not represented by figure 8.2, in which the hypothesis of Simpson's innocence fit with the most coherent story. Moreover, it is also possible that the jurors did think that the evidence supported his guilt, but not beyond a reasonable doubt. According to the legal scholar Alan Dershowitz (1997), who was also a member of the Simpson defense team, the incompetence of the police and prosecution made room for the jury to conclude that there was reasonable doubt about Simpson's guilt. Two additional Simpson lawyers, Cochran (1997) and Shapiro (1996), also suggested that it was reasonable for the jury to doubt the prosecution's case. Three of the jurors describe their conclusions as based on reasonable doubt (Cooley, Bess, and Rubin-Jackson 1995).

From the perspective of the theory of explanatory coherence, reasonable doubt might be viewed as an additional constraint on the maximization of coherence, requiring that hypotheses concerning guilt must be substantially more plausible than ones concerning innocence. In ECHO, presumption of innocence can be modeled by treating hypotheses concerning guilt as the opposite of data, so that their activation is suppressed in order to require that the hypotheses they represent is achieved only when coherence overwhelmingly requires it. In fact, simulation of the network in figure 8.2, with inhibition of the unit representing Simpson being the killer, can reject that hypothesis if the inhibition is over .065, which is stronger than the default .05 excitation value for data. I am inclined, therefore, to conclude that the jurors' decisions in favor of Simpson was not based solely on explanatory coherence and reasonable doubt, and later I will present evidence that their decisions were in part emotional. First, however, it is necessary to consider an alternative cold-cognitive explanation of the jury decision, based on probability theory rather than on explanatory coherence. Later in the chapter I consider an emotional-coherence interpretation of reasonable doubt; see also chapter 9 below.

Probability Theory

Perhaps the jury in the Simpson trial inferred that the probability that he committed the crime given the evidence was insufficient for conviction. The conditional probability that Simpson was guilty given the evidence, P(guilty/ evidence), can in principle be calculated by Bayes's theorem, which says that the posterior probability of a hypothesis given the evidence, P(H/E), is a function of the prior probability of the hypothesis, P(H), the likelihood of the evidence given the hypothesis, P(E/H), and the probability of the evidence: $P(H/E) = P(H) * P(E/H)/P(E)$. To calculate P(guilty/evidence), we need to know the prior probability that Simpson was guilty, the probability of the evidence in the trial given the hypothesis that Simpson committed the murder, and the probability of the evidence. Some legal scholars (e.g. Lempert 1986) contend that jurors do and should use probabilistic reasoning of this kind.

It is obvious that these probabilities are hard to come by. If probability is interpreted objectively as involving frequencies in a population, then the relevant probabilities are undefined, since we have no idea about the relative frequencies needed to attach a probability to propositions such as that Simpson committed the murder. Hence advocates of the application of probability theory to complex inference, often called Bayesians, have to rely on a subjective conception of probability as degree of belief. But this interpretation of probability is also problematic for legal applications, since there is no support for the view that the degrees of belief of the jurors conform to the principles of the calculus of probabilities. Indeed, there is considerable psychological evidence that people's degrees of belief violate the laws of probability theory (Kahneman, Slovic, and Tversky 1982; Tversky and Koehler 1994).

Even supposing that it were reasonable to measure degrees of belief by probabilities, there is the great practical problem of attaching meaningful probabilities to the various propositions involved in a judgment. In addition to its explanatory-coherence interpretation, figure 8.2 can be given an interpretation in terms of conditional probabilities based on causal relations. Much sophisticated work in artificial intelligence has concerned the calculation of probabilities in probabilistic causal networks, which are usually called Bayesian networks (Pearl 1988; Neapolitan 1990). For calculation of probabilities such as P(O. J. killed Nicole), such networks need a wealth of conditional probabilities such as P(blood in O. J.'s car/O. J. killed Nicole) and P(blood in O. J.'s car/O. J. did not kill Nicole). The jurors in the Simpson trial had no idea what values might be attached to such probabilities, and neither does any expert one might consult. Probability theory is an extraordinarily valuable tool for dealing with frequencies in populations, but its application to the psychology of causal reasoning is rather fanciful.

Moreover, Ronald Allen (1991, 1994) has pointed out many respects in which probability theory and Bayesian inference do not fit well with legal practice. For example, if two hypotheses H1 and H2 are independent, then P(H1 & H2) is always less than or equal to P(H1) and less than or equal to P(H2). In a trial in which the case for the prosecution involves many propositions that must be jointly evaluated, the probability of the conjunction of these hypotheses will typically drop below .5, so that it would seem that a probabilistically sophisticated jury would never have good reason to convict anyone. In addition, no one has been able within a probabilistic framework to give a plausible interpretation of reasonable doubt, which is a cornerstone of criminal law in the U.S. and elsewhere. Does "beyond a reasonable doubt" mean that the probability that a person committed a crime must be greater than .6 rather than .5 for conviction, or does it mean that the ratio of the probability of guilt to the probability of innocence must be well over 1, or what? I gave an explanatory coherence account of reasonable doubt above, but will give a fuller account below as part of the application of emotional coherence to legal inference.

A full probabilistic analysis of the 12-node network shown in figure 8.2 would require $2^{12} = 4096$ probabilities, but Bayesian networks simplify the calculation of probabilities by assuming that each variable representing the truth or falsity of a proposition is independent of most other variables. Figure 8.3 shows a Bayesian network constructed with JavaBayes, a very sophisticated and convenient Bayesian simulator due to Cozman (2001). The network in figure 8.3 has the same structure as the coherence network in figure 8.2, except that the links are unidirectional; they represent conditional probability rather than coherence. Each node represents a variable that has two possible values, *true* or *false*. The arrows typically indicate causal

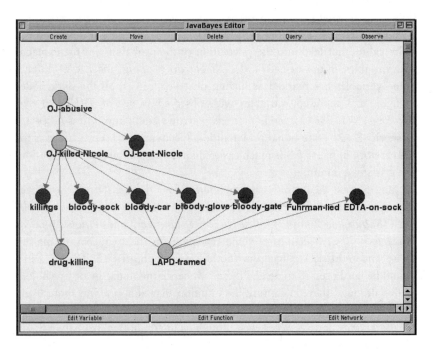

Figure 8.3
Bayesian network produced with the program JavaBayes (Cozman 2001). Dark nodes represent observed variables, while light nodes represent explanatory variables. Links indicate conditional probabilities.

relations: for example, Simpson's abusive nature was a possible cause of his killing Nicole and not vice versa. The exception to this interpretation are the link that I put in between *OJ-killed-Nicole* and the alternative explanation, *drug-killing*. This is not a causal relation, but some probabilistic connection must be represented to indicate the presumed incompatibility of these hypotheses. I drew the links *from OJ-killed-Nicole* rather than to it because doing so reduced the number of required conditional probabilities, for reasons I will now explain.

I did not, however, draw a link between *OJ-killed-Nicole* and *LAPD-framed*, which seem to me to be probabilistically independent. In ECHO, the framing hypothesis is treated as incoherent with *OJ-killed-Nicole*, not because they are logically incompatible, but because they offer competing explanations of evidence such as the bloody sock. If there is to be a connection between the two hypotheses, JavaBayes requires numbers for P(*OJ-framed*/*OJ-killed-Nicole*), P(*not-OJ-framed*/*OJ-killed-Nicole*), P(*OJ-framed*/*not-OJ-killed-Nicole*), and P(*not-OJ-framed*/*not-OJ-killed-Nicole*). I do not know what these probabilities should be, logically or psychologically.

After a network is created with JavaBayes, it is necessary to insert probability values that feed into the calculation of the probability of the explanatory variables, in this case *OJ-killed-Nicole*, *drug-killing*, and *LAPD-framed*. Some variables are marked as having observed values: all the dark nodes in figure 8.3 represent variables with observed values of TRUE, so that P(*killings*) = 1. For each node that has n arrows going into it, it is necessary to specify $2 * 2^n$ conditional probabilities. Specifying the 60 probabilities for the network in figure 8.3 is much easier than doing the full joint distribution, but it is still a daunting task.

Consider first the conditional probabilities for *OJ-killed-Nicole*. JavaBayes requires numbers for P(*OJ-killed-Nicole*/*OJ-abusive*), P(*OJ-killed-Nicole*/*not-OJ-abusive*), P(*not-OJ-killed-Nicole*/*OJ-abusive*), and P(*not-OJ-killed-Nicole*/*not-OJ-abusive*). After some reflection on the frequency of marital abuse and murder, I plugged in the following numbers: .2, .01, .8, .99. I would be hard pressed to defend these numbers either logically or psychologically, although they do capture the intuition that Simpson was more likely to have killed Nicole if he was abusive than if he was not. The specifications for the *killings* node is easier even though eight conditional probabilities are needed, because obviously the probability of *killings* given either *OJ-killed-Nicole* or *drug-killings* is 1. But specifying the conditional probabilities for the *bloody-sock* node is extremely difficult: you might be able to come up with a high number for P(*bloody-sock*/*OJ-killed-Nicole & LAPD-framed*), but what number would you estimate for such quantities as P(*not-bloody-*

sock/not-OJ-killed-Nicole & LAPD-framed)? After much reflection I inserted, for this variable and for others, some numbers that were guesses at best.

Once all the conditional probabilities had been inserted, I had JavaBayes query the different variables to calculate posterior probabilities given the evidence. The results were not unreasonable: P(*OJ-killed-Nicole*/evidence) = .72, P(*drug-killings*/evidence) = .29, and P(*LAPD-framed*/evidence) = .99. Like ECHO, JavaBayes concluded that Simpson was guilty *and* he was framed. The last probability strikes me as much too high, but it is not clear how to alter the network and probability values in order to change it.

Since JavaBayes with the input shown in figure 8.3 reached a different conclusion from the jury, we can conclude that this network is not a good model of the jurors' thinking. Of course, it is possible that they had a different set of variables and conditional probabilities than the ones I provided. Constructing the causal network was no more difficult than constructing the explanatory network for ECHO, but coming up with values for the sixty conditional probabilities was very hard, even for someone who knows more about probability than most jurors. Thus explanatory coherence provides a much simpler and psychologically natural cold-cognitive account of how jurors reach decisions. Neither account, however, appears adequate to explain the jurors' thinking.

In sum, there are psychological and legal reasons for doubting the applicability of a Bayesian analysis to the jury's decision in the Simpson trial, even if it was a rational decision based only on the plausibility of the various hypotheses given the evidence. Even more obviously, probability theory can not account for the role that hot cognition involving emotions and motivation may have played in the Simpson trial.

Wishful Thinking

There is substantial evidence that emotional bias on the part of the jurors may have contributed to their decision to acquit O. J. Simpson. His lawyers hired a jury consultant who conducted a poll in which she found that 20 percent of the sample believed Simpson innocent, and 50 percent did not *want* to believe Simpson was guilty (Schiller and Willwerth 1997, p. 220). The consultant then worked intensively with 75 people and found that black, middle-aged women were Simpson's most aggressive champions (p. 243). This was contrary to the expectations of the defense lawyers, who had thought that black women would resent O. J. Simpson for marrying a white woman, but found instead that virtually every middle-aged

African-American woman in the focus group supported Simpson and resented the murder victim (p. 244)! Accordingly, the defense team set out to get as many black, middle-aged women on the jury as possible. Further polling found that only 3 percent of 200 African Americans assumed that Simpson was guilty (p. 251), and 44 percent said that Los Angeles police had treated them unfairly at least once. Most strikingly, 49 percent of divorced black women wanted to see Simpson acquitted (p. 251). The defense was elated when juror selection produced a jury that included eight blacks, most of them middle-aged women. In accord with their strategy to impress the African-American women, the defense began its case with testimony from Simpson's daughter and mother. News polls also found that African Americans, especially women, were inclined to believe that Simpson was innocent. Bugliosi (1997, p. 74) reports that a *Los Angeles Times* poll of blacks in Los Angeles county found that 75 percent of them believed Simpson was framed. Psychological experiments have also found that blacks were more likely than whites to view Simpson as innocent (Newman et al. 1997).

It is possible that these differences between white and black attitudes were in part based on differences in personal experience: black residents of Los Angeles had probably observed or heard of more cases of people being framed by the police than white residents were aware of. But there is also reason to believe that some members of the jury in the Simpson trial were emotionally biased toward finding him not guilty. At the most extreme, one might propose that their verdict in the face of all the evidence linking Simpson with the crime was a matter of wishful thinking: the jurors found Simpson not guilty because they wanted to. Explanatory coherence, probability theory, and other cold cognitive factors had nothing to do with the jurors' decisions, which was based on their emotional attachment to Simpson and their motivation to acquit him.

It is implausible, however, to suppose that the jurors' decisions were merely a matter of wishful thinking. The defense certainly did not rely only on the fact that many of the jurors were probably predisposed toward Simpson; rather, his lawyers labored intensively to show that the LAPD was incompetent in collecting and protecting evidence and that officers such as Fuhrman had the motive and opportunity to frame Simpson. Some members of the jury may have been emotionally inclined to acquit Simpson, but they would not have done so if the evidence had been overwhelmingly against him. One of the jurors reported after the trial that if she had been aware of some of the evidence that was not presented at the trial, then she would have voted to convict Simpson (Bugliosi 1997, p. 143; see also Cooley, Bess, and Rubin-Jackson 1995, p. 198). If there had been stronger evidence against

Simpson, and if the case against the LAPD had not been so strong, then the jurors may well have found Simpson guilty despite their emotional attachments. One of the jurors, Carrie Bess, said on television (Bugliosi 1997, p. 301): "I'm sorry, O. J. would have had to go if the prosecution had presented the case differently, without the doubt. As a black woman, it would have hurt me. But as a human being, I would have to do what I had to do."

This assessment is consistent with psychological research on motivated inference. Kunda (1999, p. 224) summarizes the results of psychological experiments as follows:

Motivation can color our judgments, but we are not at liberty to conclude whatever we want to conclude simply because we want to. Even when we are motivated to arrive at a particular conclusion, we are also motivated to be rational and to construct a justification for our desired conclusion that would persuade a dispassionate observer. We will draw our desired conclusion only if we can come up with enough evidence to support it. But despite our best efforts to be objective and rational, motivation may nevertheless color our judgment because the process of justification construction can itself be biased by our goals.

This conclusion is supported by numerous experimental findings that people have reality constraints that keep them from believing whatever they want to believe (Kunda 1990; Sanitioso, Kunda, and Fong 1990). Thus the jurors in the Simpson trial may have started with an emotional bias to acquit him, but that motivation was probably not sufficient in itself. Rather, there had to be interactions between the jurors' emotional attitudes and the evidence and explanations presented by the prosecution and the defense. Such interactions can be explained by the theory of emotional coherence.

Emotional Coherence

When people make judgments, they not only come to conclusions about what to believe, they also make emotional assessments. For example, the decision to trust people is partly based on purely cognitive inferences about their plans and personalities, but also involves adopting emotional attitudes toward them (Thagard 2000, chap. 6). The theory of emotional coherence serves to explain how people's inferences about what to believe are integrated with the production of feelings about people, things, and situations. On this theory, mental representations such as propositions and concepts have, in addition to the cognitive status of being accepted or rejected, an emotional status called a *valence*, which can be positive or negative depending on one's emotional attitude toward the representation. For example, just as one can accept or reject the hypothesis that Simpson was the murderer, one can attach a positive or negative valence to it depending on whether one thinks this is good or bad.

The computational model HOTCO implements the theory of emotional coherence by expanding ECHO to allow the units that stand for propositions to have valences as well as activations. In the original version of HOTCO (Thagard 2000), the valence of a unit was calculated on the basis of the activations and valences of all the units connected to it. Hence valences could be affected by activations and emotions, but not vice versa: HOTCO enabled cognitive inferences such as ones based on explanatory coherence to influence emotional judgments, but did not allow emotional judgments to bias cognitive inferences. HOTCO and the overly rational theory of emotional coherence that it embodied could explain a fairly wide range of cognitive-emotional judgments involving trust and other psychological phenomena, but were inadequate to explain the emotional biasing of inference that seems to have taken place in the Simpson trial.

Accordingly, I have altered HOTCO to allow a kind of biasing of activations by valences. Consider, for example, the proposition that *O. J. is good*. This proposition can be viewed as having an activation that represents its degree of acceptance or rejection, but it can also be viewed as having a valence that corresponds to a person's emotional attitude toward Simpson. The predicate "good" involves both a statement of fact and an evaluation. As such, it is natural for the valence of *O. J. is good* to affect its activation. Technical details concerning explanatory and emotional coherence are provided in the appendix to chapter 3.

Now we have a natural way to simulate the emotional bias of the jurors in the Simpson case. Figure 8.4 shows figure 8.2 with the addition of units corresponding to *O. J. is good* and *LAPD is good*. Depending on a person's emotional bias, these units may have positive or negative valence associated with them. It would seem, for example, that many of the black jurors had a positive emotional attitude toward Simpson, and a negative one toward the Los Angeles Police. Hence in figure 8.4, *O. J. is good* has a positive link to the valence unit that spreads valences, while *LAPD is good* has a negative link. The activation of these units is a function not only of the activation input to them but also of the valence input to them that they receive from the valence unit. Hence *O. J is good* tends to become active while *LAPD is good* tends to be deactivated. Then these units can influence the activations of the key hypotheses in the network, that O. J. was the killer and that the LAPD framed him. There is naturally a negative link between *O. J. is good* and *O. J. killed Nicole*, so that the positive evaluation of Simpson tends to sup-

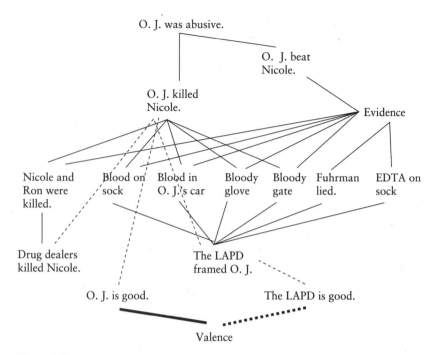

Figure 8.4
Emotional coherence analysis of the Simpson case. The thick lines are valence links. As with the other links, solid lines are excitatory and dashed lines are inhibitory.

press acceptance of the hypothesis that he killed his ex-wife. Similarly, a negative evaluation of the LAPD tends to support the hypothesis that Simpson was framed. When HOTCO 2 is run on the network shown in figure 8.4 with the default .05 valence link to *O. J. is good* and a −.05 valence link to *LAPD is good*, it rejects the conclusion that O. J. killed Nicole, just as the jury did.

But emotional coherence is not just wishful thinking, because it assumes that an inference is based in part on cognitive considerations, not just emotional bias. If the simulation just described is altered by deleting the defense's explanations of the evidence using the hypothesis that the LAPD framed Simpson, then HOTCO 2 finds Simpson guilty. If explanatory coherence supports a conclusion very strongly, then an emotional bias against the conclusion can be overcome. This fits well with the Simpson jurors' contentions that if the evidence had been stronger they would have found Simpson guilty. Valences affect activations, but do not wholly determine them. Emotional bias requires coherence between emotional attitudes and evidence, not just wishful thinking.

It therefore seems that the most plausible answer to the question *Why wasn't O. J. convicted?* is that the jurors made their decisions based on emotional coherence, which combined an emotional bias with an assessment of competing explanations of the evidence. Given the flawed case presented by the prosecution and the ingenuity of the defense lawyers in generating alternative explanations, it was natural for the jurors to go with their emotional biases and find Simpson not guilty. A stronger case might have overcome the jurors' predisposition to acquit Simpson.

It might seem that emotional matters are totally inappropriate for use in deciding guilt or innocence, and I will argue in the conclusion that the kind of emotional biasing I have just described should generally *not* be part of legal decision making. But it is accepted in criminal proceedings that an accused should be convicted only if he or she is shown to be guilty beyond a reasonable doubt, which seems to me more a matter of value than of fact. Legal practice deems that acquitting a guilty person is not as bad as convicting an innocent one. This is a matter of fairness rather than fact or probability. The purpose of the law is not only to ascertain truth, but also to achieve fairness. In HOTCO 2, reasonable doubt is implemented by having a unit for *Acquit the innocent* which has positive valence and activation. It then inhibits the acceptance of any hypothesis concerning the guilt of an accused, such as that Simpson killed Nicole. When HOTCO 2 is run with an *Acquit the innocent* unit inhibiting the unit that represents guilt, it finds Simpson innocent with less pro-Simpson bias than is otherwise required to produce a not guilty decision. If this account of reasonable doubt is correct, then judgments of guilt and innocence legitimately involve emotional as well as explanatory coherence.

The involvement of emotional coherence in jury decision making also explains another aspect of legal practice that would be puzzling if juries used only cold cognition. According to Just (1998), one way in which the common law attempts to protect accused persons against irrational jury deliberations is the exclusion of evidence which has prejudicial effect outweighing its probative value. Evidence can be prejudicial if it is of a kind to which a jury is likely to attach more importance than is deserved, or if it is likely to raise within a jury an emotional reaction to an accused that will distort calm and rational deliberation. In terms of the HOTCO 2 model, evidence is prejudicial if it attaches a negative valence to the accused in a way that would encourage acceptance of the hypothesis that the accused is guilty.

I have argued that the most plausible available explanation of Simpson's acquittal was that the mental processes of the jury involved emotional as well as explanatory coherence. What about the decision made by the jury in the civil trial initiated by the parents of Nicole Brown Simpson and Ron Goldman? The jury in this trial found Simpson to be responsible and assessed him millions of dollars in damages (Petrocelli 1998). There are several differences between the civil trial and the criminal trial that can help to explain the different outcomes. First, in a civil trial, there is no burden of proof beyond a reasonable doubt, so the jurors needed only to decide that the preponderance of evidence supported the hypothesis of Simpson's innocence. Second, the lawyers who made the case for Simpson's guilt avoided many of the mistakes made by the prosecution in the criminal trial, such as having the demonstrably racist detective Fuhrman called as a witness. Third, additional evidence had come to light by the time of the civil trial, particularly the pictures showing Simpson wearing Bruno Magli shoes. Fourth, the civil trial was conducted in Santa Monica and drew on a different population of jurors from those in the criminal trial, which was conducted in downtown Los Angeles. The lawyer for the families of Nicole Simpson and Ron Goldman was acutely aware of the pro-Simpson bias of black women, and managed to get a jury of mostly white males, with only one black woman (Petrocelli 1998, p. 376). I conjecture therefore, that the jurors in the civil trial reached their conclusions because they had different emotional biases from those of the jurors in the criminal trial, as well as because the case for Simpson's guilt had greater explanatory coherence and no burden of reasonable doubt to overcome.

Psychological Evidence for Emotional Coherence

I have argued that the emotional coherence account of juror decision making is more plausible than purely cold or hot accounts, but have presented no direct evidence that the mental processes of jurors involve emotional coherence. But the results of two recent psychological studies support the hypothesis that people's inferences involve both cognitive and emotional constraint satisfaction as implemented in the HOTCO 2 model.

Westen et al. (forthcoming) conducted three studies in 1998 during the scandals concerning U.S. President Clinton. All three studies found that people's beliefs about Clinton's guilt or innocence bore minimal relation to their knowledge of relevant data, but were strongly predicted by their feelings about Democrats, Republicans, Clinton, high-status philandering males, feminism, and infidelity. Westen et al. argue that people's inferences about the scandal involved a combination of cognitive constraints (data) and affective constraints (feelings, emotion-laden attitudes, and motives). Their views are clearly consistent with the theory of emotional coherence described above,

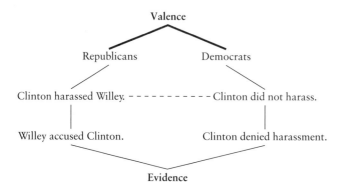

Figure 8.5
Emotional coherence in the assessment of whether President Clinton harassed Kathleen Willey. Thick lines are valence links, which may be positive or negative depending on attitudes toward Democrats and Republicans.

and HOTCO 2 can be used to simulate the inferences made by people in their studies.

Figure 8.5 shows the structure of a highly simplified HOTCO 2 simulation of central aspects of the first study of Westen et al. (forthcoming), which concerned the allegations made by Kathleen Willey that she had been sexually harassed by the President. The hypothesis to be evaluated is that Clinton was guilty of harassment, which would explain why she accused him. On the other hand, the contradictory hypothesis that he did not harass her would explain his protestations of innocence. I have not included in figure 8.5 possible alternative explanations, such as that Willey made the accusation for political reasons and that Clinton denied the accusation simply to protect his reputation. In figure 8.5, the evidence is exactly balanced, so that the explanatory coherence program ECHO finds the competing hypotheses that Clinton harassed Willey and that he did not do so equally acceptable— they get the same low activation.

HOTCO 2, however, reaches very different conclusions depending on whether the Democrats or Republicans are favored by receiving a positive valence through a link with the VALENCE unit. If Democrats are favored by means of an excitatory valence link, the Democrat evaluation unit receives positive valence and activation, which suppresses the activation of the hypothesis that Clinton was guilty, so the program concludes that Clinton did not harass Willey. On the other hand, if Republicans are favored by means of an excitatory valence link, the Republican evaluation unit receives positive valence and activation, which then supports the activation of the hypothesis that Clinton was guilty. Thus the behavior of the HOTCO 2 simulation is in accord with the findings of Westen et al. that emotional attitudes predicted people's judgments of guilt and innocence. The subjects in the Westen et al. studies obviously had many more values and beliefs than the bare-bones HOTCO 2 simulation, but it suffices to show how people's inferences about Clinton could arise from a combination of cognitive and emotional constraints. As in the Simpson simulation, HOTCO 2 is not simply engaging in wishful thinking, because if it is given a large amount of evidence against Clinton then it finds him guilty even if it has a pro-Democrat bias.

Further empirical support for emotional coherence is provided by studies of stereotype activation reported by Sinclair and Kunda (1999). They found that participants who were praised by a Black individual tended to inhibit the negative Black stereotype, while participants who were criticized by a Black individual tended to apply the negative stereotype to him and rate him as incompetent. According to Sinclair and Kunda, the participants' motivation to protect their positive views of themselves caused them either to suppress or to activate the negative Black stereotype. Another study found similar reactions from students who received low grades from women professors: the students used the negative stereotype of women to judge female professors who had given them a poor grade as less competent than male professors who had given them an equally poor grade (Sinclair and Kunda 2000).

Figure 8.6 shows the structure of a simplified HOTCO 2 simulation of aspects of the experiment in which praise and criticism produced very different evaluations of the individual who provided them. Without any evidence input that the evaluation is good or bad, the program finds equally acceptable the claims that the evaluator is competent or incompetent. However, a positive evaluation combines with the motivation for self-enhancement to generate positive judgments of the evaluator and blacks, while a negative evaluation combines with self-enhancement to generate negative judgments of the evaluator and blacks. In the simulation shown in figure 8.6, the positive valence of the *I am good* unit supports activation of the accurate-evaluation unit, which activates the competent-manager unit and suppresses the black stereotype. HOTCO 2 thus shows how thinking can be biased by emotional attachment to goals such as self-enhancement. Hence the mental mechanism of integrated cognitive and affective constraint satisfaction that is postulated by the theory of emotional coherence appears to be psychologically realistic.

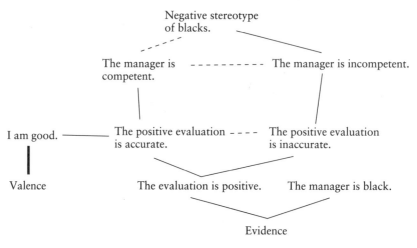

Figure 8.6
Evidential and valence associations leading to the motivated inhibition of the negative black stereotype. Solid lines are excitatory links and dashed lines are inhibitory.

Limitations of the HOTCO Model

Although the HOTCO model can simulate the results of psychological experiments as well as real-life legal decisions, it is obvious that it captures only a small part of the interactions of emotion and cognition. The theory of emotional coherence is nothing like a general theory of emotion. Both the theory and the computational model deal primarily with positive and negative valence, neglecting the many different kinds of positive and negative emotions. For example, different people's reactions to the Simpson case included being happy that he was acquitted, or angry that Mark Fuhrman had lied, or sad that Nicole had been killed. HOTCO can model general reactions of happiness and sadness as overall coherence or incoherence, but it does not provide an account of how specific emotions directed toward particular objects can arise. In contrast, the ITERA model of Nerb and Spada (2001) can differentiate between sadness and anger as emotional reactions to events. Neither HOTCO nor ITERA can differentiate between myriad other emotions experienced by people, such as shame and pride. Emotional coherence is not intended as an alternative to appraisal theory, which provides a general account of how different emotions are elicited by different evaluations of events and situations (Scherer, Schorr, and Johnstone 2001). Rather, it specifies some of the computational mechanisms by which appraisal might take place. Chapter 4 discussed some of the relations between connectionist models, dynamic systems theory, and appraisal theory.

From a biological perspective, the HOTCO model is simplistic in many respects. It uses localist representations in which a whole concept or proposition is represented by a single unit, rather than distributed representations in which multiple neurons collectively represent multiple concepts or propositions. HOTCO units spread activation to each other symmetrically, without the unidirectional action and spiking behavior of real neurons. Morever, HOTCO makes no attempt to model neuroanatomical organization, such as the arrangement of neurons in particular parts of the brain such as the neocortex and the amygdala. Brandon Wagar and I produced a much more neurologically accurate model of the interactions between emotion and cognition (Wagar and Thagard 2004, chap. 6 above). Yet another limitation of the HOTCO simulations performed so far is that they model only the thought processes of a single juror, neglecting the social interactions that are part of group decision making. See Thagard (2000, chap. 7) for a computational model of how scientists reach consensus, and chapter 5 above for a social model.

Conclusion

Despite these limitations, the theory of emotional coherence provides a psychologically plausible account of the decision made by the jurors to acquit O. J. Simpson. The two cold-cognitive explanations I considered, based on explanatory coherence and on probability theory, neglect the emotional considerations that appear to have been part of the psychological processes of the jurors. But the jurors did not engage in pure wishful thinking either: their emotional biases were integrated with considerations of explanatory coherence to produce a judgment that was in part emotion based and in part evidence based.

What *should* the jurors have been thinking? Members of a jury are supposed to be impartial, with no emotional biases for or against the accused. Hence it would seem illegitimate for the jurors to have biases that affect their interpretation of the evidence. If truth is one of the aims of legal deliberation, and if emotional bias helps to prevent the jury from arriving at true answers, then having emotions influence the assessment of evidence and explanatory hypotheses would seem to be normatively inappropriate. Moreover, if fairness is also an aim of legal deliberation, and emotional bias leads some involved parties to be treated unfairly, then the emotional part of emotional coherence seems to be doubly undesirable. Emotion only seems to be a normatively appropriate part of coherence judgments when emotional bias is inspired by fairness concerns, as in my account of reasonable doubt based on valuing acquitting the innocent over convicting the guilty.

I am not, however, trying to exclude emotion from legal thinking. Even scientific thinking is permeated by emotion (see chaps. 10–12 of this vol.), and it would be unreasonable to expect jurors to shut down the emotional reactions that are an ineliminable part of human thought (Damasio 1994). All we can hope for is that the process of jury selection should tend to avoid the inclusion of jurors with strong emotional biases, and that the conduct of trials by the prosecution, defense, and presiding judge should emphasize evidence and alternative explanations rather than emotional appeals. Juror decision making would then still be a matter of emotional coherence, but the emotional component would be minor compared to the rational assessment of the acceptability of competing hypotheses based on explanatory coherence. According to Posner (1999, p. 325): "It would be misleading to conclude that good judges are less 'emotional' than other people. It is just that they deploy a different suite of emotions in their work from what is appropriate both in personal life and in other vocational settings." Further work on the theory of emotional coherence should contribute to an understanding of how emotions can enhance rather than undermine the quality of legal and other kinds of inference.

Introduction

Descartes contended that "I am obliged in the end to admit that none of my former ideas are beyond legitimate doubt" (Descartes 1964, p. 64). Accordingly, he adopted a method of doubting everything: "Since my present aim was to give myself up to the pursuit of truth alone, I thought I must do the very opposite, and reject as if absolutely false anything as to which I could imagine the least doubt, in order to see if I should not be left at the end believing something that was absolutely indubitable" (p. 31). Similarly, other philosophers have raised doubts about the justifiability of beliefs concerning the external world, the existence of other minds, and moral principles; philosophical skepticism has a long history (Popkin 1979).

The concept of doubt is not only of philosophical interest, for it plays a central role in the legal system when jurors are instructed not to convict an accused criminal unless they are convinced of guilt beyond a reasonable doubt. Surprisingly, however, there is little consensus in the theory and practice of law concerning what differentiates reasonable from unreasonable doubt. Faust (2000a, p. 229) reports a "firestorm of controversy" concerning the proper legal meaning of the term "reasonable doubt," and furnishes an extensive annotated bibliography.

My aim in this paper is to propose (1) a descriptive theory of doubt as a cognitive-emotional mental state and (2) a normative theory of the conditions under which doubt can be viewed as reasonable. After describing previous philosophical accounts of doubt, I develop an account of doubt as emotional incoherence that provides a framework for a general account of when doubt is reasonable or unreasonable in philosophical, legal, and scientific contexts.

Cold and Hot Doubt

Social psychologists distinguish between cold cognition and hot cognition, where the latter involves emotions tied in with personal goals and motivations (Kunda 1999). Similarly, I shall distinguish between cold doubt and hot doubt, where the latter involves an attitude toward a proposition that is emotional as well as cognitive. Most philosophers and legal theorists have discussed cold doubt, but I shall follow Charles Peirce in treating doubt as hot, that is, as involving an attitude toward a proposition that has a central emotional component. First let us consider accounts of cold doubt.

Nathan Salmon (1995) proposes the following definition for the word "doubt":

A doubts $p =_{\text{def}}$ (A disbelieves p) or (A suspends judgment concerning p)
A disbelieves $p =_{\text{def}} A$ believes not-p
A suspends judgment concerning $p =_{\text{def}}$ not-(A believes p) and not-(A disbelieves p)

Salmon acknowledges that this definition constitutes a departure from standard usage in that it does not require that a believer has a grasp of a proposition and has attempted consciously to choose between the proposition and its negation. It follows from his definitions that for any proposition p, either A believes p or A doubts p. This is a very odd result: it implies that a person who has never even considered a proposition, for example, that there are more than a million trees in Newfoundland, either believes it or doubts it. Salmon's definition of doubt also does not take into account the contention of Bertrand Russell (1984, p. 142) that doubt "suggests a vacillation, an alternate belief and disbelief." For both Salmon and Russell, doubt is an entirely cognitive rather than emotional phenomenon, a matter of belief and disbelief.

Similarly, Jennifer Faust's (2000b) discussion of reasonable doubt in the law assumes that it is a purely cognitive matter. She distinguishes two senses of doubt that generate two senses of reasonable doubt:

S doubts$_1$ that $p =_{\text{def}} S$ believes that not-p.
S doubts$_2$ that $p =_{\text{def}} S$ does not believe that p.
S reasonably doubts$_1$ that $p =_{\text{def}} S$ has sufficient reason to believe that not-p.
S reasonably doubts$_2$ that $p =_{\text{def}} S$ does not have sufficient reason to believe that p.

Faust makes a convincing case that some prevalent legal instructions concerning reasonable doubt mistakenly confuse the first and second senses, so that jurors are told that acquitting an accused person requires having sufficient reason to believe that the accused was not guilty (sense 1 of "doubt" and "reasonable doubt"). The more appropriate instruction is that acquitting an accused person requires only not having sufficient reason to believe that the accused was guilty (sense 2). As for Salmon and Russell, Faust's doubt is a matter of cold cognition.

An alternative hot conception of doubt was developed by Charles Peirce in the 1860s and 1870s. He attacked Descartes's method of doubt by arguing that complete doubt is a mere self-deception: "Let us not pretend to doubt in philosophy what we do not doubt in our hearts" (Peirce 1958, p. 40). According to Peirce, beliefs are habits of mind that guide our desires and shape our actions. Doubt is not merely a matter or belief or disbelief, but is an *irritation* that causes inquiry, which is a struggle to attain a state of belief (p. 99). The Cartesian exercise of questioning a proposition does not stimulate the mind to struggle after belief, which requires a "real and living doubt" (p. 100). According to Peirce, "the action of thought is excited by the irritation of doubt, and ceases when belief is attained" (p. 118). Doubt is not the result of an internal exercise: "Genuine doubt always has an external origin, usually from surprise" (p. 207). For Peirce, doubt is intimately tied with goals and motivation to increase knowledge, as well as with emotional states involving irritation, excitement, and surprise. Doubt is a matter of hot cognition.

Doubt as Emotional Incoherence

I think that Peirce's account of doubt captures much more of the nature of real doubt than Salmon's cold account, but Peirce does not offer a general theory of what doubt is. First it is useful to have some concrete examples of what Peirce called "real and living" doubt to make it clear what needs to be explained. I am not proposing a definition of the concept of doubt, since such analyses are rarely successful or fruitful. Rather, my aim is to develop a theory about the nature and causal origins of the mental state of doubting.

Here are some real philosophical, scientific, and legal examples of doubt:

Philosophy   Many students taking their first course in philosophy of mind are surprised to learn that most work in the field adopts some form of materialism, in contrast to their religious views that assume there is a nonmaterial soul that survives death. The students doubt that mind is just the brain, and feel considerable anxiety at the possible challenge to their religious beliefs.

Science In 1983, medical researchers heard a young Australian, Barry Marshall, propose that most peptic ulcers are caused by infection by a newly discovered bacterium, now known as *Helicobacter pylori*. The researchers strongly doubted that Marshall could be right about the causes of ulcers, and were very annoyed that a beginner would propose such a preposterous theory (Thagard 1999).

Law In 1995, the jury in the O. J. Simpson trial learned that some of the evidence was sloppily handled and that one of the detectives in the case had a long history of racism. For these and other reasons they doubted that Simpson murdered his ex-wife and quickly and enthusiastically voted to acquit him (chap. 8).

In each of these cases, people encountered a proposition or set of propositions that did not fit with what they already believed, and they reacted emotionally as well as cognitively.

These cases fit the following prototype of the mental and social situation in which doubt arises. Note that this prototype is not proposed as a definition of the word "doubt," but as a description of the typical nature and origins of doubt. Typically, people doubt a proposition when:

1. Someone makes a claim about the proposition.
2. People notice that the proposition is incoherent with their beliefs.
3. The people care about the proposition because it is relevant to their goals.
4. The people feel emotions related to the proposition.
5. The emotions are caused by a combination of the claim, the incoherence, and the relevance of the proposition.

Let us examine each of these facets of doubt in more detail.

In all three of the cases I described, doubt arises by virtue of claims made by others: mind is material, ulcers are caused by bacteria, O. J. is guilty. But doubt does not have to arise by virtue of a claim made by someone else. Occasional cases of real doubt are internally engendered: I think that my gloves are in my coat pocket, but then it occurs to me that I might have forgotten to put them there. Hence Peirce exaggerated when he stated that genuine doubt always has an external cause, but he was for the most part right in understanding doubt as externally inspired, in contrast to an internal Cartesian exercise. External causes of doubt are most often the claims of others, as in my prototype above, but can also be interactions with the world, as when scientists collect data that cause them to doubt prevailing theories. In the gloves example, my doubt that my gloves are in my coat pocket may be caused by seeing something that reminds me that I put my gloves elsewhere. The typical external origins of doubt are important for the kinds of emotional states involved in doubt, such as surprise when the world does not turn out to be as it was expected to be, or annoyance that someone is making a claim incoherent with one's own beliefs.

Doubt always involves the incoherence of a proposition with the rest of what one believes. Incoherence is best understood in terms of a theory of coherence as constraint satisfaction that I have developed at length elsewhere (Thagard 2000). On this theory, inference is a matter of accepting and rejecting representations on the basis of their coherence with other representations. Coherence is determined by the constraints between representations, with different kinds of constraint and different kinds of representation for six kinds of coherence: explanatory, conceptual, perceptual, deductive, analogical, and deliberative. For example, in explanatory coherence, the representations are propositions and the constraints include positive ones that arise between two propositions when one explains another and negative ones that arise between propositions that are contradictory or in explanatory competition. Competing theories in science, law, and ordinary life can be evaluated by accepting or rejecting propositions based on the extent to which doing so maximizes satisfaction of multiple conflicting constraints. Various algorithms for maximizing coherence are available.

A proposition is incoherent with a person's belief system when the process of coherence maximization does not lead to its acceptance into that belief system. The most obvious source of incoherence is contradiction, when a claim is made that contradicts what one already believes. But incoherence can be looser, when a claim has weaker kinds of negative constraints than contradiction. For example, in the ulcer case, the claim that bacteria cause ulcers did not logically contradict the claim that excess acidity causes ulcers, yet medical researchers saw them as competing hypotheses. Doubt can even arise analogically, when a hypothesis is recognized as analogous to one such as cold fusion that has previously been recognized as dubious. So the incoherence that a doubted claim has with a belief system need not be based on contradiction. In all cases of doubt, a claim is not accepted because doing so would diminish coherence.

Just as Salmon distinguishes between disbelief and suspension of judgment, we can distinguish between *strong incoherence*, in which a proposition is rejected, and *weak incoherence*, in which a proposition is neither accepted nor rejected. This can happen with the connectionist (artificial neural network) algorithm for maximizing coherence, in which the activation of an artificial neuron representing a proposition can vary between 1 (acceptance) and −1 (rejection), with activation close to 0 signifying a state of neither acceptance nor rejection. Doubt requires nonacceptance, but it does not require rejection, for it can involve either strong or weak incoherence.

Doubt does not require the conscious recognition of incoherence: we can feel unease about a proposition without being at all aware of the source of the discomfort. Coherence calculations, like most inferences, are performed by the brain unconsciously, with only some of the results being conveyed to consciousness. Hence noticing that a proposition is incoherent with one's belief system (facet 2 in the prototype above), need not involve the conscious thought "I can't believe that because it does not fit with my other beliefs" but merely a negative emotional reaction to the claim.

Facet 3 in my doubt prototype posits that people only doubt propositions that they care about, where care is a matter of relevance to their goals, both epistemic and practical. The two main epistemic goals are truth and understanding, where the latter is achieved by unifying explanations. If your goals include the achievement of truth and understanding, then you will be provoked by someone who makes a claim that you are convinced is false. Gastroenterologists were in part annoyed by Barry Marshall because his claims about ulcers seemed to them false and inimical to understanding. But personal, practical goals can also contribute to doubt: if a claim is a potential threat to your well-being or self-esteem, then you may be motivated to look at it more critically. For example, the beginning philosophy students may doubt materialist philosophy more intensely because of its potential threat to the solace and social connections that they derive from their religious beliefs, producing a kind of motivated inference (Kunda 1999). Practical goals need not involve only personal interests, but could also be concerned with the general welfare of people or with questions of fairness. As I will discuss further below in connection with reasonable doubt, inference in science and law are not merely aimed at acquiring truths. Science also often has a practical goal of increasing human welfare through useful technology, for example using antibiotics to cure ulcers. And the law is concerned not only to find out the truth, but also to ensure that the accused gets a fair trial and is presumed to be innocent until proven otherwise. Epistemic and practical goals must be relevant to a claim, for there is no point in wasting your time doubting (or even entertaining) a claim that you do not care about.

There are a wide variety of emotions involved with the feeling of doubt, most of them negative. The mildest negative emotions associated with doubt include Peirce's irritation and the unease and discomfort that I mentioned.

These emotions can be sufficiently vague and ill defined that it is not even obvious what their objects are, for example whether you are irritated by the claim that aroused doubt or by its proponent. If a claim is not strongly incoherent with your belief system, so that rejection is not obviously called for, the tension between accepting and rejecting the proposition may cause anxiety, especially if it is highly relevant to your personal goals.

Intense negative emotions can also be associated with doubt. If someone makes a claim that is both strongly incoherent with your belief system and highly relevant to your epistemic and practical goals, then doubting the claim can involve emotions such as annoyance, outrage, and even anger. Believing that the proposed claim is to be rejected is tied in not only with disliking the claim but also with disliking the proponent of the claim. For example, the medical researchers who challenged Barry Marshall called him crazy and irresponsible, and were angry that he kept defending claims that they thought were absurd. According to the seventeenth-century philosopher John Wilkins (1969), doubt is a kind of fear. This claim is not generally true, but there are cases where fear may be part of doubt, as when a scientist fears that new data may show a favored theory to be false.

There are also unusual cases in which doubt is associated with positive emotions. Suppose you are told by a doctor that you need open heart surgery, but you read on the Internet that your condition might be treated less invasively by a new drug. Then you doubt that you should have the surgery, and are happy at the prospect of avoiding a risky procedure. In this case, you are happy to doubt that you need surgery. However, if you are unsure of which treatment to pursue, you may feel strong negative emotions such as anxiety because you have doubts about not getting surgery as well as about getting surgery.

The five facets of my doubt prototype do not deductively imply that Cartesian and Humean doubts are not real, since the facets are typical features rather than necessary conditions. But it is clear that skeptical questions about the external world, other minds, and induction fail to fit the prototype. These claims have not been made seriously by anyone who believes them, they are too fanciful to be relevant to anyone's goals, and concern with them is an intellectual exercise rather than an emotional reaction.

We now have the ingredients of the causal network that produces the emotions associated with doubt. Because someone makes a claim that is incoherent with what you believe and that is relevant to your goals, you respond emotionally to the claim and sometimes also to the claimant. Prototypically, doubt is emotional incoherence.

Reasonable Doubt

If doubt is a cognitive-emotional state caused by the incoherence of a claim relevant to a person's goals, then what is reasonable doubt? This question is of philosophical, legal, and scientific importance. In philosophy, we can ask whether the doubts raised by Descartes, Hume, and other skeptics, in ethics as well as epistemology, are reasonable. Is it reasonable to doubt whether there is an external world, whether the future will be like the past, and whether there is an objective difference between right and wrong? In the law, the issue of what constitutes reasonable doubt has been vexing, for practical as well as theoretical reasons. For example, the Supreme Court of Canada recently overturned a number of convictions on the grounds that the judges in the original trial had given an incorrect instruction to the jury concerning the nature of reasonable doubt. Psychological experiments have found that whether mock jurors decide to convict an accused can be influenced by what they are told about the nature of reasonable doubt (Koch and Devine 1999). In science, there are not only epistemic issues about whether scientists are reasonable in doubting a newly proposed theory, but also practical issues about when it is reasonable to doubt the desirability of technological applications of science. For example, were gastroenterologists in 1983 reasonable in doubting the truth of the bacteria theory of ulcers and the efficacy of treatment of ulcers by antibiotics? I will propose a general account of reasonable doubt as *legitimate* emotional incoherence, and then discuss its application to philosophy, law, and science and technology.

On my view, the reasonableness of doubt is both an epistemic and a practical matter, involving epistemic standards concerning truth and understanding and also practical standards concerning welfare and fairness. In keeping with the prototype of doubt that I advanced in the last section, I will specify that doubt in a proposition is *reasonable* when:

1. A claim about the proposition has been made.
2. The noticed incoherence of the proposition with other beliefs is based on a legitimate assessment of coherence.

First, the aptness of doubt requires that a claim about a proposition has been made, normally by someone other than the person who doubts it. This rules out the fanciful, imaginary cases of doubt that Peirce rightly derided. The second condition is much more demanding, requiring that, when people come to doubt something because it is incoherent with their beliefs, they have performed a legitimate calculation of coherence.

Legitimacy depends on the kind of coherence involved. For explanatory coherence, which is the kind most relevant to factual claims in metaphysics, law, and science, the requirements of legitimacy include:

1. The available relevant evidence has all been taken into account.
2. The available alternative hypotheses have all been taken into account.
3. The available explanatory relations have all been used to establish constraints among the hypotheses and evidence.
4. Constraint maximization has been performed, consciously or unconsciously, producing a coherence judgment about what propositions to accept or reject.

Doubt can fail to be reasonable according to these legitimacy conditions when people make their judgments of incoherence without taking into account all the available relevant information.

It is tempting to say that a *set* of propositions can be reasonably doubted if there is reasonable doubt about one of the members of the set. But from a coherence perspective, it is better not to aggregate propositions by mere conjunction. In real legal and scientific cases, groups of propositions can form wholes through interconnections by explanation relations, as when one hypothesis explains another or two hypotheses together provide an explanation. We should therefore maintain that it is reasonable to doubt a group of propositions when a claim about the group has been made and when the noticed incoherence of the group with other beliefs is based on a legitimate assessment of coherence.

This discussion has been rather abstract, so let me now relate it to philosophical, legal, and scientific cases of reasonable and unreasonable doubt. The philosophy students' initial doubts about materialist theories of mind strike me as reasonable, at least initially. They encounter the claim that there is no soul in lectures or reading, and the claim is indeed incoherent with their religious and metaphysical beliefs. Because they care for both theoretical and personal reasons whether there is a soul, they feel negative emotions such as discomfort arising from the materialist claim. Of course, the doubt will remain reasonable only if, as they learn more about the evidence for materialism and against mind–body dualism, they continue to perform a legitimate coherence calculation. My own view is that, once all the available evidence and explanations are taken into account, materialism has more explanatory coherence than dualism (Thagard 2000). But students initially do not have all this information available to them, so their doubt is reasonable. In contrast, Cartesian doubt about whether one exists is not reasonable: no one claims nonexistence, and the hypothesis is not incoherent with other beliefs.

The same is true for Humean doubt about whether the future will be like the past. There are no negative emotions involved in these philosophical exercises; if there were any people seriously worried about whether they exist, we would judge them to be mentally ill.

In legal trials, the reasonableness of doubt depends on the kind of legal investigation. It is of crucial importance that the standard of "beyond reasonable doubt" that applies in criminal trials is not used in civil trials, where jurors' conclusions need only be based on a preponderance of evidence. A crucial aspect of criminal trials in the English tradition is that there is a presumption of innocence. This is clearly not related to the epistemic goal of truth: there is no reason to believe that the prior probability of innocence is greater than that of guilt, and in fact the conditional probability of guilt given arrest is usually much higher than the conditional probability of innocence given arrest. Rather, the presumption of innocence is maintained in order to ensure that trials are fair, not just in the sense that the accused and prosecution are treated equally, as the plaintiff and defendant are supposed to be in civil trials, but in the stronger sense that we place a high moral value on not convicting the innocent. Because fairness is a goal of criminal trials in addition to truth, negative emotions concerning claims about the guilt of the accused can arise that are more intense than would be inspired by explanatory coherence alone. Convicting the innocent is a moral as well as an epistemic mistake, and appropriately provokes outrage.

Finally, consider the reasonableness of doubt in scientific and technological contexts. It might be assumed that scientific doubt is a purely epistemic matter, but Richard Rudner (1961, pp. 32–33) has convincingly argued otherwise:

Since no scientific hypothesis is ever completely verified, in accepting a hypothesis on the basis of evidence, the scientist must make the decision that the evidence is sufficiently strong or that the probability is sufficiently high to warrant the acceptance of the hypothesis. Obviously, our decision with regard to the evidence and how strong is "strong enough" is going to be a function of the importance, in the typically ethical sense, of making a mistake in accepting or rejecting the hypothesis. Thus, to take a crude but easily manageable example, if the hypothesis under consideration stated that a toxic ingredient of a drug was not present in lethal quantity, then we would require a relatively high degree of confirmation or confidence before accepting the hypothesis—for the consequences of making a mistake here are exceedingly grave by our moral standards. In contrast, if our hypothesis stated that, on the basis of some sample, a certain lot of machine-stamped belt buckles was not defective, the degree of confidence we would require would be relatively lower. How sure we must be before we accept a hypothesis depends on how serious a mistake would be.

Thus doubt in science is in part a function of our practical goal of avoiding harm that might result from premature acceptance of a hypothesis. In theoretical astrophysics, the risk of harm is trivial, so doubt can be based largely on epistemic goals, but doubts can have a partially practical basis in areas like medicine (relevant to treating the sick) and nuclear physics (relevant to the construction of power plants and bombs). Just as the concern to acquit the innocent can intensify doubts in legal contexts, so the concern to avoid technological harm can intensify doubts in scientific contexts.

Medical doubts can be reasonable for both epistemic and practical reasons. When gastroenterologists first encountered the bacterial theory of ulcers, they had strong negative emotional reactions in part because it was incoherent with their beliefs about the causes of ulcers and the absence of bacteria in the stomach, but also because of their concern about people being treated inappropriately. Their doubts about Barry Marshall's views were reasonable in 1983, because there was little evidence then that bacteria cause ulcers and none that killing the bacteria could cure ulcers. By 1994, however, the situation had changed dramatically as the result of carefully designed studies that showed that many people's ulcers had been cured by the right combination of antibiotics. At this point, coherence with the relevant medical information required acceptance of the bacterial theory of ulcers, so doubt was unreasonable.

Many epistemologists think that rational belief fixation is a probabilistic rather than a coherence-based process, so that reasonable doubt depends on the probability of a claim. For example, Davidson and Pargetter (1987) give three requirements for a guilty verdict:

(a) the probability of guilt given the evidence is very high,
(b) the evidence on which the probability is based is very reliable, and
(c) the probability of guilt is highly resilient relative to any possible evidence.

But there are powerful reasons why probability theory is not the appropriate tool for understanding reasonable doubt.

First, the interpretation of probability is problematic in legal, scientific, and philosophical contexts. It is obvious that the probability of guilt given the evidence is not the objective, statistical sense of probability as a frequency in a population: we have no data that allow us to say in a particular trial that the accused would be guilty in a specifiable proportion of such trials. So probability must be either some kind of logical relation that has never been clearly defined, or a subjective degree of belief.

Second, there is considerable psychological evidence that people's degrees of belief do not obey the rules of the probability calculus (Kahneman, Slovic, and Tversky 1982; Tversky and Koehler 1994). Many psychological experiments have shown that the degrees of confidence that people place in propositions are often not in keeping with the rules of probability theory. Probability theory is a relatively recent invention, having been developed only in the seventeenth century (Hacking 1975). Yet people have been making judgments of uncertainty for thousands of years, without the aid of probability theory. Coherence provides a much more plausible descriptive and normative account of nonstatistical human inference than does probability theory.

Third, probability theory is often orthogonal to the aims and practice of law. Cohen and Bersten (1990) argue that high probability is not even a necessary condition of finding someone guilty, which requires satisfying a number of legal rules that must be followed in order to ensure that the accused is given the benefit of the presumption of innocence. Allen (1991, 1994) has described numerous ways in which deliberation in legal trials much better fits a coherence account than a probabilistic one.

Fourth, there are technical reasons why probabilities are difficult to compute in real-life cases in law and other areas. A full probability calculation is impossible in cases involving more than a handful of propositions, because the size of a full joint distribution increases exponentially with the number of propositions. Powerful computational tools have been developed for the calculation of probabilities in Bayesian networks, but they require more conditional probabilities than are usually available and strong assumptions of independence that are rarely satisfiable. Computing probabilities in legal and similar cases is much more difficult than coherence computations based on maximization of constraint satisfaction (Thagard 2004). Hence incoherence is a more plausible basis for reasonable doubt than low probability.

Finally, probability does not provide the basis for understanding reasonable doubt because it is not directly tied in with emotion. I have argued that doubt is a mental state that usually involves negative emotions such as discomfort and fear, whereas probability judgments are purely cognitive. In contrast, coherence judgments routinely give rise to positive emotions such as feelings of satisfaction and even beauty, whereas incoherence judgments give rise to negative emotions such as anxiety (Thagard 2000). If doubt is emotional incoherence, then there must be more to reasonable doubt than just a probability calculation.

Conclusion

This paper has advanced and defended several novel claims about the nature of doubt and reasonable doubt. First, doubt is not just a cold cognitive matter of belief and disbelief, but also involves a hot, emotional reaction to a claim that has been made. Second, doubt is not based on the low probability of a claim, but on its incoherence with a thinker's beliefs and goals, where coherence can be computed in a psychologically realistic manner by parallel satisfaction of multiple constraints. Third, what makes a doubt reasonable is not a probability calculation, but a coherence computation that takes into account constraints based on the full available range of evidence, hypotheses, and explanatory and other relations. Reasonable doubt is legitimate emotional incoherence.

Introduction

This chapter discusses the cognitive contributions that emotions make to scientific inquiry, including the justification as well as the discovery of hypotheses. James Watson's description of how he and Francis Crick discovered the structure of DNA illustrates how positive and negative emotions contribute to scientific thinking. I conclude that emotions are an essential part of scientific cognition.

Since Plato, most philosophers have drawn a sharp line between reason and emotion, assuming that emotions interfere with rationality and have nothing to contribute to good reasoning. In his dialogue the *Phaedrus*, Plato compared the rational part of the soul to a charioteer who must control his steeds, which correspond to the emotional parts of the soul (Plato 1961, p. 499). Today, scientists are often taken as the paragons of rationality, and scientific thought is generally assumed to be independent of emotional thinking.

But current research in cognitive science is increasingly challenging the view that emotions and reason are antagonistic to each other. Evidence is accumulating in cognitive psychology and neuroscience that emotions and rational thinking are closely intertwined (see, e.g., Damasio 1994; Kahneman 1999; and Panksepp 1998). My aim in this chapter is to extend that work and describe the role of the emotions in scientific thinking. If even scientific thinking is legitimately emotional, then the traditional division between reason and emotion becomes totally unsupportable.

My chapter begins with a historical case study. In his famous book, *The Double Helix*, James Watson presented a review of the discovery of the structure of DNA. Unlike the typical dry and scientific biography or autobiography, Watson provided a rich view of the personalities involved in one of the most important discoveries of the twentieth century. I will present a survey and analysis of the emotions mentioned by Watson and use it and quotations from other scientists to explain the role of the emotions in scientific cognition. My account will describe the essential contributions of emotions in all three of the contexts in which scientific work is done: investigation, discovery, and justification. Initially, emotions such as curiosity, interest, and wonder play a crucial role in the pursuit of scientific ideas. Moreover, when investigation is successful and leads to discoveries, emotions such as excitement and pleasure arise. Even in the third context, justification, emotions are a crucial part of the process of recognizing a theory as one that deserves to be accepted. Good theories are acknowledged for their beauty and elegance, which are aesthetic values that are accompanied by emotional reactions.

The Discovery of the Structure of DNA

In 1951, James Watson was a young American postdoctoral fellow at Cambridge University. He met Francis Crick, a British graduate student who was already in his mid-thirties. Both had a strong interest in genetics, and they began to work together to identify the structure of the DNA molecule and to determine its role in the operations of genes. The intellectual history of their work has been thoroughly presented by Olby (1974) and Judson (1979). My concern is with emotional aspects of the thinking of Watson and Crick and of scientific thinking in general; these aspects have been largely ignored by historians, philosophers, and even psychologists. The primary question is: What role did emotions play in the thinking of Watson and Crick that led to the discovery of the structure of DNA and the acceptance of their model?

In order to answer this question, I read carefully through *The Double Helix*, looking for words that refer to emotions. Watson described not only the ideas and the hypotheses that were involved in the discovery of the structure of DNA, but also the emotions that accompanied the development of the new ideas. In Watson's (1969) short book, whose paperback edition has only 143 pages, I counted a total of 235 emotion words. Of the 235 emotion episodes referred to, more than half (125) were attributed by Watson solely to himself. Another 35 were attributed to his collaborator Francis Crick, and 13 emotions were attributed by Watson to both of them. There were also 60 attributions of emotions to other researchers, including various scientists in Cambridge and London. I coded the emotions as having either positive valence (e.g., happiness) or negative valence (e.g., sadness), and found that more than half of the emotions (135) had positive valence. Of course, there

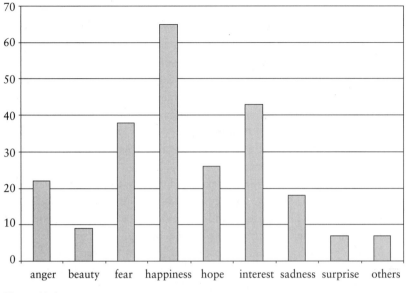

Figure 10.1
Frequency of classes of emotion words in Watson 1969.

is no guarantee that Watson's reports of the emotions of himself and others are historically and psychologically accurate, but they provide a rich set of examples of possible emotional concomitants of scientific thinking.

In order to identify the kinds of emotions mentioned by Watson, I coded the emotion words in terms of what psychologists call *basic* emotions, which are ones taken to be culturally universal among human beings (Ekman 1992). The usual list of basic emotions includes happiness, sadness, anger, fear, disgust, and sometimes surprise. To cover classes of emotion words that occurred frequently in the book but did not fall under the six basic emotions, I added three additional categories: interest, hope, and beauty. Figure 10.1 displays the frequency with which these categories of emotions appear in Watson's narrative. Happiness was the most frequently mentioned emotion, occurring 65 times with many different words referring to such positive emotional states as excitement, pleasure, joy, fun, delight, and relief. The next most frequently mentioned classes of emotions were: interest, with 43 emotion words referring to states such as wonder and enthusiasm; and fear, with 38 emotion words referring to states such as worry and anxiety.

The point of this study, however, was not simply to enumerate the emotion words used by Watson in his story. To identify the role that emotions played in the thinking of Watson and Crick, I coded the emotion words as occurring in three different contexts of the process of inquiry: investigation, discovery, and justification. Most scientific work occurs in the context of investigation, when scientists are engaged in the long and often difficult attempt to establish empirical facts and to develop theories that explain them. Much preparatory experimental and theoretical work is usually required before scientists are able to move into the context of discovery, in which new theoretical ideas and important new empirical results are produced. Finally, scientists enter the context of justification, when new hypotheses and empirical results are evaluated with respect to alternative explanations and the entire body of scientific ideas.

The distinction between the contexts of discovery and justification is due to Reichenbach (1938). I use it here not to demarcate the psychological and subjective from the philosophical and rational, as Reichenbach intended, but merely to mark different stages in the process of inquiry, all of which I think are of both psychological and philosophical interest. I further divide Reichenbach's context of discovery into contexts of investigation and discovery, in order to indicate that much work is often required before actual discoveries are made. In scientific practice, the contexts of investigation, discovery, and justification often blend into each other, so they are best viewed as rough stages of scientific inquiry rather than as absolutely distinct.

Most of Watson's emotion words (163) occurred in the context of investigation. Fifteen words occurred in the context of discovery, 29 in the context of justification, and 28 emotion words occurred in other more personal contexts that had nothing to do with the development of scientific ideas. In the rest of this chapter, I will provide a much more detailed account of how the many different kinds of emotions contribute to scientific thinking in the three contexts. I will offer not only a correlational account of what emotions tend to occur in what contexts, but also a causal account of how emotions produce and are produced by the cognitive operations that occur in the different stages of scientific inquiry.

Emotions in the Context of Investigation

Discussions of scientific rationality usually address questions in the context of justification, such as when is it rational to replace a theory by a competing one. But scientists engage in a great deal of decision making that precedes questions of justification. Students who are interested in pursuing a scientific career must make decisions that answer questions such as the following: What science (e.g., physics or biology) should I concentrate on? What area of the science (e.g., high-energy physics or molecular biology) should I focus on? What particular research topics should I pursue? Which questions should I attempt to answer? What methods and tools should I use in attempting to answer those questions?

On the traditional view of rational decision making familiar from economics, scientists should attempt to answer these questions by calculating how to maximize their expected utility. This involves taking into account scientific goals such as truth and understanding, and possibly also taking into account personal goals such as fame and financial gain, as well as considering the probabilities that particular courses of research will lead to the satisfaction of these goals. Some philosophers (e.g., Goldman [1999] and Kitcher [1993]) describe scientists as choosing projects based on maximizing epistemic goals such as truth.

I would like to propose an alternative view of scientific decision making in the context of investigation. Decisions concerning what topics to research are much more frequently based on emotions than on rational calculations. It is rarely possible for scientists to predict with any accuracy what choice of research areas, topics, and questions will pay off with respect to understanding, truth, or personal success. The range of possible actions is usually ill specified, and the probabilities of success of different strategies are rarely known. Because rational calculation of maximal utility is effectively impossible, it is appropriate that scientists rely on cognitive emotions such as interest and curiosity to shape the direction of their inquiries. See chapter 2 above for a model of decision making as informed intuition based on emotional coherence.

Watson's narrative makes it clear that he and Crick were heavily motivated by interest. Watson left Copenhagen where his postdoctoral fellowship was supposed to be held because he found the research being done there boring: the biochemist he was working with there "did not stimulate me in the slightest" (Watson 1969, p. 23). In contrast, he reacted to questions concerning the physical structure of biologically important molecules such as DNA with emotions such as excitement: "It was Wilkins who first excited me about X-ray work on DNA" (p. 22); "Suddenly I was excited about chemistry" (p. 28). Crick similarly remarks how he and Watson "passionately wanted to know the details of the structure" (Crick 1988, p. 70). Much later, Watson (2000, p. 125) stated as one of his rules for succeeding in science: "Never do anything that bores you."

Once interest and curiosity direct scientists to pursue answers to particular questions, other emotions such as happiness and hope can help motivate them to perform the often laborious investigations that are required to produce results. It was clearly important to Watson and Crick that they often became excited that they were on the right track. Watson (1969, p. 99) wrote that "On a few walks our enthusiasm would build up to the point that we fiddled with the models when we got back to our office." Both took delight in getting glimpses of what the structure of DNA might be. They were strongly motivated by the hope that they might make a major discovery. Hope is more than a belief that an event might happen—it also the emotional desire and joyful anticipation that it will happen. I counted 26 occurrences where Watson mentioned the hopes of himself or others for scientific advance.

In addition to positive emotions such as interest and happiness, scientists are also influenced by negative emotions such as sadness, fear, and anger. Sadness enters the context of investigation when research projects do not work out as expected. Watson and Crick experienced emotions such as dismay when their work faltered. Such emotions need not be entirely negative in their effects, however, because sadness about the failure of one course of action can motivate a scientist to pursue an alternative and ultimately more successful line of research.

Fear can also be a motivating emotion. Watson and Crick were very worried that the eminent chemist Linus Pauling would discover the structure of DNA before they did, and they also feared that the London researchers, Rosalind Franklin and Maurice Wilkins, would beat them. Watson wrote that when he heard that Pauling had proposed a structure, "my stomach sank in apprehension at learning that all was lost" (Watson 1969, p. 102). Other worries and anxieties arose from setbacks experienced by Watson and Crick themselves. Watson was initially very excited by a proposal that was shown by a crystallographer to be unworkable, but tried to salvage his hypothesis: "Thoroughly worried, I went back to my desk hoping to salvage the like-with-like idea" (1969, p. 122).

The other negative emotion that Watson mentions frequently in the context of investigation is anger. To himself, Watson ascribes only weak forms of anger, such as annoyance and frustration, but he describes Crick as experiencing fury and outrage when his senior professors wrote a paper that failed to acknowledge his contributions. According to Oatley (1992), people experience anger when the accomplishment of their goals is blocked by people or events. Most of the anger-related episodes mentioned by Watson are directed at people, but some concern facts, as when Watson and Crick both become annoyed at the complexity of DNA bonds. I do not get the impression from Watson's chronicle that anger was ever a motivating force in the scientific

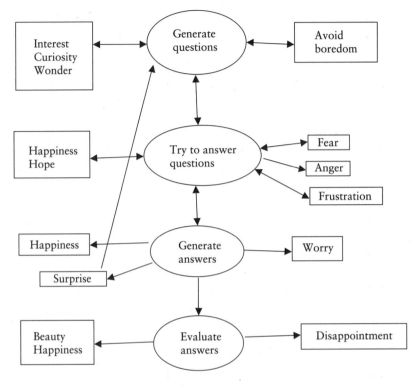

Figure 10.2
A model of the causal interconnections of cognitive processes of inquiry and emotional states. Arrows indicate causal influences.

work he described, but we can see it as an effect of undesirable interactions with other people and the world.

A general model of the role of emotions in the context of scientific investigations is shown in figure 10.2. Interest, wonder, curiosity, and the avoidance of boredom are key inputs to the process of selecting scientific questions to investigate. I have made the causal arrows between emotions and the process of question generation bidirectional in order to indicate that emotions are outputs as well as inputs to the generation of questions. Coming up with a good question can increase curiosity and interest, and produce happiness as well. Once questions have been generated, the cognitive processes involved in trying to generate answers to them can also interact with emotions such as interest and happiness, as well as with negative emotions such as fear. For convenience, I have organized positive emotions on the left side of figure 10.2, and negative emotions on the right side. The causal arrows connecting processes of question generation, question answering, and answer evaluation are also bidirectional, indicating interconnections rather than a linear operation. For example, the attempt to answer a question can generate subordinate questions whose answers are relevant to the original question. For a discussion of the process of question generation in science, see Thagard (1999).

The emotions that Watson attributed to himself and his colleagues are commonly found in other scientists, as evident in a series of interviews conducted by the biologist Lewis Wolpert for BBC Radio (Wolpert and Richards 1997). Wolpert elicited frank descriptions of leading researchers' intense emotional involvement in their work. For example, the distinguished biologist Gerald Edelman stated: "Curiosity drives me. I believe that there is a group of scientists who are kind of voyeurs, they have the splendid feeling, almost a lustful feeling, of excitement when a secret of nature is revealed ... and I would certainly place myself in that group" (Wolpert and Richards 1997, p. 137). Similarly, the eminent physicist Carlo Rubbia said of scientists: "We're driven by an impulse which is one of curiosity, which is one of the basic instincts that a man has. So we are essentially driven not by ... how can I say ... not by the success, but by a sort of passion, namely the desire of understanding better, to possess, if you like, a bigger part of the truth" (Wolpert and Richards 1997, p. 197).

According to Kubovy (1999, p. 147), to be curious is to get pleasure from learning something that you did not previously know. He contends that curiosity has its roots in animal behavior, having evolved from the need to search for food. Many mammals prefer richer environments over less complex ones. Humans can be curious about a very wide range of subjects, from the trivial to the sublime, and scientists direct their intense drive to learn things that are unknown not just to themselves, but to people in general. Loewenstein (1994) defends a more cognitive account of curiosity as the noticing of knowledge gaps, but underplays the emotional side of curiosity. There are many knowledge gaps that scientists may notice, but only some of them arouse an emotional interest that spurs them to the efforts required to generate answers.

Emotions in the Context of Discovery

The discovery of the structure of DNA occurred after Maurice Wilkins showed Watson new X-ray pictures that Rosalind Franklin had taken of a three-dimensional form of DNA. Watson reports: "The instant I saw the picture my mouth fell open and my pulse began to race" (Watson 1969, p. 107). This picture moved Watson from the context of investigation into the context of discovery, in which a plausible hypothesis concerning the structure of DNA could be generated. While drawing, Watson got the idea that each DNA molecule might consist of two chains, and he became very excited about the possibility and its biological implications. Here is a passage that describes his resulting mental state; I have highlighted in boldface the positive emotion words and in italics the negative emotion words.

> As the clock went past midnight I was becoming more and more **pleased**. There had been far too many days when Francis and I *worried* that DNA structure might turn out to be superficially very *dull*, suggesting nothing about either its replication or its function in controlling cell biochemistry. But now, to my **delight** and **amazement**, the answer was turning out to be profoundly **interesting**. For over two hours I **happily** lay awake with pairs of adenine residues whirling in front of my closed eyes. Only for brief moments did the *fear* shoot through me that an idea this good could be wrong. (Watson 1969, p. 118)

Watson's initial idea about the chemical structure of DNA turned out to be wrong, but it put him on the track that quickly led to the final model that Watson and Crick published.

Most of the emotions mentioned by Watson in his discussion of discoveries fall under the basic emotion of happiness; these include excitement, pleasure, and delight. The chemist who helped to invent the birth control pill, Carl Djerassi, compares making discoveries to sexual pleasure. "I'm absolutely convinced that the pleasure of a real scientific insight—it doesn't have to be a great discovery—is like an orgasm" (Wolpert and Richards 1997, p. 12). Gopnik (1998) also compares explanations to orgasms, hypothesizing that explanation is to cognition as orgasm is to reproduction.

The pleasure of making discoveries is effusively described by Gerard Edelman:

> After all, if you have been filling in the tedium of everyday existence by blundering around a lab, for a long time, and wondering how you're going to get the answer, and then something really glorious happens that you couldn't possibly have thought of, that has to be some kind of remarkable pleasure. In the sense that it's a surprise, but it's not too threatening, it is a pleasure in the same sense that you can make a baby laugh when you bring an object out of nowhere ... Breaking through, getting various insights is certainly one of the most beautiful aspects of scientific life. (Wolpert and Richards 1997, p. 137)

Carlo Rubbia reports that "The act of discovery, the act of being confronted with a new phenomenon, is a very passionate and very exciting moment in everyone's life. It's the reward for many, many years of effort and, also, of failures" (Wolpert and Richards 1997, p. 197).

François Jacob (1988, pp. 196–197) describes his first taste of the joy of discovery as follows: "I had seen myself launched into research. Into discovery. And, above all, I had grasped the process. I had tasted the pleasure." Later, when Jacob was developing the ideas about the genetic regulatory mechanisms in the synthesis of proteins that later won him a Nobel Prize, he had an even more intense emotional reaction: "These hypotheses, still rough, still vaguely outlined, poorly formulated, stir within me. Barely have I emerged that I feel invaded by an intense joy, a savage pleasure. A sense of strength, as well, of power" (Jacob 1988, p. 298). Still later, Jacob describes the great joy that came with experimental confirmation of his hypotheses. Scheffler (1991, p. 10) discusses the joy of verification, when scientists take pleasure when their predictions are found to be true. Of course, predictions sometimes turn out to be false, producing disappointment and even gloom.

It is evident from Watson and the other scientists that I have quoted that discovery can be an intensely pleasurable experience. In figure 10.2, I have shown surprise and happiness as both arising from the successful generation of answers to pursued questions. The prospect of being able to experience such emotions is one of the prime motivating factors behind scientific efforts. Richard Feynman proclaimed that his work was not motivated by a desire for fame or prizes such as the Nobel that he eventually received, but by the joy of discovery: "The prize is the pleasure of finding a thing out, the kick of the discovery, the observation that other people use it [my work]—those are the real things, the others are unreal to me (Feynman 1999, p. 12). Discoveries are usually pleasant surprises, but unpleasant surprises also occur, for example when experiments yield data that are contrary to expectations. Disappointment and sadness can also arise when the evaluation stage leads to the conclusion that one's preferred answers are inferior or inadequate, as shown in figure 10.2.

Kubovy (1999) discusses virtuosity, the pleasure we have when we are doing something well. He thinks that humans and also animals such as monkeys and dolphins enjoy working and take pleasure in mastering new skills. Scientists can achieve virtuosity in many diverse tasks such as designing experiments, interpreting their results, and developing plausible theories to explain the experimental results. According to physicist Murray Gell-Mann, "Understanding things, seeing connections, finding explanations, discovering beautiful, simple principles that work is very, very satisfying" (Wolpert and Richards 1997, p. 165).

Emotions in the Context of Justification

Although many would concede that the processes of investigation and discovery are substantially emotional, it is much more radical to suggest that even the context of justification has a strong emotional component. In Watson's writings, the main sign of an emotional component to justification is found in his frequent description of the elegance and beauty of the model of DNA that he and Crick produced. Watson wrote:

We only wished to establish that at least one specific two-chain complementary helix was stereoochemically possible. Until this was clear, the objection could be raised that, although our idea was aesthetically elegant, the shape of the sugar-phosphate backbone might not permit its existence. Happily, now we knew that this was not true, and so we had lunch, telling each other that a structure this pretty just had to exist. (Watson 1969, p. 131)

Thus one of the causes of the conviction that they had the right structure was its aesthetic, emotional appeal. Other scientists also had a strong emotional reaction to the new model of DNA. Jacob (1988, p. 271) wrote of the Watson and Crick model: "This structure was of such simplicity, such perfection, such harmony, such beauty even, and biological advances flowed from it with such rigor and clarity, that one could not believe it untrue."

In a similar vein, the distinguished microbiologist Leroy Hood described how he takes pleasure in coming up with elegant theories:

Well, I think it's a part of my natural enthusiasm for everything, but what I've been impressed with in science over my twenty-one years is the absolute conflict between, on the one hand, as we come to learn more and more about particular biological systems there is a simple elegant beauty to the underlying principles, yet when you look into the details it's complex, it's bewildering, it's kind of overwhelming, and I think of beauty in the sense of being able to extract the fundamental elegant principles from the bewildering array of confusing details, and I've felt I was good at doing that, I enjoy doing that. (Wolpert and Richards 1997, p. 44)

Many other scientists have identified beauty and elegance as distinguishing marks of theories that should be accepted (McAllister 1996).

From the perspective of traditional philosophy of science, or even the perspective of traditional cognitive psychology that separates the cognitive and the emotional, the fact that scientists find some theories emotionally appealing is irrelevant to their justification. My own previous work is no exception: I have defended the view that scientific theories are accepted or rejected on the basis of their explanatory coherence with empirical data and other theories (Thagard 1992, 1999). But my theory of emotional coherence shows how cognitive coherence judgments can generate emotional judgments (Thagard 2000, chap. 6).

As I described in previous chapters, coherence is not just a matter of accepting or rejecting a conclusion, but can also involve attaching a positive or negative emotional assessment to a proposition, object, concept, or other representation.

On this account, a theory is justified if inferring it maximizes coherence, but assessment can also involve an emotional judgment. Theories consist of hypotheses which are comprised of concepts. According to the theory of emotional coherence, these representations not only have a cognitive status of being accepted or rejected, they also have an emotional status of being liked or disliked. In keeping with Bower's (1981) account of the psychology of emotions, I use the term *valence* for the emotional status of a representation. A representation receives its valence as the result of its connections with other representations. The valence of a theory will flow from the valences of the hypotheses that constitute it, as well as from the overall coherence that it generates.

Overall coherence requires a judgment about how everything fits together. Such judgments can be made by the computational model HOTCO ("hot coherence"), which not only simulates the spread of valences among representations, but also simulates how the coherence of the representations with each other can generate a "metacoherence" inference which is associated with happiness. I will not repeat the computational details (Thagard 2000), but merely want here to give the general flavor of how the model works. A proposition is highly coherent with other propositions if its acceptance helps to maximize the satisfaction of constraints, such as the constraint that if a hypothesis explains a piece of evidence, then the hypothesis and the evidence should be either accepted together or rejected together. If a group of propositions can be accepted together in such a way that the individual propositions each tend to satisfy a high proportion of the constraints on them, the overall system of proposition gets a high metacoherence rating.

Figure 10.3 diagrams how judgments of coherence and other emotions can arise. Units are artificial neurons that represent propositions, and their assessment by neural network algorithms for maximizing constraint satisfaction leads to them either being accepted or rejected. In addition, the extent to which the constraints on a unit are satisfied affects a unit representing a judgment of coherence, which produces happiness. For example, if the acceptance of a hypothesis makes possible satisfaction of numerous constraints that tie the hypothesis with the evidence it explains, then a unit representing the hypothesis will strongly activate the coherence node and thence the hap-

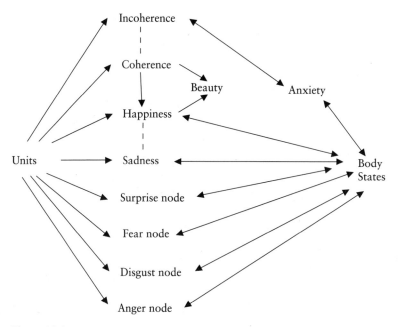

Figure 10.3
Interactions of cognitive units (neurons or neuronal groups) with emotions and bodily states. Reprinted from Thagard 2000 by permission of MIT Press.

piness node. At the other end of the emotional distribution, incoherence tends to produce unhappiness or even fear-related emotions such as anxiety.

This sketch of the theory and computational model of emotional coherence shows how it is possible for a mind simultaneously to make cognitive judgments and emotional reactions. Watson and Crick's hypothesis concerning the structure of DNA was highly coherent with the available evidence and with the goals of biologists to understand the genetic basis of life. This high coherence generated not only a judgment that the hypothesis should be accepted, but also an aesthetic, emotional attitude that the hypothesis was beautiful. Coherence made Watson, Crick, Jacob, and others very happy.

Conceptual Change as Emotional Change

Discovering the structure of DNA was a major scientific breakthrough, but it was not a major case of conceptual change. The discovery brought about additions to the concepts of a gene and DNA, but did not require revisions of previous components of the concepts. New hypotheses were adopted, but there was no rejection of previously believed hypotheses. In contrast, scientific revolutions involve both major alteration of concepts and revision of previously held hypotheses (Thagard 1992). I will now argue that conceptual changes also often involve emotional change.

Consider, for example, Darwin's theory of evolution by natural selection. When he proposed it in the *Origin of Species* in 1859, some scientists such as Huxley quickly realized the strength of the theory and adopted it. But others continued to maintain the traditional view that species arose by Divine creation, and viewed Darwin's theory as not only false but repugnant. Even today, there are creationists who view the theory of evolution as not only false but evil, since they see it as undermining religious beliefs and values. Most biologists, in contrast, feel that Darwin's theory is profound and elegant. Thus for a creationist to become a Darwinian, or for a Darwinian to become a creationist, thinkers must undergo emotional as well as cognitive changes. In addition to rejecting some hypotheses already held and accepting new ones, thinkers who are changing theories are also changing their emotional attitudes toward propositions, concepts, and even people: there are different emotions associated with Darwin-as-scientific-hero and Darwin-as-heretic.

Consider also the more recent historical case of the initial rejection and eventual acceptance of the bacterial theory of ulcers (Thagard 1999). When Marshall and Warren (1984) proposed that most peptic ulcers are caused by the newly discovered bacterium now known as *Helicobacter pylori*, their hypothesis was initially viewed as not only implausible, but even crazy! Marshall's persistent advocacy of the unpopular hypothesis led people to view him as brash and irresponsible. But annoyance turned to respect as evidence mounted that eradicating the bacteria brought many people a permanent cure of their ulcers. Not only did attitudes change toward Marshall but also toward the bacterial theory of ulcer and toward the concept of ulcer-causing bacteria. What was ridiculed became appreciated as an important part of medical theory and practice.

I propose that these changes come about through the process of achieving emotional coherence. At the same time that decisions concerning what to believe are made by a process that maximizes explanatory coherence (fitting hypotheses with data and each other), attitudes are formed by a process that spreads valences through the representational system in accord with existing valences and emotional constraints. For example, scientists who come to appreciate the explanatory power of Darwin's evolutionary hypotheses will come to believe them and to attach a positive emotional valence to them, to the concept of evolution, and to Darwin. On the other hand, scientists (if there are any) who adopt religious fundamentalism and decide that the Bible is to be revered will reject the hypothesis and concept of evolution and view it as odious. Our beliefs are revised by a holistic process of deciding what fits with what, and our emotions are similarly adjusted.

If conceptual change in science is often emotional change, what about science education? Often, science education will not require emotional change because students do not have any emotional attachments to prescientific ideas. For example, learning to use Newton's laws of motion to understand the behavior of projectiles does not seem to require abandoning any emotional attachment on the part of the students to Aristotelian ideas. But learning in biology and the social sciences may involve much more emotional adjustment. Biology students learning about genetics and evolution may have to abandon beliefs that they not only hold but value about the nature of the universe. Similarly, social and political beliefs may be factual, but they are closely intertwined with strongly emotional values. A microeconomist who is convinced that laissez-faire capitalism is the best economic system differs in beliefs and also emphatically in values from a macroeconomist who favors socialism. Hence educators should be alert for cases where resistance to conceptual change derives from emotional as well as cognitive factors. Normally, emotional change is more the province of psychotherapists than science teachers, but teaching emotionally laden scientific issues such as the theory of evolution may require therapeutic techniques to identify valences as well as beliefs. Appreciation of radically different conceptual frameworks, for example traditional Chinese medicine from the perspective of Western medicine, may require emotional as well as conceptual flexibility (Thagard and Zhu 2003).

Should Scientists Be Emotional?

But should it not be the job of science educators to help students aspire to what scientists are supposed to be: objective and nonemotional reasoners? Even if emotions are associated with scientific thinking, perhaps the aim of scientific education, from grade school through the Ph.D., should be to inculcate in students the necessity of eradicating subjective emotions in order to improve their scientific thinking by insulating it from bias. It is not hard to find cases where emotions have distorted science, such as Nazis rejecting Einstein's theory of relativity because they hated Jews, and researchers fabricating data because they wanted to be famous.

While recognizing that there are many such cases in which emotions have undermined scientific objectivity and truth seeking, I think it would be a mistake to demand that scientists strive to eliminate emotions from the cognitive processes that enable them to do science. First, severing the cognitive from the emotional is probably impossible. As I mentioned in the introduction, there is abundant evidence from psychology and neuroscience that cognitive and emotional processes are intimately intertwined. The ethical principle that *ought implies can* applies: we cannot insist that a person's thinking should be emotion free when it is biologically impossible for people to think that way. Mitroff (1974, p. 99) found in his study of Apollo moon scientists that they held strongly emotional views, especially of other researchers, but concluded that "the existence of such strong emotions does not prevent scientists from doing excellent scientific work."

Second, even if scientists could become free of the sway of emotions, it is likely that science would suffer as a result. The discussion above of emotions in the contexts of investigation and discovery showed that positive emotions such as happiness and even negative emotions such as anxiety play an important role in motivating, energizing, and directing science. Given that science is often difficult and frustrating, why would anyone do it if it were not also sometimes exciting and satisfying? According to Mitroff (1974, p. 248): "To eliminate strong emotions and intense commitments may be to eliminate some of science's most vital sustaining forces." Moreover, emotions help to focus scientific research on what is important. According to Polanyi (1958, p. 135): "Any process of inquiry unguided by intellectual passions would inevitably spread out into a desert of trivialities." Because major discoveries require breaking the rules that govern mundane research, "originality must be passionate" (p. 143).

Even in the context of justification, there is a useful cognitive contribution of feelings of elegance and beauty, because they are attached to theories that excel in explanatory coherence, which, I would argue, is what scientific theory is intended most immediately to maximize. An interesting open question is how the training of scientists might be expanded to include enhancement of the kinds of emotional responses that foster good scientific research. I suspect that most such training occurs implicitly during the interactions between budding researchers and their mentors, through a kind of contagion of taste and enthusiasm. It is possible, however, that scientists individually possess sets of inherited and learned emotional dispositions that are impervious to emotional training.

In conclusion, I would emphatically not urge that scientists aim to become robotically unemotional. Despite dramatic increases in computer speed and intelligent algorithms, computers currently are no threat to replace scientists. A key aspect of intelligence that is rarely recognized is the ability to set new goals, not just as ways of accomplishing other existing goals, but as novel ends in themselves. There is no inkling in the field of artificial intelligence of how computers could acquire the ability to set goals for themselves, which is probably just as well because there is no guarantee that the goals of such artificially ultra-intelligent computers would coincide with the goals of human beings. In humans, the development of noninstrumental goals is intimately tied with emotions such as interest, wonder, and curiosity, which are just the goals that spur scientists on. As the eminent neurologist Santiago Ramón y Cajal (1999, p. 7) asserted: "All outstanding work, in art as well as in science, results from immense zeal applied to a great idea." A scientist without passion would be at best a mediocre scientist.

Curing Cancer? Patrick Lee's Path to the Reovirus
Treatment

Introduction

People usually think of viruses as dangerous germs that cause diseases like colds, flu, and AIDS. Some viruses even cause cancer, like the herpes virus that produces Kaposi's sarcoma in people with deficient immune systems. Recently, however, medical researchers have found that some kinds of viruses can actually kill cancer cells, and there is much excitement about the prospects of using viruses to treat a wide variety of cancers in people. It is too soon to say whether the new viral treatments will be medically effective, but important scientific discoveries have been made in the past decade about the interactions of viruses and cancer cells.

One of the most intriguing discoveries was made in 1995 by Dr. Patrick Lee, a Canadian virologist. He realized that the reovirus, a medically benign virus that he has investigated for more than two decades, could infect and kill cells with an activated Ras pathway. Ras is a gene crucial for cell growth that, when mutated, can contribute to the uncontrolled cell growth found in cancerous tumors. Most cancer cells have an activated Ras pathway, and the reovirus has been successful in killing in test tubes many kinds of cancer cells, including ones from brain, prostate, breast, ovarian, pancreatic, and colorectal tumors. Moreover, injection of reovirus into mice has produced dramatic elimination of many kinds of tumors, as Lee and his colleagues reported in the journal *Science* in 1998 (Coffey et al. 1998). Several clinical trials are now (2005) under way to see whether reovirus injections can also reduce or eliminate cancers in humans. Because there have been many cancer treatments that worked well with mice but failed with humans, it is unrealistic to expect the reovirus to provide *the cure* for cancer. But even if the reovirus treatment does not provide the major medical breakthrough that many people are hoping for, its development is an interesting episode in the history of science that illustrates important aspects of scientific discovery.

After providing some background on the history of research on cancer treatments and reoviruses, I will describe the unusual path that led Lee and his colleagues to the discovery that reoviruses can destroy cancer cells. I will then discuss what this case tells us about the nature of scientific discovery, including experimental design, reaction to failed experiments, hypothesis formation, and the role of emotions and aesthetic judgments in scientific thinking.

Cancer Treatments

Although many refinements have been made, the main kinds of treatment for cancer have remained the same for several decades: surgery, radiation, and chemotherapy. Cancer was recognized as a disease by the ancient Greeks and Romans, who were aware that it could sometimes be treated by surgically removing cancerous tumors, although cancers were usually fatal (Olson 1989). After the invention of anesthesia in the mid-nineteenth century, surgery for cancer became more common, and was found to be sometimes successful when the tumors removed were small. For example, by 1900 the radical mastectomy was the treatment of choice for breast cancer.

X-rays were discovered by Wilhelm Roentgen in 1895, and radiation treatment of cancer began almost immediately. In the 1930s, Geoffrey Keynes pioneered the use of radiotherapy instead of or in addition to radical surgery for breast cancer. Today, radiation is used to kill many types of cancer cells such as those in bone tumors.

Chemical treatment for cancer goes at least as far back as A.D. 1000, when Avicenna gave arsenic to cancer patients. Modern chemotherapy originated in 1942, when Alfred Gilman and Louis Goodman were attempting to develop antidotes to mustard gas chemical warfare. They found that rapidly growing lymphatic tissues were especially vulnerable to mustard gases, and proposed that nitrogen mustard could be used to treat malignant lymphoma. By 1956, ten kinds of cancer were known to be treatable by drugs. Less toxic kinds of chemicals have been used to kill cancer cells, but they always have the side effect of killing ordinary cells as well—the usual ratio cited is six cancer cells for every one normal cell. Hence there is a limit on the strength of chemotherapy that can be used because of the large numbers of normal cells that are destroyed. Moreover, cancer cells often become resistant to different kinds of chemotherapy by mutating, so in many cases chemotherapy has only temporary benefits. The same is true for hormonal treatments often used in prostate and breast cancers.

In the 1980s, there was dramatic progress in understanding how cancers originate. According to the "two hit" theory, cancer occurs when (1) normal genes involved in cellular functions are transformed by mutation into oncogenes that excessively stimulate cell growth and (2) there is a mutation in a tumor-suppressor gene that then fails to perform its function of controlling growth. Disappointingly, the dramatic advances in understanding the molecular biology and biochemistry of cancer have been slow to yield effective treatments for the hundred or so kinds of cancers that afflict people.

Today, there are a number of novel kinds of cancer treatment in early stages of investigation. In 1960, Judah Folkman discovered that cancer tumors require a blood supply in order to grow and spread, and he began the search for drugs that would prevent this process of angiogenesis (Cooke 2001). Numerous anti-angiogenesis drugs are now being tested in clinical trials. In a very different approach, viruses such as variants of the herpes virus have been found to have cancer-killing capabilities. Bischoff et al. (1996) discovered that an adenovirus (similar to the viruses that cause colds) can be genetically engineered to kill cells deficient in the activity of p53, which is one of the most important tumor-suppressor genes. Clinical trials are now underway to see whether these viruses can be successful in treating humans with cancer. More recently, another virus has been found to have cancer-killing potential.

The Reovirus

The term *virus* originally meant "poison," and any cause of disease could be referred to as a virus. In the 1890s, researchers found that an extract from diseased tobacco plants that had been filtered to remove bacteria could nevertheless cause disease in previously healthy plants, and it was soon found that many other diseases were associated with "filterable viruses." During the 1930s, the electron microscope was developed and it became possible to identify and describe the appearance of particular viruses. Unlike bacteria, viruses cannot reproduce on their own but are parasitic on living cells. By 1950, the field of virology had split off from bacteriology.

The first reovirus was isolated in 1951 from the feces of an Australian aboriginal child (White and Fenner 1994). It is now recognized to be one of three serotypes of mammalian reoviruses belonging to the genus *Orthoreovirus* and the family *Reoviridae*. The term "reovirus" was coined in 1959 by Albert Sabin, known for his work on the oral polio vaccine. He formed the prefix "reo" to abbreviate "respiratory enteric orphan" because the virus was found in the body's respiratory and enteric tracts and because it was an orphan in the sense that it was not identified as the cause of any human disease. Initially, there was considerable interest in the reovirus because of its similarities with the polio virus. But ethically dubious experiments in which prisoners were injected with reovirus found that infection caused at most mild flu-like symptoms. Many people have been infected by reovirus as children with little effect more than a runny nose.

Even though the reovirus turned out to be of low medical significance, it continued to be a popular topic of research for leading virologists. Reoviruses are easy to grow and have biologically interesting properties such as consisting of double-stranded RNA. The reovirus has only ten genes, and the proteins produced by each have been isolated and characterized with respect to their effects on virulence. For example, the gene S1 produces a protein that enables reoviruses to attach to cells in the first stage of infection, but different types of reovirus attach to different kinds of cells. Reoviruses were a major focus of investigation in the Duke University laboratory of Wolfgang Joklik, where Patrick Lee arrived as a postdoctoral fellow in 1978.

Patrick Lee

Patrick W. K. Lee was born in China in 1945, but grew up in Hong Kong. In 1967 he moved to Edmonton, Canada, to attend the University of Alberta, receiving a B.Sc. in 1970 and a Ph.D. in biochemistry in 1978. His doctoral research concerning the biochemistry of the mengo encephalomyelitis virus was supervised by John Colter, a leading expert on that virus. Lee then received a postdoctoral fellowship from the Medical Research Council of Canada that he took to work with another leading researcher in the biochemistry of viruses, Wolfgang (Bill) Joklik, who had come to Duke University as chair of the Department of Microbiology and Immunology. Because Lee had his own funding from the Canadian government, and because Joklik was supervising numerous other postdocs and graduate students on top of his duties as department chair, Lee was given a relatively free rein to work on topics that interested him. Joklik was an intimidating supervisor, and Lee was taken aback when Joklik was not enthusiastic about Lee's proposal to do an experiment to determine which protein produced by the reovirus allows it to attach to cells. Joklik said that the experiment was not worth doing: others must have tried it already and found that it did not work. But Lee did the experiment anyway and found the reovirus cell attachment protein, a result that Lee and Joklik published in the journal *Virology* in 1981.

In that same year, Lee returned to Alberta as an assistant professor in the Department of Microbiology and Infectious Diseases at the University of Calgary. In collaboration with a series of graduate students, he continued to work on the biochemistry of reoviruses. Lee published extensively on such topics as the genetic structure of reovirus attachment gene S1 and the nature of the receptors in cells that enable reoviruses to attach to them. His research addressed fundamental questions about the biochemical mechanisms of viral development, completely independent of questions about the genesis and treatment of cancer. Lee was strongly motivated to do research equal to that of the top virologists, and became engaged in controversies with leading figures such as Bernard Fields over the nature of viral attachment. By 1991, Lee was a full professor.

Discovering the Reovirus-Cancer Connection

The finding that started the long path to the discovery that reoviruses can kill cancer cells came in 1992, when a graduate student, Damu Tang, proposed an experiment that Lee still describes as "silly" and "stupid." The student was interested in the role of sialic acid as a receptor on the plasma membrane of a cell. In order to attach to a cell, a virus uses attachment proteins to bind itself to such receptors. The student proposed to use an enzyme to cleave sialic acid from cells and predicted that this would block infection by reoviruses. Lee thought that the experiment would not work and would not be very interesting even if it did.

Fortunately, just as Lee had ignored Joklik's opinion of the experiment Lee had proposed as a postdoctoral fellow, Tang ignored Lee's opinion and did the experiment anyway. Because viruses reproduce rapidly—reovirus progeny are detectable in under ten hours—experiments like the one proposed by Tang can be done in a day or two, with very little cost in equipment. Tang found, as Lee had predicted, that the sialic acid manipulation did not produce less viral infection than occurred in the control cell medium not receiving the enzyme. The big surprise, however, was that the viral infection was reduced in the control cells! Lee was sure that the student had just made a mistake, and told him to repeat the experiment with no changes. When the student repeated the experiment with the same results, Lee told him to do it again. Yet another replication of the results convinced Lee that there was something genuinely odd going on in the control cell medium, and he began to suspect that something in it was blocking virus reproduction. He dropped everything and went to the library to try to find an answer to the question of what might be going on in the control cells.

From a journal article, Lee learned that the cells used in the experiment secrete epidermal growth factor receptor (EGFR). The cells were from the human epidermoid carcinoma cell line A431, which Lee had used in previous experiments to show that beta-adrenergic receptors, possessed in large numbers by A431 cells, are not receptors for reovirus binding. The difference between the enzyme and control conditions was not the cell lines, which were both A431, but that the control cells had been sitting around for a few days, which gave them time to secrete something that blocked viral replication. Lee initially hypothesized that reoviruses were binding to EGFR in solution in the control cell medium, which prevented them from binding to EGFR on cells that they were supposed to infect.

Lee and his students then did experiments that showed that two mouse cell lines previously known to express no EGFR were relatively resistant to reovirus infection, whereas the same cell lines became susceptible to infection with the insertion of the gene encoding EGFR. In papers published in *Virology* in 1993, they concluded that the process of reovirus infection is closely coupled to the cell signal pathway mediated by the EGFR (Strong, Tang, and Lee 1993; Tang, Strong, and Lee 1993). As is common in scientific publications, this paper gave no indication of the serendipitous origins of the finding that the epidermal growth factor pathway is involved in reovirus reproduction.

At this time, Lee had not yet considered any possible connection between reovirus and cancer. He was still thinking that the virus might bind to an epidermal growth factor receptor, but further reflection about the mechanisms of reovirus binding raised doubts about whether reoviruses bind to EGFR. Lee was forced to rethink the situation, and it occurred to him that the virus might infect cells that were already prepared for infection because of an already activated chemical pathway. In a paper written in 1995, Strong and Lee lay out two alternative explanations for the augmentation of reovirus infection by functional EGFR:

The first possibility is that reovirus plays an active role by first binding to EGFR, thereby activating the tyrosine kinase activity of the latter and triggering a cell signaling cascade which is somehow required for subsequent steps of the infection process.... The second possibility is that reovirus takes advantage of an already activated signal transduction pathway conferred by the presence of functional EGFR on the host cell. (Strong and Lee 1996, p. 612)

To choose between these possibilities, Strong and Lee designed an experiment using a cell line that they heard about from a visiting speaker at the University of Calgary, H. J. Kung. Kung provided them with a cell line,

NIH 3T3, which had been used extensively to assess the transforming activities of oncogenes, which are genes whose transformation can lead to cancer. Lee was still not thinking about cancer, but rather focusing on the question of whether an oncogene introduced into NIH 3T3 cells could transform them internally in a way that would show the correctness of the second possibility that reovirus infection exploits an already activated pathway.

In their experiment, Strong and Lee used the v-*erbB* oncogene known to be related to a growth factor receptor similar to EGFR. Decisively, it turned out that addition of this oncogene to the NIH 3T3 cells did indeed make cells that are normally resistant to reovirus infection become susceptible to infection. This result showed that the role of EGFR in the 1992 experiment was fortuitous and inconsequential: what mattered was not the attachment process of reoviruses, but the internal modification of cells that allowed the reovirus to reproduce rapidly.

The crucial question then concerned the nature of the activated signal transduction pathway within the cells that made them susceptible to infection by reovirus. Answering this question was made easier by the availability of a number of NIH 3T3-derived cell lines transformed with active oncogenes. At the end of their paper, Strong and Lee reported (1996, p. 615): "We have obtained preliminary data which suggest that activated ras alone also confers enhanced reovirus infectibility." The research motivation was still basic virology, to understand the intracellular mechanisms that promote viral replication. Ras was investigated because it was widely known to be downstream from EGFR: there is a biochemical mechanism in which EGFR affects Ras.

Patrick Lee was quoted in 1999 as saying: "I can still remember the day we found out that the reovirus could have a cancer connection. It was the most exciting day of my life" (AHMFR 1999). The connection came from the nature of reovirus reproduction, which, as in many other viruses, leads to the destruction of the infected cells. After a reovirus gains access to a cell, it reproduces itself by using the cell's internal chemistry to replicate viral RNA which is then assembled into thousands of new viruses. These viruses then cause the cell to burst, a process called *lysis*, enabling the viruses to spread out to infect many other cells. The discovery that the reovirus is prone to infect cells that have an activated Ras pathway suggested immediately that the virus might be *oncolytic*, that is, capable of killing cancer cells by infecting and bursting them. Thus by the end of 1995, Lee had the hypothesis that there might be a reovirus treatment for cancer.

Lee did not, however, immediately try to test whether reovirus could cure cancer in animals. First, he and his students set out to identify the mechanism which made cells with an activated Ras pathway susceptible to reovirus infection. The crucial protein was found to be the double-stranded RNA-activated enzyme, PKR. Inhibition of PKR activity drastically enhanced reovirus protein synthesis, and it was found that Ras-activated cells depress the activity of this protein, permitting the reproduction of reoviruses and the destruction of the cells. By 1998, Lee's team understood why reoviruses are potentially oncolytic (Strong et al. 1998). More recent research has demonstrated that a similar mechanism explains the oncolytic properties of the herpes simplex virus.

It was relatively easy to do studies that showed that reoviruses could kill many different kinds of cancer cells in test tubes, but answering the question of whether they could be effective in animals required a dramatic shift in Lee's research methodology. He launched a new line of research to determine whether injecting cancerous mice with cells infected by reovirus would have any effect on their tumors. The results were excellent, demonstrating the eradication of many tumors, even in mice with competent immune systems (Coffey et al. 1998). Another investigator got significant results in reducing tumor growth in dogs. Because reovirus is not associated with any major human diseases, it has substantial promise for treating cancers in humans, but results of the first clinical trial are not yet available. In 1998, Lee helped to start a company, Oncolytics Biotech, which has patented the use of reovirus, trademarked as Reolysin, to treat cancer in humans. In May 2001, the company announced that it was seeking approval for phase 2 clinical trials concerning effects of Reolysin on prostate cancer and a type of brain cancer, glioblastoma. Health Canada granted approval for the prostate cancer trial in October 2001.

To summarize, Patrick Lee's path to the reovirus treatment of cancer was very indirect, and involved the following key steps:

1. The odd experimental result that reovirus infection was inhibited in a control cell medium.
2. The determination that epidermal growth factor receptor in cells encouraged viral reproduction.
3. The determination that EGFR was not so important, but that what mattered was an internal pathway.
4. The determination that the Ras pathway was involved.
5. The realization that the reovirus could kill cancer cells.

We can now consider what these developments can tell us about the nature of scientific discovery.

Serendipity and the Economy of Experimental Research

Charles Peirce, who was an active scientist as well as a philosopher, coined the phrase "economy of research" to indicate that scientific method is not just a logical matter of what to believe, but also a practical matter of what to investigate. He emphasized the need to form hypotheses that can be tested by means of economical experiments, that is, ones that do not require an excess of money, time, thought, and energy (Peirce 1931–1958, vol. 5, secs. 5.598–600). The economy of experiments varies dramatically from field to field. At one extreme, there is high-energy physics where an experiment can require hundreds of person-years of work and millions of dollars. Clinical trials in medicine that evaluate the efficacy of drugs can take months or years and cost hundreds of thousands of dollars. In experimental psychology, a typical experiment requires weeks of planning, weeks of running subjects, and weeks of data analysis. Monetary costs include stipends for graduate students who run the experiments and payments to subjects. Given the high cost of conducting experiments, researchers must be very careful concerning the experiments on which they expend their resources.

In virology, the economy of research is very different. Experiments can often be done in one or two days with materials already on hand. Under such circumstances, it is not unusual for graduate students and postdoctoral fellows to ignore the advice of their supervisors concerning whether an experiment is worth doing or not. T. H. Huxley said that every now and again a scientist should perform an outrageous experiment, like blowing a trumpet at a tulip, just to see what happens. But if an experiment requires a great deal of time and expensive equipment, then outrageous experiments are out of the question.

Many discoveries in science are serendipitous, coming about even though no one was looking for them. An example is the discovery that the human stomach often contains bacteria, *Helicobacter pylori*, that cause ulcers. When the bacteria were discovered by an Australian physician, Robin Warren, in 1979, it was not part of a research project to find improved treatment for ulcers, but merely arose in his everyday work as a pathologist (Thagard 1999). The finding by Warren and Barry Marshall that presence of the bacteria is highly correlated with peptic ulcers was an exciting surprise. Kevin Dunbar (2001b) reports that in the scientific research groups he has studied more than half of the results of experiments were unexpected. Unexpected results do not reflect just the failure of hypotheses to survive experimental tests, but often serve to initiate new hypotheses and new experiments.

Lee's path to the reovirus treatment for cancer began with the unexpected finding that viral reproduction was inhibited in a control cell medium. Another important biological experiment where the control condition produced surprising results led to the discovery that lithium can be used to treat manic depression disorder. The researcher thought that uric acid might be involved, so he was treating guinea pigs with lithium urate. As a control, he used lithium carbonate, and was surprised to find that it calmed the guinea pigs down, showing that lithium was the key—and totally unexpected—factor (van Andel 1994, p. 641; see also Roberts 1989 and Campanario 1996).

Judah Folkman's research on cancer angiogenesis also began serendipitously (Cooke 2001, chap. 4). After his surgery training at Harvard, Folkman was drafted in 1960 by the U.S. Navy and assigned to work on finding a blood substitute that could be used on aircraft carriers that spend months at sea. Working with a pathologist, Fred Becker, Folkman was using rabbit thyroid glands to test the effectiveness of a hemoglobin solution as a blood substitute. They implanted cancer cells in the glands because malignant cells grow rapidly and would therefore reveal the effectiveness of the substitute. Initially, tumors implanted in the thyroids grew rapidly, but then Folkman and Becker noticed something very odd: the little tumors stopped growing as soon as they reached a size of about one millimeter in diameter. They then realized that the tumors had become dormant because they did not have any connection to the circulatory system. This was the serendipitous beginning of research on angiogenesis that has led, forty years later, to the current investigation of dozens of anti-angiogenesis drugs as potential cancer treatments. Like Patrick Lee, Judah Folkman's interest in cancer arose because of an unplanned finding in an unrelated field of biomedicine.

A field like virology, in which experiments are very economical, allows the carrying out of numerous experiments, which can in turn lead to serendipitous findings. This is what happened in the experiment that initiated the path to the reovirus treatment of cancer. Because experiments with reovirus require little time and expense, Tang was able to perform what Lee viewed as an unpromising experiment. Reoviruses do not cause serious disease, so working with them does not require the extensive safety precautions required for working with dangerous viruses such as HIV and Ebola. Thus the economy of research, in this case the ease of doing dubious experiments, contributed to the serendipitous beginning of the path to the reovirus treatment. However, as Pasteur said, chance favors the prepared mind, and I discuss below the mental mechanisms by which the surprising result of Tang's experiment was turned into a series of hypotheses and experiments.

Another serendipitous aspect of Lee's research was the hypothesis that reoviruses bind to EGFR. This hypothesis turned out to be a red herring, but it was very useful theoretically because it helped to move Lee's theorizing away from questions of reovirus attachment toward questions about chemical processes internal to cells. It is interesting that Lee's doubts about this hypothesis arose not from experimental tests of it but from reflection on its incompatibility with what he knew about the biochemical mechanisms of reovirus attachment.

How do scientists decide what experiments to do? Peirce's idea of the economy of research suggests that such decisions might involve some kind of cost–benefit calculation, with steps such as the following:

1. Estimate the benefits of an experiment with respect to potential contribution to scientific knowledge and (perhaps) personal career advancement.
2. Estimate the costs of the experiment with respect to time, money, and energy.
3. Compare the cost–benefit ratio of the experiment with ratios for other possible experiments, and decide whether the experiment is worth doing.

However, this strikes me as an implausible model of what productive scientists actually do. For one thing, it is extremely difficult to calculate the expected benefits of an experiment. As the experiment that began the path to the reovirus treatment shows, it is often very difficult to know where an experiment will lead. Therefore, it is difficult to compare the cost–benefit ratios of different experiments. Below, in the section on emotions, I will offer a different model of experimental decisions based on emotional intuitions.

A very interesting question that has received very little attention in the history, philosophy, and psychology of science is how scientists come up with ideas for experiments. For example, how did Tang come up with the idea of using an enzyme to cleave sialic acid from cells in order to block reovirus reproduction? Sometimes, mundane experiments can originate analogically, when a scientist is familiar with the design of an existing experiment and adapts it to do a similar experiment. More generally, experimental design can be thought of as a kind of means–ends problem solving, in which there is a given end, for example to test a newly generated hypothesis, from which the scientist works backward to figure out what kind of experiment might accomplish that end. Most important experiments come about, I suspect, because they are devised to answer some important theoretical question. For example, Strong and Lee devised the v-erbB experiment to find out whether reovirus reproduction takes advantage of an already activated pathway.

Cognitive Mechanisms: Hypothesis Formation

A central task of scientific thinking is to generate hypotheses that explain the results of observation and experiment. Peirce called the generation of scientific hypotheses *abduction*, which he defined as studying facts and devising a theory to explain them (Peirce 1931–1958, vol. 5, sec. 5.145). An abductive inference starts with a surprising and interesting fact that needs explanation, then uses background information to generate a hypothesis that provides a potential causal explanation of the interesting fact. The path to the reovirus treatment involved numerous instances of abductive inference. When Tang's experiment produced its odd result that reovirus replication was reduced in the control condition, Lee's first hypothesis was that the student had made some kind of mistake. The structure of this abductive inference was something like:

Fact to be explained   Odd experimental result—reovirus replication reduced.
Background information   When students make mistakes in performing experiments, they often get odd results.
Hypothesis   Maybe the student made a mistake in performing the experiment.

The background information came from Lee's years of experience as an experimenter and teacher, and might have been in the general form stated here, or might have been at a lower, more particular level in the form of specific cases of students who had got odd results because of erroneous experiments.

The hypothesis that there was some mistake in Tang's experiment could easily be tested by running it again and again. Replication ruled out the mistake hypothesis, so Lee was forced to come up with the alternative hypothesis that there was something unusual going on in the control cells. The odd experimental result was anomalous, but it only became a really interesting anomaly when the initial hypothesis of experimental error was ruled out. The exciting abductive inference was something like:

Fact to be explained   Odd experimental result—reovirus replication reduced.
Background information   Cell secretions can block viral reproduction.
Hypothesis   There is some secretion in the cell medium that is blocking viral reproduction.

Lee had no idea what the secretion might be, but found by reading journals that A431 cells secrete EGFR so it became a candidate to fill in the hypothesis. This kind of abductive inference to the existence of an unknown entity is called *existential* abduction (Thagard 1988). It is common in science, for example when nineteenth-century astronomers inferred from the orbit of Uranus that there exists another planet which was later identified as Neptune.

Another major abductive mental leap came later with the formation of hypotheses to explain why EGFR in host cells enhances viral reproduction. Here there were two abductive inferences:

Fact to be explained   EGFR in host cells increases reovirus reproduction.
Background information   If binding of viruses to cells is increased, then viral reproduction increases.
Hypothesis 1   Reoviruses might bind to EGFR.

However, reflection about biochemical mechanisms made this hypothesis implausible, so Lee had to generate another:

Fact to be explained   EGFR increases reovirus reproduction.
Background information   If some chemical process downstream from EGFR encourages viral reproduction, then viral reproduction increases.
Hypothesis 2   There is some chemical process downstream from EGFR encouraging viral reproduction.

As in the abductive inference that there was something in the control cell medium blocking viral reproduction, this was an existential abduction. Identification of the postulated agent came from further experiments that filled in the Ras pathway as the downstream chemical process involved in enhancing viral reproduction.

Lee's last major mental leap was more deductive than abductive. It involved the following steps:

1. Reovirus kills the cells it infects.
2. Reovirus infects cells with activated Ras pathways.
3. Cancer cells often have activated Ras pathways.
4. Therefore, reovirus may be able to kill cancer cells.

Laying the steps out like this makes the leap seem obvious, but remember that Lee was a virologist, not a cancer researcher, so he was not particularly concerned with the oncogenic properties of Ras. The big breakthrough came when Lee and his students determined that Ras pathway activation enhanced reovirus infection, which directly suggested that reoviruses might be used to treat cancer.

Emotional Mechanisms

We often think of scientists as paragons of cool rationality, but they are as emotional as anyone else, and their emotionality is often a major contributor to their success (Thagard 2002; chap. 10 above). Emotions are an important factor in all the phases of scientific thinking, including planning of experiments, recognition of anomalies, formation of hypotheses, and evaluation of competing theories. Aesthetic judgments that a theory or experiment is beautiful or ugly are an important class of emotional reactions (Thagard 2000, pp. 199–203). McAllister (1996) has discussed the contribution of aesthetics to theory appraisal, and Parsons and Rueger (2000) analyze the relevance of aesthetics to experimental science.

Consider first the economy of research discussed above. I argued that the explicit cost–benefit model of choice of experiments is psychologically unrealistic. A more plausible model is the account of decision making as *informed intuition* (see chap. 2). Intuitions are emotional judgments that arise from unconscious processes that balance various cognitive and emotional constraints. For example, if I need to buy a car, I may have the feeling that I should buy a particular model because it satisfies my most important goals such as its being reliable and well equipped. Decision making involves both positive constraints, such as that I want the car to furnish reliable transportation, and negative constraints such as that I cannot afford to buy more than one car. These constraints include ones that are cognitive, based on the interrelations of various compatible and incompatible beliefs that I have about cars, and also ones that are emotional, reflecting how I feel about the various factors such as style and equipment that factor into my decision. I will be intuitively satisfied in choosing a particular model of car when the choice is coherent in the sense that it maximizes satisfaction of the various cognitive and emotional constraints (see Thagard 2000 for a theory and computational model of this kind of coherence).

Of course, intuitions may produce poor decisions, if the decisions neglect crucial cognitive and emotional constraints. For example, my decision making may be temporarily swamped by a single factor, such as seeing a car with a gorgeous color. More effective decision making requires *informed* intuition, in which a person has taken care to collect information about the factors relevant to the decision so that the intuitive judgment that emerges to consciousness as an emotional reaction is based on maximizing satisfaction of all the relevant constraints.

I conjecture that decisions about what experiments to do are typically made on the basis of informed intuition. When a researcher generates an idea about a possible experiment, it comes with an intuitive judgment about whether the experiment is worth doing. This intuition may be based on considerable knowledge of the relevant field and experience with similar experiments, or it may merely reflect a newcomer's need to get some research going. The intuitive judgment of the scientist who first considers the experiment may be quite different from the judgments of others, for example a supervisor or a reviewer of a grant application. Regardless of who is making the judgment, it does not come out as a cold estimate such as "This experiment has a probability of success of .7," but rather as an emotional judgment such as "This experiment is exciting" or "This experiment is pointless." Lee has been quoted as saying: "The most exciting thing about science is you wake up in the morning and say to yourself, 'Gee, what I am going to find out today?'" (AHMFR 1999).

I described earlier how two of the important episodes in Patrick Lee's career involved an emotional mismatch between the judgments of junior and senior researchers. Experienced researchers react emotionally to proposed experiments on the basis of their substantial experience with previous successful and unsuccessful experiments, as well as on the basis of their sense of the research goals of the field. The distinguished social psychologist Richard Nisbett learned about doing experiments from the reactions he got in discussions with his supervisor, Stanley Schacter. Nisbett says (personal communication, Feb. 23, 2001) "He let me know how good my idea was by grunts: non-committal (hmmm...), clearly disapproving (ahnn...) or (very rarely) approving (ah!)." Interestingly, many of Schacter's students went on to become very successful social psychologists, as have many of Nisbett's students. So when a senior researcher tells a junior one that an experiment is stupid, as Joklik did to Lee and Lee did to Tang, it is an emotional judgment based on substantial experience. Of course, such judgments are not always right, and in both those cases the youthful exuberance of the junior researchers, coupled with the relative ease of doing the experiments, led to the experiments being done anyway. Regardless of the status of the researcher, the decision whether to do or not to do an experiment is not based on any explicit cost–benefit calculation, but on an emotional reaction to the proposed plan. Depending on its simplicity and its coherence with prevailing beliefs, a researcher may make the aesthetic judgment that a proposed experiment is beautiful or ugly.

I suggested earlier that experiments are often designed to answer questions, but how are questions generated? Figure 11.1 is a model of the origins of scientific questions. On this model, questions arise because of curiosity about some phenomena, serendipitous findings that produce surprise, or

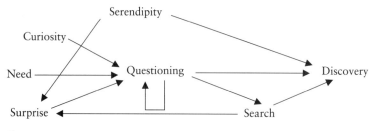

Figure 11.1
Origins of scientific questions. From Thagard 1999, p. 47. Reprinted by permission.

concern with some practical need. In addition, some questions are formed because they potentially provide answers to other questions, as shown by the feedback loop connecting questioning with questioning. Patrick Lee's path to the reovirus treatment displays all these ways of generating questions. He had a long-standing curiosity about the biochemical mechanisms of viral attachment and reproduction. Serendipity was a factor when Tang's experiment produced surprising results from the control cells unexpectedly displaying reduced viral infection. Surprise is an emotion that arises from addition of information to a cognitive system that is incoherent with the representations previously in the system (Thagard 2000, p. 194). Lee found the results of Tang's initial experiment very "odd," which I take to mean that they were surprisingly incompatible with what he already knew about reoviruses. Practical need entered into the picture later when Lee realized that reoviruses might be oncolytic and therefore relevant to the great demand for improved cancer treatments. (Lee's father had died of pancreatic cancer, which usually involves an activated Ras pathway.) Note that the inputs to the questioning process—curiosity, need, and surprise—are inherently emotional.

The questioning process is crucial to the focusing of inquiry that makes useful abductions possible. Scientists do not form hypotheses about randomly chosen facts, but rather about facts that cry out for explanation through questioning driven by curiosity, need, or surprise. Figure 11.1 shows discovery downstream (to use the biochemists' term) from questioning, and this is certainly true of the abductive inferences described in the above section on cognitive mechanisms. Abduction is a cognitive process, but it has emotional inputs via the way that questioning helps to select the facts that are worthy of being explained. Manifestly, abduction also has emotional outputs, since the formation of a promising new hypothesis can be an intensely exciting event in the life of a scientist. When I interviewed Patrick Lee, he used words like "amazing," "excited," "astounding," and "this is it" to describe his reaction to the new ideas that emerged in the course of his research between 1991 and 1996.

Figure 10.2 in the previous chapter showed a more general model of the role of emotion in scientific thinking. As the story of Patrick Lee and the reovirus illustrates, the mental mechanisms by which scientific discoveries are made include emotional as well as cognitive processes. Lee's interest and curiosity led him to generate questions such as what was going on in the control medium in Tang's surprising experiment. The attempt to generate answers sometimes led to surprises such as the implausibility of the initial hypothesis about reoviruses binding to EGFR. The evaluation of answers sometimes led to happiness, as when Lee determined that the Ras pathway crucially influenced reovirus reproduction.

Conclusion

In sum, Patrick Lee's path to the reovirus treatment provides a fine illustration of the complex process of scientific development. It was not a simple matter of having an idea and testing it, but required a series of developments that combined experiments (both failed and successful), information acquisition, and hypothesis generation. The mental mechanisms involved in this study were diverse, ranging from decision processes for deciding what experiments are worth doing to abductive processes by which hypotheses are generated to explain surprising facts. Emotional processes were not just a byproduct of the cognitive processes, but were an essential contributor to those processes. The mental mechanisms of scientific thinkers involve interconnected cognitive-emotional processes that support anomaly recognition, experiment planning, and hypothesis formation.

At this writing (June 2005), it is impossible to say whether the research of Lee and his students will constitute a breakthrough in treating human cancers. It may turn out that the difficulty of delivering reoviruses to cancerous tumors and the robustness of the human immune system will render the reovirus treatment of cancer ineffective. But it is also possible that clinical trials over the next year or two will show that the reovirus treatment provides a useful weapon in the war against cancer. In either case, Patrick Lee's discoveries about the mechanisms of reovirus infection stand as valuable additions to scientific knowledge. This chapter has combined historical, philosophical, and psychological perspectives to describe how those additions came about.

Introduction

Studies in the history, philosophy, sociology, and psychology of science and technology have gathered much information about important cases of scientific development. These cases usually concern the most successful scientists and inventors, such as Darwin, Einstein, and Edison. But case studies rarely address the question of what made these investigators more accomplished than the legions of scientific laborers whose names have been forgotten.

This chapter is an attempt to identify many of the psychological and other factors that make some scientists highly successful. I explore two sources of information about routes to scientific achievement. The first derives from a survey that Jeff Shrager conducted at the Workshop on Cognitive Studies of Science and Technology at the University of Virginia in March 2001. He asked the participants to list "7 habits of highly creative people," and after the workshop he and I compiled a list of habits recommended by the distinguished group of historians, philosophers, and psychologists at the workshop. My second source of information about the factors contributing to scientific success is advice given by three distinguished biologists who each won a Nobel prize: Santiago Ramón y Cajal, Peter Medawar, and James Watson. These biologists provide advice that usefully supplements the suggestions from the workshop participants.

Habits of Highly Creative People

When Jeff Shrager asked the workshop participants to submit suggestions for a list of "7 habits of highly creative people," I was skeptical that they would come up with anything less trite than *work hard* and *be smart*. But the suggestions turned out to be quite interesting, and Jeff and I compiled and

Table 12.1
Habits of highly creative people

---

1. Make new connections.
Broaden yourself to more than one field.
Read widely.
Use analogies to link things together.
Work on different projects at the same time.
Use visual as well as verbal representations.
Don't work on what everyone else is doing.
Use multiple methods.
Seek novel mechanisms.

2. Expect the unexpected.
Take anomalies seriously.
Learn from failures.
Recover from failures.

3. Be persistent.
Focus on key problems.
Be systematic and keep records.
Confirm early, disconfirm late.

4. Get excited.
Pursue projects that are fun.
Play with ideas and things.
Ask interesting questions.
Take risks.

5. Be sociable.
Find smart collaborators.
Organize good teams.
Study how others are successful.
Listen to people with experience.
Foster different cognitive styles.
Communicate your work to others.

6. Use the world.
Find rich environments.
Build instruments.
Test ideas.

---

organized them into the list shown in table 12.1. Not surprisingly, we did not end up with 7 habits, but rather with 27 organized into 6 classes.

The first class of habits concerns ways to make new connections, recognizing the fact that creativity in science and technology usually involves putting together ideas in novel combinations (Ward, Smith, and Vaid 1997). Many successful scientists do not restrict their reading to the particular area of research that they are currently focused on, but instead read widely, including work outside their own field. This enables them to grasp analogies between current problems they face and established ones that may suggest new solutions (Holyoak and Thagard 1995; Dunbar 2001). Visual representations may facilitate analogical and other kinds of inference (Giere 1999; Nersessian 1992). Working on multiple projects with multiple methods may make possible new approaches to those projects. As Herbert Simon often recommended, researchers should not follow the crowd and work on what everyone else is doing, because it is difficult to do anything novel in such situations. Because scientific explanations and technological breakthroughs often involve the discovery and manipulation of mechanisms, seeking novel mechanisms is often a good strategy (Bechtel and Richardson 1993; Machamer, Darden, and Craver 2000).

The second class of habits recognizes the fact that work in science and technology often does not proceed as expected. When anomalous experimental results arise, it is important for investigators to take them seriously and not brush them aside. There is then the possibility of learning from failed expectations, not by giving up, but by recovering from the local failure and moving on to research suggested by the anomalous findings. Much can be learned from both successful and unsuccessful experiments (Gooding 1990; Gooding, Pinch, and Schaffer 1989).

Given the frequent difficulties and setbacks in research in science and technology, it is important that investigators have a third class of habits involving persistence. They need to focus on key problems rather than being distracted by peripheral issues, and they need to pursue their research systematically, keeping detailed records about successes and failures. The injunction to "confirm early, disconfirm late" goes against the methodological advice of Karl Popper (1959) that scientists should set out to refute their own ideas. But it allows a research project to develop without being destroyed prematurely by apparent disconfirmations that may arise from difficulties in getting good experimental research underway.

The first three classes all involve cognitive habits, that is ones tied to basic thinking processes of problem solving and learning. The fourth class suggests that successful scientists are ones who also possess a set of emotional habits that get them intensely involved with their research projects (Feist and Gorman 1998). It is rarely possible for scientists to do a cost–benefit analysis of what projects to pursue, but following their noses to work on projects that are fun and exciting can keep them motivated and focused. Scientific research is not just a matter of doing experiments and forming hypotheses, but in its early stages requires formulating a project that will answer a question that is interesting for theoretical or practical reasons. Interest, excitement, and the avoidance of boredom provide motivation to work hard and do work that is creative rather than routine. Playing with ideas and instruments can be inherently enjoyable. Taking risks to do nonstandard research can provoke fear of failure, but this emotion must be managed if a scientist is to move in highly novel directions. For further discussion of the role of emotion in scientific thinking, see the previous two chapters and Wolpert and Richards (1997).

Cognitive and emotional habits both concern individual psychology, but no scientist is an island. The fifth class of habits is social, concerning ways in which working with others can foster a scientific career. Most scientific research today is collaborative, so that having smart collaborators organized into effective teams is crucial (Galison 1997; Thagard 1999). Teams should not be homogeneous, but should have members who combine a variety of areas of knowledge and methodologies (Dunbar 1995). Scientists can also benefit from observing how other researchers have managed to be successful and by listening to the advice of mentors about how to conduct their research. Finally, there is little point to doing research if you do not devote time to communicating it effectively to others by well-written articles and interesting presentations.

The sixth and final class of habits acknowledges that science is not just a psychological and sociological process, but also involves interactions with the world (Thagard 1999). Scientists can benefit from finding rich environments to study and building instruments to detect features of those environments. Testing ideas is not just a logical matter of working out the consequences of hypotheses, but involves interacting with the world to determine whether it has the properties that the hypotheses ascribe to it (Hacking 1983).

It would take an enormous amount of empirical research to establish that the above habits really are ones that lead to scientific success (see the discussion below of Feist and Gorman 1998). One would have to produce a substantial database of scientists, ordinary as well as illustrious, with records of the extent to which they exemplify the different habits and degrees of professional success. Here I can attempt only a much more modest kind of validation of the list of habits of successful scientists, by comparing it with the advice given by three distinguished biologists.

Ramón y Cajal

Santiago Ramón y Cajal was a Spanish biologist who won a Nobel prize in medicine and physiology in 1906 for important discoveries about nerve cells. While still an active scientist, he wrote in 1897 *Reglas y Consejos sobre Investigacion Cientifica*, which was translated into English with the title:

Advice for a Young Investigator (Ramón y Cajal 1999). The book is rich with many kinds of recommendations for pursuing a career in biology.

Ramón y Cajal's book begins by rejecting advice from philosophers such as Descartes and Bacon, insisting that "the most brilliant discoveries have not relied on a formal knowledge of logic" (Ramón y Cajal 1999, p. 5). Rather, they arose from an "acute inner logic that generates ideas." In chapter 2, he warns beginning scientists against traps that impede science, including excessive admiration for the work of great minds and a conviction that the most important problems are already solved. He also recommends cultivating science for its own sake, without considering its application (p. 9). Ramón y Cajal doubts that superior talent is required for good scientific work. Even those with mediocre talent can produce notable work if they concentrate on information pertinent to an important question.

Concentration is one of the intellectual qualities that Ramón y Cajal describes in chapter 3 as being indispensable for the researcher worker: "all great work is the fruit of patience and perseverance, combined with tenacious concentration on a subject over a period of months or even years" (p. 38). Other intellectual qualities include independent judgment, taste for scientific originality, passion for reputation, and patriotism. Concentration and taste for originality are partly cognitive qualities, but they are also emotional, since they involve desire and motivations. Ramón y Cajal strongly emphasizes the emotional side of scientific thought: "two emotions must be unusually strong in the great scientific scholar: a devotion to truth and a passion for reputation" (p. 40). The passion for reputation is important because eagerness for approval and applause provides a strong motivational force; science requires people who can flatter themselves that they have trodden on completely virgin territory. Similarly, Ramón y Cajal sees patriotism as a useful motivating force, as researchers strive to make discoveries in part for the glory of their countries. Most motivating qualities, however, are more local: "Our novice runs the risk of failure without additional traits: a strong inclination toward originality, a taste for research, and a desire to experience the incomparable gratification associated with the act of discovery itself" (p. 48). Discovery is an "indescribable pleasure—which pales the rest of life's joys" (p. 50).

Chapter 4 is of less general interest, as it is directed primarily at newcomers to research in biology. Ramón y Cajal points to the value of having a general education, with philosophy particularly useful because it "offers good preparation and excellent mental gymnastics for the laboratory worker" (p. 54). But specialization is also necessary if a researcher is to master a particular scientific area. Ramón y Cajal also provides advice about the importance of learning foreign languages, reading monographs with special attention to research methods and unsolved problems, and mastering experimental techniques. Ramón y Cajal stresses the "absolute necessity of seeking inspiration in nature" (p. 62), and urges patient observations designed to produce original data. Researchers should choose problems whose methodology they understand and like.

Chapter 5 provides negative advice—qualities to avoid because they militate against success. Evocatively, the chapter is entitled "Diseases of the Will," and it divides unsuccessful scientists into a number of types: contemplators, bibliophiles and polyglots, megalomaniacs, instrument addicts, misfits, and theorists. For example, theorists are wonderfully cultivated minds who have an aversion to the laboratory, so that they can never contribute original data. According to Ramón y Cajal, "enthusiasm and perseverance work miracles" (p. 94).

Chapter 6 describes social factors beneficial to scientific work, including material support such as good laboratory facilities. Ramón y Cajal also makes recommendations about marriage that presuppose that researchers are male: "We advise the man inclined toward science to seek in the one whom his heart has chosen a compatible psychological profile rather than beauty and wealth" (p. 103).

Chapter 7 returns to more cognitive advice, concerning the operations in all scientific research: observation and experimentation, working hypotheses, and proof. Observation is not to be done casually. "It is not sufficient to examine; it is also necessary to observe and reflect: we should infuse the things we observe with the intensity of our emotions and with a deep sense of affinity" (p. 112). Experiments should be carried out repeatedly using the best instruments. Once data have been gathered, it is natural to formulate hypotheses that try to explain them. While hypotheses are indispensable, Ramón y Cajal warns against "excessive attachment to our own ideas" (p. 122). Hypotheses must be tested by seeking data contrary to them as well as data that support them. Researchers must be willing to give up their own ideas, as excessive self-esteem and pride can prevent improvements.

Chapters 8 and 9 return to more practical advice concerning how to write scientific papers and how to combine research with teaching.

Peter Medawar

To my knowledge, the only other book-length advice for scientists written by a distinguished scientist is Peter Medawar's (1979) *Advice to a Young Scientist*. The title is similar to the English translation of Ramón y Cajal's much earlier book, but the translators must have been mimicking Medawar rather than Medawar mimicking Ramón y Cajal, whose original title lacked the word "young." Medawar was a British biologist who shared the Nobel prize in 1960 for work conducted in 1949, when he was still in his thirties. There is no indication in Medawar's book that he had read the much earlier book by Ramón y Cajal.

Medawar begins by asking the question: How can I tell if I am cut out to be a scientific research worker? He says that most able scientists have a trait he calls "exploratory impulsion" (p. 7), which is a strong desire to comprehend. They also need intellectual skills, including general intelligence and particular abilities required for specific sciences, such as manipulative skills necessary for many experimental sciences.

Medawar's next chapter provides advice concerning: What shall I do research on? His main recommendation is to study important problems, ones whose answers really matter to science generally or to humankind. Young scientists must beware of following fashion, for example by picking up some popular gimmick rather than pursuing important ideas.

Medawar's chapter 4 concerns how scientists can equip themselves to be better scientists. He recognizes that the beginner must read the literature, but urges reading "intently and choosily and not too much" (p. 17). The danger is that novices will spend so much time mastering the literature that they never get any research done. Experimental researchers need to get results, even if they are not original at first. The art of research is the "art of the soluble," in that a researcher must find a way of getting at a problem, such as a new measuring technique, that provides a new way of solving the problem.

Whereas Ramón y Cajal assumed that scientists were male, Medawar includes a chapter on sexism and racism in science. Medawar sees no difference in intelligence, skill, or thinking style between men and women, and has little specific advice for women scientists. Similarly, he sees no inborn constitutional differences in scientific prowess or capability between different races or nationalities.

Medawar states that nearly all his scientific work was done in collaboration, and emphasizes the importance of *synergism*, when a research team comes up with a joint effort that is greater than the sum of the several contributions to it. Young scientists who have the generosity of spirit to collaborate can have much more enjoyable and successful careers than loners. Scientists should be willing to recognize and admit their mistakes: "I cannot give any scientist of any age better advice than this: the intensity of the conviction that a hypothesis is true has no bearing on whether it is true or not" (p. 39). Medawar suggests that creativity is helped by a quiet and untroubled life. Scientists concerned with priority may be inclined toward secretiveness, but Medawar advises telling close colleagues everything you know. Ambition in young scientists is useful as a motive force, but excess of ambition can be a disfigurement.

Like Ramón y Cajal, Medawar encourages scientists to make their results known through publications and presentations. He recommends a policy generally followed in the sciences (but not, unfortunately, in the humanities) that presentations should be spoken from notes rather than read from a script. Papers should be written concisely and appropriately for the intended audience.

Medawar also provides advice about the conducting and interpretation of experiments. He advocates "Galilean" experiments, ones that do not simply make observations but rather discriminate between possibilities in a way that tests hypotheses. He warns against falling in love with a pet hypothesis. Young scientists should aim to make use of experiments and theories to make the world more understandable, not just to compile information. A scientist is a "seeker after truth" (p. 87), devising hypotheses that can be tested by practicable experiments. Before scientists set out to convince others of their observations or opinions, they must first convince themselves, which should not be too easily achieved. Medawar prefers a Popperian philosophy of science based on critical evaluation to a Kuhnian philosophy based on paradigms.

James Watson

My third eminent biologist is James Watson, who shared a Nobel prize in 1962 for his role in the discovery of the structure of DNA. In 1993 Watson gave an after-dinner talk at a meeting to celebrate the fortieth anniversary of the double helix, and later published the talk in a collection of occasional pieces (Watson 2000). The published version, titled "Succeeding in Science: Some Rules of Thumb," is only four pages long, much more concise than the books by Ramón y Cajal and Medawar. Watson says that to succeed in science you need a lot more than luck and intelligence, and he offers four rules for success.

The first rule is to learn from the winners, avoiding dumb people. To win at something really difficult, you should always turn to people who are brighter than you are. The second rule is to take risks, being prepared to get into deep trouble. Big success requires taking on a very big goal that you are not prepared to pursue and ignoring people, including your mentors, who tell you that you are not ready for it. Watson's third rule, however, is to have someone as a fallback when you get into trouble. He describes how important it was to his career to have John Kendrew and Salvador Luria behind him at critical moments.

Watson's final rule is: "Never do anything that bores you" (Watson 2000, p. 125). It is much easier to do well things that you like. Watson also remarks on the importance of having people around you that care about you and that you can go to for intellectual help. It is also valuable to have people with whom you can expose your ideas to informed criticism; Watson suggests that his main competitors in the search for the structure of DNA, Rosalind Franklin and Linus Pauling, both suffered from a lack of people who could usefully disagree with them. People should not go into science as a way of avoiding dealing with other people, because success in science requires spending time with other scientists, both colleagues and competitors. Watson's success was partly the result of knowing everyone he needed to know.

Discussion

To what extent does the advice offered by the three distinguished biologists coincide with the habits of creative scientists summarized in table 12.1? There is clearly some overlap, for example with Watson's suggestion to take risks and Medawar's suggestion to have good collaborators. But the three biologists also made many recommendations that were not reported by the participants in the 2001 Workshop on Cognitive Studies of Science and Technology. I have listed the additional recommendations in table 12.2, which should be read as a supplement rather than as a replacement for table 12.1.

The three biologists do not add a lot to the cognitive advice in table 12.1, although there are valuable nuggets such as Medawar's advice about new techniques making problems soluble, Ramón y Cajal's and Medawar's concerns about giving up one's own ideas when necessary, and Ramón y Cajal's recommendation to concentrate tenaciously. The emotional additions are more interesting, particularly Ramón y Cajal's and Medawar's discussion of the kinds of passion that foster scientific success, such as strong desires for truth, reputation, discovery, and comprehension. The correlate of table 12.1's advice to have fun is Watson's advice to avoid boredom, which was a major impetus behind his own work on the double helix (Watson 1969; see also chap. 10 of this vol.).

The three biologists also have a wealth of social and environmental advice that goes well beyond that found in table 12.1. Ramón y Cajal, Medawar,

Table 12.2
More habits of successful scientists

1. *Make new connections.*
Find new ways of making problems soluble, e.g. by new techniques (Medawar).
2. *Expect the unexpected.*
Avoid excessive attachment to your own ideas (Ramón y Cajal).
Be willing to recognize and admit mistakes (Medawar).
3. *Be persistent.*
Concentrate tenaciously on a subject (Ramón y Cajal).
4. *Get excited.*
Have a devotion for truth and a passion for reputation (Ramón y Cajal).
Have an inclination toward originality and a taste for research (Ramón y Cajal).
Have a desire for the gratification of discovery (Ramón y Cajal).
Have a strong desire to comprehend (Medawar).
Never do anything that bores you (Watson).
5. *Be sociable.*
Marry for psychological compatibility (Ramón y Cajal).
Tell close colleagues everything you know (Medawar).
Communicate research results effectively (Ramón y Cajal, Medawar).
Learn from winners. (Watson).
Have people to fall back on when you get into trouble (Watson).
6. *Use the world.*
Seek inspiration in nature (Ramón y Cajal).
Have good laboratory facilities and use them (Ramón y Cajal).
Observe and reflect intensely (Ramón y Cajal).
Perform experiments that rigorously test hypotheses. (Medawar)
7. *Other*
Avoid excessive admiration for the work of great minds (Ramón y Cajal).
Cultivate science for its own sake (Ramón y Cajal, Medawar).
Study important problems (Medawar).
Don't read too much (Medawar).
Have a quiet and untroubled life (Medawar).

and Watson all have useful social recommendations summarized in table 12.2, ranging from marrying appropriately to communicating well with colleagues and the general scientific community. Ramón y Cajal and Medawar were more emphatic than philosophers, psychologists, and historians of science usually are about the importance of using experiments and instruments to interact effectively with the world. Whereas the workshop participants did an excellent job of identifying cognitive factors in scientific success, the three biologists who have provided advice seem stronger on the relevant emotional, social, and environmental factors.

Table 12.2 also lists a set of other factors that do not seem to fit into any of the six classes in table 12.1. Both Ramón y Cajal and Medawar recommend studying science for its own sake without worrying too much about practical applications. Ramón y Cajal's counsel to avoid being too impressed with great minds fits with Watson's injunction to take risks by deviating from established opinion. Medawar's suggestion not to read too much seems to contradict the suggestion in table 12.1 to read widely. Studying important problems and avoiding life's disruptions seems like good general advice.

Another possible source of information about what makes scientists successful comes from psychological studies of personality. Feist and Gorman (1998) review a large literature that compares personality characteristics of scientists to nonscientists. Their major conclusions are:

- Scientists are more conscientious.
- Scientists are more dominant, achievement oriented, and driven.
- Scientists are independent, introverted, and less sociable.
- Scientists are emotionally stable and impulse controlled.

They also reviewed literature that compares eminent and creative scientists with less eminent and creative ones, concluding:

- Creative scientists are more dominant, arrogant, self-confident, or hostile.
- Creative scientists are more autonomous, independent, or introverted.
- Creative scientists are more driven, ambitious, or achievement oriented.
- Creative scientists are more open and flexible in thought and character.

From this literature, we could conclude that to become a successful scientist it helps to be dominant, independent, driven, and flexible.

Even without the personality findings, between tables 12.1 and 12.2 we now have assembled close to fifty pieces of advice for scientific success. Surely some of these recommendations are much more important than others for fostering the creative breakthroughs that contribute most to scientific success, but we have no way of knowing which ones are most influential. Perhaps a large-scale psychological and/or historical survey might be able to provide some ideas about which factors are most important (cf. Feist 1993).

There is also the possibility of providing practical advice about how to conduct a scientific career at a much more low level, for example how to deal with career choices, work–family conflicts, and becoming an aging scientist (see e.g., Darley, Zanna, and Roediger 2004; Sindermann 1985). This chapter has not attempted to provide a definitive list of what traits and activities it takes to become a creatively successful scientist, but I hope it has provided both a framework and set of factors for understanding scientific success.

The broad range of the factors for scientific success discussed in this chapter demonstrates the great diversity of what needs to be taken into account in explanations of the growth of scientific knowledge. Science studies need to go beyond the traditional concerns of particular discipline, such as philosophical attention to modes of reasoning, psychological attention to cognitive processes, and sociological attention to social interactions. All these concerns are legitimate, but need to be complemented by understanding how emotions, personality, and intelligent interactions with the world also contribute to the development of science.

Baljinder Sahdra and Paul Thagard

Introduction

Skeptics such as Paluch (1967) and Haight (1980) think that the very notion of self-deception is implausible. However, there is empirical evidence that self-deception is not only possible but also highly pervasive in human life. It accounts for positive illusions of opponents in battle and their belief that they will win (Wrangham 1999). It is involved in denial in physical illness (Goldbeck 1997). It has been shown to account for unrealistic optimism of the self-employed (Arabsheibani et al. 2000). It has been observed in traffic behavior of professional drivers (Lajunen et al. 1996). And it has been shown to mediate cooperation and defection in a variety of social contexts (Surbey and McNally 1997).

What is self-deception? How do we deceive ourselves? Researchers have attempted to answer these questions in various ways. Some thinkers argue that self-deception involves a division in the self where one part of the self deceives the other (Davidson 1985; Pears 1986; Rorty 1988, 1996). Others, however, maintain that such division is not necessary (Demos 1960; Elster 1983; Johnston 1988; McLaughlin 1988; Rey 1988; Talbott 1995; Mele 2001). Some consider self-deception to be intentional (Sackeim and Gur 1978; Davidson 1985; Pears 1986; Rorty 1988; Talbott 1995), while others insist that it is non-intentional (Elster 1983; Johnston 1988; McLaughlin 1988, 1996; Lazar 1999; Mele 2001). Some think that self-deception is a violation of general maxims of rationality (Pears 1982; Davidson 1985), while others argue that self-deception is consistent with practical rationality (Rey 1988; Rorty 1988).

We propose that self-deception can result from emotional coherence directed to approach or avoid subjective goals. We will show this by modeling a specific case of self-deception, namely that of Dimmesdale, the minister in Hawthorne's *The Scarlet Letter* (1850). The model has two parts, namely, a "cold" or non-emotional model and a "hot" or emotional model. The emotional aspect of self-deception may be implicit in some accounts, but no one has brought it to the forefront of the discussion. Two notable exceptions are Ronald de Sousa (1988) and Ariela Lazar (1999). Our computational account is more precise than de Sousa's. Lazar (1999) argues that self-deceptive beliefs are partially caused by emotions whose effects are not mediated by practical reasoning. Our account differs from Lazar's in that we show that self-deception can arise even in those cases in which self-deceivers are highly motivated to be rational; the effects of emotions are just as mediated by rational thought as the effects of rational thought are by emotions. In other words, we will show that it is the interaction of cognitive and emotional factors that plays the pivotal role in self-deception.

After giving our model, we will also compare it to two other models of self-deception, namely Rey's (1988), and Talbott's (1995). We will argue that our model is more psychologically plausible than their models.

What Is Self-Deception?

Self-deception involves a blind or unexamined acceptance of a belief that can easily be seen as "spurious" if the person were to inspect the belief impartially or from the perspective of the generalized other (Mitchell 2000, p. 145). Consider an example from Mele (2001, p. 26): Don deceives himself into believing the belief p that his research paper was wrongly rejected for publication. Indubitably, there are two essential characteristics of Don's self-deception:

1. Don *falsely* believes p.
2. Either someone other than Don, or he himself at a later *impartial* examination, observes (or accuses) that he is deceiving himself into believing p.

The two points are related. The reason we know that Don falsely believes p is that an impartial examination of evidence suggests that Don ought to believe $\sim p$. Most of the time, "the impartial observer," to use Mele's (2001) term, is someone other than the self-deceiver, but it is also possible that the self-deceiver herself may realize the spuriousness of and self-deception involved in her beliefs, at a later careful examination.

In (2) above, one might even use the term "interpretation" instead of observation or accusation. Goldberg notes, "accusations of self-deception are only as strong as the interpretation of ... [the] behavior" (Goldberg 1997). Thus, one might say that the model of Dimmesdale's self-deception that we will present shortly is based on *our* interpretation of his speech and beliefs as they are revealed in the narrative. But we cannot have just any interpretation. The best interpretation is the one that is consistent with all the available information.

The minimal description of self-deception that we have given above is not finely tuned to distinguish self-deception from wishful thinking and denial. We will make such distinctions after we give a much more precise account of self-deception in our computational model. Given these remarks, we can begin the impartial or external analysis of the self-deception of Dimmesdale, the minister in *The Scarlet Letter*.

Dimmesdale's Self-Deception

Before we present our analysis, we must clarify that our purpose is not to morally judge Dimmesdale. Some theorists hold that self-deception is intrinsically wrong in that it is a sort of spiritual failure (Sartre 1958; Fingarette 1969). At the same time, many philosophers also argue that self-deception is not always wrong, and may even be beneficial; for example, see Rorty (1996) and Taylor (1989). Nevertheless, in the era in which Hawthorne wrote *The Scarlet Letter*, it was taken for granted that being dishonest with oneself was somehow always wrong. Hawthorne gives us the famous advice: "Be true! Be true! Be true! Show freely to the world, if not your worst, yet some trait whereby the worst may be inferred!" (Hawthorne 1850, p. 260). For Hawthorne, self-deception, like hypocrisy, is morally wrong because self-deceivers are largely out of touch with the true selves within them and mistakenly place their trust in what the reader recognizes to be a false outer appearance (Harris 1988, p. 21). We think that the issue of moral reprehensibility of self-deception is important. However, our objective is much humbler in that we only aim to *explain* how Dimmesdale deceived himself, and thus suggest a new way of conceiving of self-deception.

The Scarlet Letter is particularly attractive for a study of self-deception because of the richness of detail of the self-deceiving characters in it. This degree of detail is invariably missing in the philosophical literature on self-deception; the most commonly cited case is Elster's (1983) example of sour grapes. In *The Scarlet Letter*, almost everybody is a hypocrite. More importantly, Hawthorne's hypocrites are almost always self-deceivers as well. The reader easily infers that from the narrative. On one occasion, however, the narrator explicitly informs us that Dimmesdale, the minister, had deceived himself; and later, Dimmesdale himself unfolds his character to reveal the complexity of his self-deception. See figure 13.1 for a pictorial analysis of

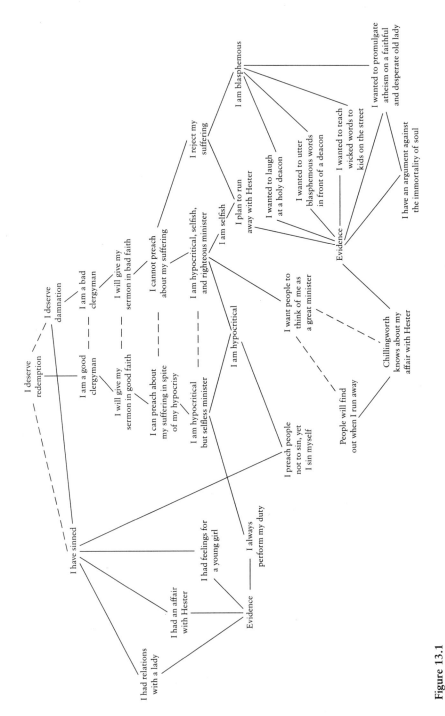

Figure 13.1
ECHO analysis of Dimmesdale's self-deception. Solid lines represent positive associations. Dotted lines represent negative representations.

Dimmesdale's self-deception. The solid lines in the figure represent positive associations, and the dotted lines represent negative associations.

The narrator informs us that Dimmesdale deceives himself when he tells himself that his satisfaction at knowing he can still preach the Election Day sermon before running off with Hester arises from his wish that people will think of him as an admirable servant of the Church. He says to Hester: People "shall say of me ... that I leave no public duty unperformed, nor ill performed" (Hawthorne 1850, p. 215). "Sad, indeed," the narrator tells us, "that an introspection so profound and acute as this poor minister's should be so miserably deceived!" (p. 215). Dimmesdale deceives himself in not wanting to have it said that he failed to carry out his "public duty," even if it were to be revealed almost immediately, as it obviously would, to the same public that his dutiful service to them was sheer hypocrisy. In other words, his self-deception consists in believing that he can fill his sacramental office and still be a hypocrite.

Dimmesdale deceives himself in believing that he is no more hypocritical now than he has been for seven years. Previously, he has known that he has been hypocritical because of his hidden sinfulness. However, at one point during his conversation with Chillingworth, he concedes that a priest who knows he is guilty may still have the obligation to continue as a priest, and in that sense he would not necessarily be a hypocrite. He claims that some people, "by the very constitution of their nature," may be forced to live with the "unutterable torment" of hidden guilt and still carry out ministerial, even sacramental functions (p. 132). Therefore, as Harris puts it, "in the past, Dimmesdale has been a good clergyman not only in spite of his hidden guilt and his consciousness of his hypocrisy, but precisely *because* of those very factors—because of his excruciating situation" (Harris 1988, p. 84). He has been a hypocrite because he has allowed people to think that he is a saint; but his motive in doing that has been to fulfill his duty. Thus, he was a good clergyman in spite of his hypocrisy because his motives were selfless.

The situation is different however, when he deceives himself. His motives have changed and he deceives himself in believing that his motives are the same. This time, his motive is to pass himself off as righteous. His main concern is that people say of him that he "leaves no public duty unperformed, nor ill performed!" (Hawthorne 1850, p. 215). In the past, Dimmesdale has been a hypocrite but still a good clergyman. Now, he is a hypocrite and a bad clergyman because his motives are selfish. He believes that he can still sincerely preach about his suffering even though he rejects his suffering now. In short, he deceives himself in believing that he is a good clergyman now as he was in the past.

The fact that Dimmesdale's self-deception is intertwined with his hypocrisy causes him much confusion. Harris thinks that his self-deception is of the "deepest, most unconscious sort, compounded by deliberate hypocrisy, and the prognosis calls for an ever-increasing confusion of identity" (Harris 1988, p. 75). The narrator in the novel describes this complexity: "No man, for any considerable period, can wear one face to himself, and another to the multitude, without getting bewildered as to which may be the true" (Hawthorne 1850, pp. 215–216). In the chapter, "The Minister in a Maze," as Dimmesdale's identity unravels, his impulses seem to be "at once involuntary and intentional: in spite of himself, yet growing out of a profounder self than that which opposed the impulse" (p. 217). This "profounder self" incites him into blaspheming in front of a deacon; laughing at the good and holy deacon; promulgating atheism to a helpless old lady who has nothing but faith in God to sustain her; teaching "some very wicked words" to a few kids playing on a street; and giving a "wicked look" to a young girl with a spiritual crush on him.

His "profounder self" has much to do with his sexuality as manifested in three things: first, his impulsive affair with Hester; second, his likely relations with "the many blooming damsels, spiritually devoted to him" from his congregation (p. 125). Third, as mentioned previously, when he meets one young girl while he is lost in his private "maze," the reader is informed, "that the minister felt potent to blight all the field of innocence with but one wicked look" (p. 220).

It is important to note that Dimmesdale is able to end his self-deception. This will factor significantly in our model, as we will explain later. Throughout the novel, Hawthorne is very sarcastic and scornful of Dimmesdale for his hypocrisy and self-deception, but in the end he makes him appear as a kind of a hero or saint. Dimmesdale, while giving the sermon, "stops deceiving himself into thinking that he could preach about his suffering at the same time he was planning to reject his suffering" (Harris 1988, p. 86). He preaches in the same spirit as before and to the same effect. Thus, he returns to his earlier state of hypocrisy. He escapes his hypocrisy at the time of his death when he declares it in front of all the people of his congregation. The reason he is able to escape his self-deception and his hypocrisy is that he knows, more than anybody else, that he is unworthy of redemption.

General Description of Our Model of Dimmesdale's Self-Deception

We used the simulators, ECHO and HOTCO 2 to computationally model Dimmesdale's self-deception. The two sections following this one contain the detailed descriptions of these simulators. In this section, we give a general description of our model.

The model has two parts: (1) Cold Clergyman, a cold or emotionless explanation, and (2) Hot Clergyman, an emotional explanation. The first part is the test to see what Dimmesdale *would* believe given the evidence. This experiment would serve as a rational baseline. In other words, this would be the impartial or external observation of the situation. The second part is the model of what he *does* believe in spite of the evidence, given his goals and emotional preferences.

In the first experiment, Cold Clergyman, the input is simply the observed propositions (that is, the evidence), and the negative and positive associations between propositions. See figure 13.1. After the experiment is run, we expect that Dimmesdale would believe the belief-set A:

1. I am a bad clergyman.
2. I will give my sermon in bad faith.
3. I cannot preach about my suffering.
4. I am hypocritical, selfish, and a righteous minister.

In the second experiment, Hot Clergyman, in addition to the evidence, propositions, and all the associations, he is given two goals: (1) approach redemption, and (2) avoid damnation. Also, he is given "likes" and "dislikes," based on whether a proposition has negative or positive emotional valence. See table 13.1. For example, he likes being a good clergyman and dislikes being a bad clergyman. In this experiment, he should be able to deceive himself into believing the belief-set B:

1. I am a good clergyman.
2. I will give my sermon in good faith.
3. I can preach about my suffering in spite of my hypocrisy.
4. I am hypocritical but selfless.

Cold Clergyman is run in the explanatory coherence program, ECHO. Hot Clergyman is run in the emotional coherence program, HOTCO 2. We devote the following two sections to describe ECHO and HOTCO 2 in detail.

ECHO and Explanatory Coherence

ECHO is an implementation of the theory of explanatory coherence discussed at length elsewhere (Thagard 1992, 2000; chap. 8 above). ECHO shows precisely how coherence can be calculated. Hypotheses and evidence are represented by units, which are highly simplified artificial neurons that can have

Table 13.1

	Propositions	Goals	Likes	Dislikes
1	I am a good minister.		*	
2	I am a bad minister.			*
3	I deserve redemption.	Approach redemption		
4	I deserve damnation.	Avoid damnation		
5	I will give my sermon in good faith.		*	
6	I will give my sermon in bad faith.			*
7	I can preach about my suffering in spite of my hypocrisy.		*	
8	I am hypocritical but selfless.			*
9	I always perform my duty.		*	
10	I cannot preach about my suffering.			
11	I am hypocritical, selfish, and righteous minister.			
12	I reject my suffering.			*
13	I am blasphemous.			*
14	I am hypocritical.			*
15	I am selfish.			*
16	I have sinned.			*
17	I preach people not to sin, yet I sin myself.			*
18	I had an affair with Hester. (E)			*
19	I had feelings for a young girl. (E)			*
20	I had relations with a lady. (E)			*
21	I want people to think of me as a great minister. (E)			
22	People will discover my guilt.			*
23	Chillingworth knows about my affair with Hester. (E)			*
24	I plan to run away with Hester. (E)			*
25	I wanted to laugh at a holy deacon. (E)			
26	I wanted to utter blasphemous words in front of a deacon. (E)			
27	I wanted to teach wicked words to kids. (E)			
28	I wanted to promulgate atheism on an old lady. (E)			
29	I have an argument against the immortality of soul. (E)			

(E) = Evidence

excitatory and inhibitory links with each other. When two propositions cohere, as when a hypothesis explains a piece of evidence, then there is an excitatory link between the two units that represent them. When two propositions are incoherent with each other, either because they are contradictory or because they compete to explain some of the evidence, then there is an inhibitory link between them. Standard algorithms are available for spreading activation among the units until they reach a stable state in which some units have positive activation, representing the acceptance of the propositions they represent, and other units have negative activation, representing the rejection of the propositions they represent. Thus algorithms for artificial neural networks can be used to maximize explanatory coherence, as can other kinds of algorithms (Thagard and Verbeurgt 1998; Thagard 2000).

HOTCO and Emotional Coherence

When people make judgments, they not only come to conclusions about what to believe, but they also make emotional assessments. For example, the decision to trust people is partly based on purely cognitive inferences about their plans and personalities, but also involves adopting emotional attitudes toward them (Thagard 2000, chap. 6). The theory of emotional coherence serves to explain how people's inferences about what to believe are integrated with the production of feelings about people, things, and situations. On this theory, mental representations such as propositions and concepts have, in addition to the cognitive status of being accepted or rejected, an emotional status called a *valence*, which can be positive or negative depending on one's emotional attitude toward the representation. For example, just as one can accept or reject the proposition that Dimmesdale committed adultery with Hester, one can attach a positive or negative valence to it depending on whether one thinks this is good or bad.

The computational model HOTCO implements the theory of emotional coherence by expanding ECHO to allow the units that stand for propositions to have valences as well as activations. Valences are affective tags attached to the elements in coherence systems. Valences can be positive or negative. In addition, units can have input valences to represent their intrinsic valences. In the original version of HOTCO (Thagard 2000), the valence of a unit was calculated on the basis of the activations and valences of all the units connected to it. Hence valences could be affected by activations and emotions, but not vice versa: HOTCO enabled cognitive inferences such as ones based on explanatory coherence to influence emotional judgments, but did not allow emotional judgments to bias cognitive inferences. HOTCO and the overly rational theory of emotional coherence that it embodied could explain a fairly wide range of cognitive-emotional judgments involving trust and other psychological phenomena, but could not adequately explain Dimmesdale's self-deception.

As we saw in chapters 3 and 8, HOTCO 2 allows biasing for all units. For instance, consider the proposition, "I will be redeemed." This proposition can be viewed as having an activation that represents its degree of acceptance or rejection, but it can also be viewed as having a valence that corresponds to Dimmesdale's emotional attitude toward redemption. Since he deems redemption as of great importance, this proposition has a positive valence. In HOTCO 2, therefore, the truth and desirability of a proposition become interdependent. Technical details concerning explanatory and emotional coherence are provided in the appendix to chapter 3.

Results of Cold Clergyman and Hot Clergyman

As expected, in the cold experiments run in ECHO, the system yields acceptance of all four propositions of the belief-set A:

1. I am a bad clergyman.
2. I will give my sermon in bad faith.
3. I cannot preach about my suffering.
4. I am hypocritical, selfish, and a righteous minister.

Also, the system rejects the belief-set B:

1. I am a good clergyman.
2. I will give my sermon in good faith.
3. I can preach about my suffering in spite of my hypocrisy.
4. I am hypocritical but selfless.

On the other hand, in the hot experiments run in HOTCO 2, given that the weight of the input valence is equal to or greater than 0.06, the system successfully self-deceives; that is, the belief-set B is accepted and A is rejected (except for proposition 4 in A). The ideal solution to model Dimmesdale's self-deception, however, is when the weight is 0.07. At this degree of input valence, Dimmesdale successfully deceives himself into believing the belief-set B while he rejects the proposition that he will be redeemed. In other words, self-deception occurs, but the proposition that he will be redeemed has a negative activation, that is, it is rejected. Also, Dimmesdale fully accepts that he has sinned. This is consistent with the novel, *The Scarlet Letter*, in which Dimmesdale never denies that he has sinned and experiences much pain due to his guilt. The result is also consistent with the fact that Dimmesdale is able to escape his self-deception, and admit his sin in front of his congregation before he dies with a cry for forgiveness. Thus, HOTCO 2 successfully models that although Dimmesdale is trying to approach redemption while deceiving himself, he never fully approaches it. This allows him to get out of his self-deception later in the novel when he realizes that he can never be redeemed unless he escapes his self-deception and hypocrisy.

Self-Deception and Subjective Well-Being

According to our model, self-deception occurs via emotional biasing of people's beliefs, while people attempt to avoid or approach their subjective goals. This account is consistent with Erez et al.'s (1995) psychological theory of subjective well-being according to which dispositional tendencies, such as, affective disposition and locus of control, influence subjective well-being through self-deception. According to this theory, certain individuals tend to use self-deception in order to maintain their happiness. Such individuals are either positively disposed or they have high expectations of control. They tend to ignore failure, for instance, if they are positively disposed. They unrealistically think that they control their environment, if they have high expectations of control. Also, individuals who tend to evaluate stimuli in a positive manner or tend to think they can control their environment do so by actively searching for positive and desirable cues while denying negative and undesirable ones (Erez, Johnson, and Judge 1995). See figure 13.2.

Thus, focusing on the bottom section of Erez et al.'s hypothesized causal model, two things may cause self-deception: affective disposition, and locus of control. However, we hypothesize that there is a two-way causal link between self-deception and subjective well-being. See figure 13.3.

We think that the causal link is bidirectional because:

(a) There is evidence that self-deception causes subjective well-being:

• Self-deception is one of the mental mechanisms that increases the subjects' positive assessments of situations (ignoring minor criticisms, discounting failure, and expecting success) (Zerbe and Paulhus 1987).
• Self-deceivers continually distort daily events to build positive esteem (Paulhus and Reid 1991).
• Self-deception improves motivation and performance of competitors by reducing their stress and bolstering their confidence by repressing their knowledge of the self-interests and confidence of their competitors (Starek and Keating 1991).

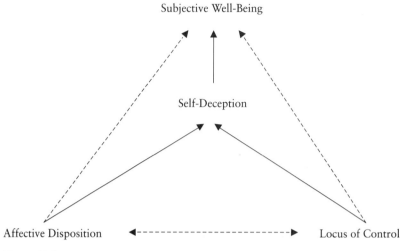

Figure 13.2
The Psychological Causal Model of Self-Deception. Adapted from Erez et al. 1995.

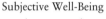

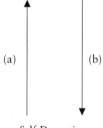

Figure 13.3
The two-way causal link between self-deception and subjective well-being.

(b) Also, subjective well-being causes self-deception:

• The positive esteem, when sufficiently strong, may act as a buffer to soften the impact of negative information (Erez, Johnson, and Judge 1995). Thus, having high subjective well-being may cause one to self-deceive by causing one to ignore negative information.

• When threatening or "harmful-to-the-self" information is presented to ego enhancers, they turn to their assets and emphasize them to neutralize the threat (Taylor 1989). Thus, an enhanced ego can cause one's self-deception in that it neutralizes the influence of any evidence that diminishes ego.

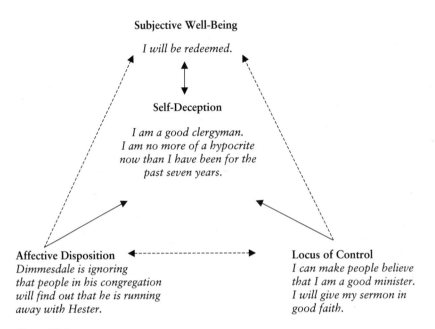

Figure 13.4
Causal Model of Dimmesdale's self-deception. Adapted from Erez et al. 1995.

In our model described in the previous sections, self-deception is directed toward approaching or avoiding certain subjective goals, which presumably increase or decrease subjective well-being if approached or avoided. For instance, in Dimmesdale's case, the causal model can be depicted as follows:

As shown in figure 13.4, Dimmesdale's subjective well-being depends on his prospect of being redeemed. Being a good clergyman is essential for redemption. He may be disposed to ignore any evidence that may suggest that he is a bad clergyman. This is consistent with HOTCO 2 experiments in which the proposition that people will know when he runs away with Hester is rejected. Also, he may have a false sense of control that he will give his sermon in good faith, and make people believe that he is a good minister. His false sense of control and his disposition to ignore certain evidence cause his self-deception which in turn, causes his subjective well-being which feeds back into his self-deception.

One might argue that the notion of cause is ambiguous or mysterious. We are suggesting a way to disambiguate or demystify the causal relations involved in self-deception by proposing that the mechanism of the causal relations is emotional coherence. Thus, the causal links in self-deception may be as depicted in figure 13.4, but the way different causes lead to self-deception is through emotional coherence. The successful modeling of Dimmesdale's self-deception in HOTCO 2, an implementation of emotional coherence, supports this conclusion.

Wishful Thinking, Denial, and Self-Deception

Wishful thinking is importantly different from self-deception. In wishful thinking an agent believes whatever he or she wants. Elster (1983), Mele (2001), and Johnston (1988) propose that at least some cases of self-deception can be explained in terms of wishful thinking. Although, it is important that the agent desires that p to self-deceive herself into believing that p, we think that self-deception is not just wishful thinking. In HOTCO 2, the valence input can be varied so as to make the system less or more emotional. After a certain degree of valence input, the system becomes so emotional that it models an agent who believes every single proposition that he or she deems as important. In a sense, emotions completely override reason. At such a degree of emotional input, the model shows that Dimmesdale not only believes that he is a good minister, he also believes that he will be redeemed. However, he does not think of himself as worthy of redemption in the experiments in which he successfully deceives himself into believing that he is a good clergyman.

Thus, in wishful thinking, people believe everything that they want to believe. Self-deception, however, is a "weaker" state in that we may successfully deceive ourselves into believing something, but not everything that we wish to believe. This claim is supported by psychological studies on motivated inference (Kunda 1999; Sanitioso, Kunda, and Fong 1990); psychologists have shown that our judgments are colored by our motivations because the process of constructing justifications is biased by our goals. Nevertheless, we cannot believe whatever we want to believe (Kunda 1999; chap. 8 above). There are constraints on what we can believe. In self-deception, we succeed in believing some (false) beliefs but not in believing everything we want to believe. Because some wishes remain unfulfilled, anxiety or internal conflict typically but not necessarily accompanies self-deception (as we will discuss in a coming section), but not wishful thinking.

Denial is also different from self-deception in that it is a kind of direct lie that self-deception is not. In denial, a person knowingly or consciously lies that $\sim p$. In self-deception, however, the person really *believes* that $\sim p$. Both claim something false, but in self-deception the correct belief (that p) is "held" nonconsciously, whereas in denial, it is believed consciously. Also, in addition to denial, self-deception contains a very strong ego-enhancement component (Paulhus and Reid 1991). Thus, self-deception and denial are importantly different.

Debates

In the beginning of our chapter, we mentioned the debates over whether self-deception is intentional or not, and whether it involves a divided self or not. In this section we briefly comment on these debates. We also discuss the issue of whether the desire that p has to be "anxious" or not.

Regarding the issue of whether self-deception is intentional or not, we think that the debate is misplaced. To the extent that Dimmesdale intends to be redeemed, his self-deception can be seen as intentional. However, it would be absurd to claim that he intends to have the emotional preferences that he does. He may not have any control over his emotions at all. Emotional coherence occurs unconsciously. In their classic experiment pioneering the psychological studies of self-deception, Sackeim and Gur found that there were discrepancies in subjects' conscious misidentifications and nonconscious correct identifications (as indicated by galvanic skin responses) of voices as their own or others (Sackeim and Gur 1979). They found that such discrepancies were a function of the subjects' independent manipulation of their self-esteem. (The subjects misidentified their own voices as others' when they thought ill of themselves, and others' voices as their own when they thought well of themselves.) We are proposing that the unconscious mechanism behind self-deception is emotional coherence. The subjective goal of redemption, in Dimmesdale's case for instance, may be a conscious goal. However, the goal is approached through nonconscious emotional coherence. Is having the intent to be redeemed sufficient to call Dimmesdale's self-deception intentional? No, for self-deception is not just approaching or avoiding one's goals. *How* the goal is approached or avoided is crucially a part of self-deception. One may fully intend to do whatever is necessary to achieve the desired goal, but at the same time, one does not *intend* to achieve emotional coherence in the approach of the goal. Therefore, until there is a good account of the relation between intentions and emotions, we cannot decide whether self-deception is intentional or not.

On the issue of a possible division of self involved in self-deception, we think that the issue arises from a misunderstanding of the notion of the self itself. Researchers have mainly focused on the deception side of self-deception, while rarely talking about the self of self-deception. What is the self that is deceived? In Dimmesdale's case, the narrator informs us of a tension between his "profounder self" and his presentational or outer self.

However, this does not imply that there is necessarily a Freudian split in his self. It is not that Dimmesdale has two selves, self-A and self-B, and that self-A deceives self-B. There is a sense in which the self has a kind of continuity or oneness to it. However, the self is a "decentered, distributed, and multiplex" phenomenon that is "the sum total of its narratives, and includes within itself all the equivocations, contradictions, struggles and hidden messages that find expression in personal life" (Gallagher 2000, p. 20). It is *because* the self is multiplex and devoid of any center, that self-deception is possible. Thus, if there is a "split" in the self, it is not at one place, but all over the place, and even in the self that does not deceive itself.

There is another debate worth paying attention to. Everybody agrees that in self-deception the agent, say, A is motivationally biased to believe *p*. Mele (2001) holds that the biasing role is played by A's desire that *p*. However, following Johnston (1988), Barnes (1997) insists that the desire that *p* must be anxious in that the person is uncertain of the truth of *p*. We can easily think of Dimmesdale's case as involving the desire to be redeemed. There is no doubt that he wants to be redeemed. We can also say that he desires to be a good clergyman, and successfully deceives himself into believing that he is a good clergyman. Hawthorne makes it clear that Dimmesdale's self-deception causes him so much confusion that he experiences profound identity crises. It appears that in Dimmesdale's case his desire is anxious. However, we are inclined to agree with Mele that in self-deception the desire that *p* does not *have to* be an anxious desire.

There is good, although not conclusive computational evidence from our model that has inclined us to say that Mele is probably right on this issue. We conducted several hot experiments with varying degrees of emotional (valence) input in the system. The general trend was that the greater the valence input, that is, the more emotional the system, the easier (that is, faster) it was for the system to model self-deception. This suggests that the "influence" of emotions on the system was a matter of degree. The same may be true in humans. There is psychological evidence to suggest that self-deception is a dispositional tendency (Sackeim and Gur 1979). It is plausible to hypothesize that this tendency is due to emotions and that depending on the degree to which people are emotional, they may be less or more disposed to deceive themselves.

Our Model Compared to Other Computational Models of Self-Deception

Rey (1988) gives a computational model based on the distinction between "central" and "avowed" attitudes of a self-deceiver. According to Rey, self-deception arises due to the discrepancies between the two kinds of attitudes. However, as Rey correctly notes, it is crucial that the discrepancies be motivated (p. 281). Otherwise, the agent would be self-ignorant and not self-deceiving. What is missing in Rey's model is any detailed account of what plays the motivated biasing role essential for self-deception. Our model shows that emotional coherence involving goals can provide the necessary motivated biasing.

Another notable model is Talbott's Bayesian model (1995). Insofar as Talbott bases his model on the assumption of the self as a practically rational Bayesian agent, Talbott's model inherits the problems of a probabilistic approach to human thinking. The problems with probabilistic models of human thinking are discussed at length in Thagard (2000, chap. 8). Such accounts assume that quantities that comply with the mathematical theory of probability can adequately describe the degrees of belief that people have in various propositions. However, there is much empirical evidence to show that human thinking is often not in accord with the notions of probability theory (see, e.g., Kahneman, Slovic, and Tversky 1982; Tversky and Koehler 1994). On the other hand, as discussed in detail in Thagard (2000), coherence-based reasoning (on which our model is based) is pervasive in human thinking, in domains such as perception, decision making, ethical judgments, and emotion. Thus, our model is much more psychologically realistic than Talbott's model. In addition, Talbott fails to note the role of emotions in self-deception, whereas we have shown that emotions play a pivotal role in this phenomenon.

Conclusion

We have given a detailed analysis of a complex case of self-deception, namely, that of Dimmesdale in *The Scarlet Letter*. We have shown, by modeling Dimmesdale's self-deception in HOTCO 2, that self-deception can be seen as resulting from emotional coherence involving beliefs and goals. We have also compared our model to other models and have argued that our model is more psychologically realistic.

Introduction

More than 85 percent of the world's people adhere to some religion, including Christianity with around two billion and Islam with more than one billion (Adherents 2003). Why is religious belief so widespread? Why do so many people adopt and retain their religious doctrines, attitudes, and practices? This chapter attempts to answer these questions by examining the role of emotion in human cognition. In particular, it offers an explanation of religious faith as a kind of emotional coherence in which people adopt religious beliefs that fit with their emotional needs as well as with their other beliefs. Emotional thinking involves both individual thought processes and social processes that transmit and help to maintain religious attitudes.

Before discussing cognitive and social mechanisms, I will provide evidence of the importance of emotion to religious thought, drawing on both primary and secondary sources. I then review current evidence from cognitive science that emotion is inherently part of cognition, and sketch some of the psychological and social mechanisms of emotional cognition. I then apply these mechanisms to explain aspects of religious belief and practice, including ritual. Finally, I discuss the limitations of explanations of religion based on evolutionary biology.

By "emotional cognition" I do not mean some special kind of thinking that involves emotions. I will argue that all thinking has an emotional component, so that emotional cognition comprises all of cognition viewed from the perspective that emphasizes the integration of traditional cognitive processes such as reasoning with emotional processes that attach values to mental representations.

Religion Is Emotional

Perusal of religious texts shows that they are often highly emotional. For example, Psalm 23 proclaims "I will fear no evil.... Thy rod and thy staff they comfort me." Saint Paul's letters to the Corinthians contain many emotion concepts, including fear, love, shame, faith, hope, charity, comfort, consolation, sorrow, anguish, joy, grief, affection, cheerfulness, and jealousy. Different religions emphasize different balances between positive emotions such as love and comfort and negative emotions such as fear and shame.

Many commentators have noted the centrality of emotions to religion. The eighteenth-century theologian Jonathan Edwards (2003/1746) asserted that "True religion in great part consists in the affections." William James (1948, p. 95) remarked that the will to religious belief is based on people's "passional nature," and that "feeling is the deeper source of religion" (James 1958, p. 329). Whitehouse (2000) noted that what he calls the "imagistic mode" of religiosity is emotionally intense. McCauley and Lawson (2002) described how religious rituals enliven our emotions. Boyer (2001) observed that religious concepts are connected to emotional systems, and Atran (2002) described how existential anxieties motivate religious belief and practice. None of these authors, however, provides a detailed account of the psychological and social mechanisms that foster religion.

Cognition Is Emotional

It is commonly believed that emotions are inherently irrational, so that there is a sharp divide between emotional thought and rational cognition. This divide has been challenged by philosophers such as de Sousa (1988), economists such as Frank (1988), and neuroscientists such as Damasio (1994). Recent reviews of human decision making have emphasized the role of emotions in choosing among relevant actions and inferences (Loewenstein et al. 2001). There is a large body of psychological experiments showing that most concepts have attached emotional attitudes (Fazio 2001). Neurological studies have revealed the close integration between emotional areas of the brain such as the amygdala and the areas for high-order thought in the prefrontal cortex (Rolls 1999; Wagar and Thagard 2004, chap. 6 above). Even scientific thinking is highly emotional (chaps. 10–12).

In order to explain some of the ways that emotion and cognition interact, I have developed a theory of emotional coherence (Thagard 2000, chap. 7; chaps. 3 and 8 above). This theory builds upon a cognitive theory of inference as explanatory coherence that has been applied to many cases of scientific and legal reasoning. Here I will describe its theological application. Two of the main arguments for the existence of God, the cosmological argument and the argument from design, can both be understood as supporting a kind of reasoning called inference to the best explanation. In this kind of reasoning, which is common in science and everyday life, a theory is accepted because it provides a better explanation of the evidence than competing theories. The cosmological argument says that the best explanation of the origin of the universe is that God created it. Similarly, the argument from design says that the best explanation of the complexity of the physical and biological world is that God designed and created them. In my view, the most powerful argument for the hypothesis of the existence of God combines these by saying that it explains both the existence and design of the world. It can then be argued that an assessment of the explanatory coherence of all the hypotheses and evidence requires acceptance of this hypothesis (Swinburne 1990).

With inference to the best explanation, however, it is crucial to consider alternative explanations of the evidence. The argument from biological design was dealt a massive blow by Darwin's theory of evolution by natural selection, which provided an alternative account of how biological complexity could arise. Similarly, the cosmological argument must contend with alternative materialist explanations of the origin and nature of the universe. Assessing the explanatory coherence of competing hypotheses with respect to all the available evidence is a complex process, but I have developed a computer program called ECHO that maximizes explanatory coherence and performs inference to the best explanation (Thagard 1992, 2000). ECHO has been used to simulate a very broad competition between theistic and dualist (mind is separate from body) beliefs, on the one hand, and materialist beliefs on the other (Thagard 2000, chap. 4). Figure 14.1 shows in highly simplified form the structure of the competition between theism and materialism. My simulation ends by accepting the materialist hypotheses and rejecting the theist/dualist ones.

This simulation is obviously a poor model of the beliefs of the vast majority of human beings who believe in God, but a better model can be achieved by incorporating emotional coherence. When people make decisions, they choose actions that produce outcomes that have positive and negative evaluations. Here positive/negative is not a purely cognitive calculation of relative utilities, but requires attaching emotional attitudes to the outcomes. For example, disease and death are emotionally negative, while health and pleasure are emotionally positive. According to the theory of emotional coherence, inferences about what to do and believe are affected not only by hypotheses

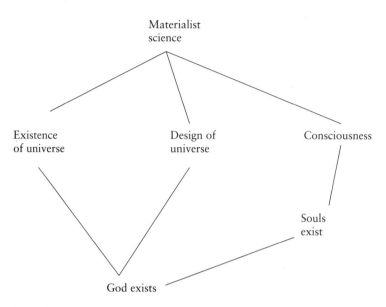

Figure 14.1
Approximate structure of the inference to the best explanation that God does or does not exist. The lines indicates that an explanatory relation exists between a hypothesis and evidence. The model in Thagard 2000 is much more detailed, with 35 propositions.

and evidence, but also by the emotional values that are attached to representations whose coherence is assessed.

I have extended the computer model ECHO into a model HOTCO that assesses emotional as well as explanatory coherence. The HOTCO simulation of belief in the existence of God adds into the coherence calculation four of the emotionally desirable outcomes of religion: comfort, social belonging, ethics, and eternal life. When these are marked as emotionally valued, and the hypothesis of the existence of God is indicated to be conducive to them, then the HOTCO simulation reverses the ECHO result and accepts the existence of God. From this perspective, religious beliefs are both cognitive and emotional, incorporating both explanatory reasoning and the satisfaction of desires. These desires include avoiding anxiety, maintaining social connections with other religious people, having a basis for distinguishing right from wrong, and hoping for a blissful afterlife.

Figure 14.2 expands figure 14.1 to display how the explanatory structure of the materialism versus theism conflict can be supplemented with an emotional structure that takes into account the nonexplanatory appeal of reli-

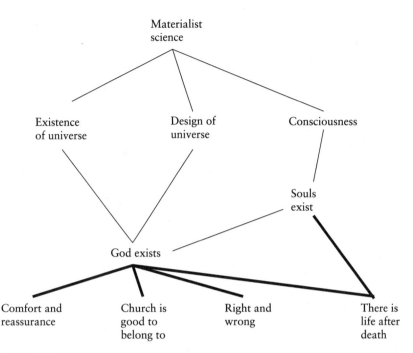

Figure 14.2
Approximate structure of the emotional coherence that God does or does not exist. The thin lines indicate explanatory relations between a hypothesis and evidence. The thick lines indicate the connection of a hypothesis with an emotionally appealing factor.

gion. It captures part of the explanatory/emotional appeal of religion, and shows how an inference can be made that incorporates both explanatory information and emotional content. It is consistent with current views in neuroscience that judgments integrate cognitive and emotional information. In line with the research of Damasio (1994) on defective decision making in people with brain damage, Wagar and Thagard (2004) present a neurocomputational model of how networks of spiking neurons can integrate cognition and emotion. On this model, effective decisions emanate from interactions between the brain's prefrontal cortex, which carries cognitive representations, and the amygdala and the nucleus accumbens, which process negative and positive emotions. Most inferences that people make, concerning what to believe as well as what to do, involve such cognitive-emotional interactions. It is therefore not surprising that religious inference should also be both intellectual and emotional, arriving at beliefs that possess emotional as well as explanatory coherence. From this perspective, religious faith is based on emotional coherence.

Faith

My account of religious faith is more psychologically plausible than alternative accounts, including those reviewed by Hick (1967). The traditional Catholic view, due to Thomas Aquinas, is that faith is an act of the intellect assenting to divine truth by the grace of God. This view assumes that divine grace somehow moves the will to voluntarily choose religious belief. It obviously begs the question of the existence of God, and leaves unexplained the means by which grace can be psychologically effective. Moreover, it fails to answer the question of which religious views to adopt in the face of conflicting claims by Catholics, Protestants, Muslims, Jews, Hindus, Buddhists, and advocates of other religions. They cannot all be right, and faith seems impotent to adjudicate among them.

The most prominent modern view of faith is William James's discussion of the "will to believe." He asserts: "Our passional nature not only lawfully may, but must, decide an option between propositions, whenever it is a genuine option that cannot by its nature be decided on intellectual grounds" (James 1948, p. 95). According to James, we have a living, forced, and momentous option to choose or reject religious beliefs, but lack the evidence to make this choice rationally. He suggests that the possible gain of belief in God outweighs the risk of acquiring a false belief, so it is legitimate to choose such a belief.

The main problem with James's view is that it makes religious belief a kind of wishful thinking, a leap with no rational basis at all. In real life, people can have many evidential reasons for choosing religious beliefs, including traditional arguments about the existence and design of the world and the apparent occurrence of miracles. They also have many emotional reasons, including desires for comfort, belonging, ethics, and immortality. My emotional coherence account of faith says that people adopt and maintain religious beliefs for a combination of evidential and emotional reasons that satisfy both cognitive and emotional constraints. Thus religious faith is not just wishful thinking or Pascal's wager, but an intuitive judgment that fits compellingly with a person's beliefs and goals.

My discussion of faith and the emotional appeal of religion assumes that notions of God and heaven are positively valenced, as they are in Christian and Muslim traditions. For religions in which gods are primarily objects of fear, and in which the afterlife is an object of dread, there is not the same kind of emotional appeal. An alternative explanation of the prevalence of such religious beliefs would therefore be necessary, perhaps based on the need for practices that reduce anxiety by placating vengeful deities. It is interesting, however, that the three religions that have been most successful by far in terms of global membership—Christianity, Islam, and Hinduism—all present a fairly positive view of gods and the afterlife. Gods are not as malicious and capricious as they used to be.

The main gap in my psychological account of faith is that it neglects important social mechanisms for the transmission of cognitive and emotional information. I will now describe some of these mechanisms and show how they contribute to religious beliefs in individual and groups.

Social Mechanisms

It is obvious that the major predictor of religious faith of children is the religion of their parents. My discussion of faith and emotional coherence misleadingly suggested that each individual has to make a judgment of which religious beliefs to choose, but most people grow up with a set of beliefs that they may or may not come to question later on. We need a broader, more social account of the acquisition and maintenance of beliefs and attitudes.

Philosophers such as Coady (1992) have noticed that most of what people know is based on testimony rather than personal experience. My belief that Arnold Schwarzenegger became governor of California in 2003 is based on news reports from reliable sources, not on any observations of my own. Children acquire innumerable beliefs from their parents, including a great many that they never have subsequent cause to doubt. It is not surprising, therefore, that most children take it for granted that their parents are a reliable source of information, so that they can quickly infer from "Parent says X" to "X is true." Hence, when a child is told by parents that God made the world and established a doctrine as the true religion, it is natural for the child to believe them. Participation in a religious organization or school in which children encounter other authoritative people with the same beliefs will provide further testimony that supports those beliefs. Thus the repeated testimony that a child encounters from parents and other people is a main cognitive source of religious belief. See Thagard (forthcoming d) for further discussion of testimony.

The structure of this kind of explanatory inference is shown in figure 14.3. The hypothesis that God really does exist can explain for the child why the parents and other relatives and teachers say that God exists. Because

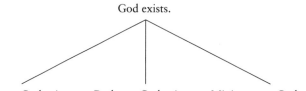

God exists.

Mom says God exists.   Dad says God exists.   Minister says God exists.

Figure 14.3
Example of how testimony supports religious beliefs. For the child, the hypothesis that God exists explains why parents and others say that he does.

young children are usually not aware of competing religious and non-religious beliefs, nor of sociological and psychological explanations of the sources of religious belief, it is natural for them to accept religious beliefs on the basis of testimony.

But religion is as much a matter of emotional attitudes as it is a matter of beliefs. For example, a Catholic child learns to attach positive emotional values to such representations as God, the Blessed Virgin Mary, the Pope, and good deeds; and negative emotional values to the devil, sin, Protestants, and so on. How are emotional values transmitted?

One method of emotional communication is explicit argumentation, although it may not be very common or effective. An example is means–ends argument, which has the form: You like Y, and X is a means to acquire Y, so you should like X too. Pascal's wager is a sort of means–ends argument for belief in God, saying that people should choose such belief because it improves their chances of acquiring a happy afterlife.

Another form of argument that can affect emotions is analogical, which has the form: You like Y, and X is like Y, so you should like X too. Many political arguments use emotional analogies (see chap. 3). Parables are a major kind of emotional analogy in religion, when a story such as the good Samaritan is used to inspire emotional reactions that are then transferred to ordinary life. Emotional analogies may supplement religious education, but they and other arguments are less psychologically crucial than other methods that are more emotionally direct.

I propose that one of the most powerful social mechanisms of transmission of emotional values is *emotional contagion*, which is "the tendency to automatically mimic and synchronize facial expressions, vocalizations, postures, and movements with those of another person and, consequently, to converge emotionally" (Hatfield, Cacioppo, and Rapson 1994, p. 5). People tend to catch the emotions of others because unconscious imitation of physical states contributes to their own emotional judgments. For example, the abrupt and shrill behavior of a nervous person may make an observer feel nervous.

Emotional contagion enables children to pick up emotional values associated with religious ideas from their parents and other close associates. Parents who speak and behave warmly and enthusiastically about their deities and religious institutions will tend to inspire similar attitudes in their children. This happens not just because of their utterances and arguments, but because children naturally mimic their parents' facial expressions and body language and thereby come to associate the same values with religious concepts and institutions. Emotional contagion can also transfer negative emotions toward evil beings such as the devil and toward sinful behavior. We tend to assume that moral education consists largely of inculcating principles such as the Ten Commandments, but principles without attendant emotional attitudes are ineffective. Psychopaths, who have no sense of responsibility for their actions, are fully familiar with moral principles; they just do not care about them or other people.

Marvin Minsky (2003) has developed the concept of *attachment-based learning*. He suggests that basic goals arise in children as the result of praise from people to whom the children are emotionally attached. For example, when young children share their toys with their playmates, they often receive praise from their parents or other caregivers. The parents have positive values for the act of sharing, and the children may also acquire a positive emotional attitude toward sharing as the result of seeing that it is something cared about by people whom they care about and who care about them. It is not just that sharing becomes a subgoal to accomplish the goal of getting praised by parents; rather, being kind to playmates becomes an internalized goal that has intrinsic emotional value to the children. Minsky does not tie attachment-based learning to emotional contagion, but it is plausible that a major reason why children pick up the emotional values of their parents, including religious values, is that people have a tendency to mimic the expressions and behavior of the people to whom they are closely attached.

Additional mechanisms of emotional transmission include empathy and altruism. Altruism is the unselfish regard for the welfare of others. If you care about a person, your altruism may lead you to acquire an emotional attitude toward something that is valued by that person. For example, if you feel for a child, and the child wants a toy, then you may acquire a positive attitude toward the toy because it will make the child happy. Empathy is more complicated, in that it involves a kind of emotional analogy in which people understand the emotional states of others by comparison to their own (Barnes and Thagard 1997; see also chap. 3 above). For example, if you are distressed because you just had a grant proposal rejected, I can understand your emotional state by remembering how I felt when I had a proposal rejected. Empathy does not guarantee emotional transmission, because it is possible for a person to understand another's distress without caring about it, but empathic understanding is often a path to altruism and compassion. Once you have gone to the effort to understand ways in which people are emotionally like you, you are likely to become able to care about them and hence altruistically to adopt some of their goals as your own. Transmission mechanisms such as altruism and emotional contagion can lead to emotional consensus in group decision making (see chap. 5).

Religious emotions can be highly damaging to individuals and groups. If one group adopts extremely negative attitudes toward another, then the result can be hatred and even violence. Examples are Christian anti-Semitism and extreme Muslim fundamentalist attitudes toward infidels. Less extremely, some religious groups use emotional tactics such as shunning to discourage people from deviating from their beliefs and practices. Emotional transmission is essential for moral education and social cohesion, but it can be used for immoral purposes such as hatred and persecution. Social transmission of emotion-laden religious values can be facilitated by rituals.

Ritual

As many writers have observed, religious rituals have a strong emotional component (Whitehouse 2000; McCauley and Lawson 2002). Whitehouse (2000) contrasts rituals that are infrequent and emotionally intense, such as weddings and funerals, with ones that have low emotional intensity, such as everyday prayer. What do emotional coherence and emotion transmission tell us about the nature of ritual?

Different emotions are associated with different kinds of ritual. Weddings are usually associated with joy and the commitment of the spouses. At funerals, the dominant emotion is grief. Coming of age rituals such as Christian confirmation and the Jewish Bar Mitzvah are often associated with pride. The expectation of divine forgiveness furnished to Catholics who go to confession can provide relief from fear of punishment. Hence rituals can generate experiences of positive emotions and relief from negative ones, and thus reinforce the association between religious beliefs and emotionally desirable goals such as comfort and hope for eternal life.

Public rituals such as church services can serve to encourage the transmission of values by emotional contagion. For example, a group of people singing or reciting together can adopt similar bodily postures and expressions that bring the people performing them into emotional synchrony with each other, encouraging common attitudes and beliefs. Often a minister or other religious leader will provide a physical model that others can imitate, thereby encouraging the achievement of a common emotional state and socially unified values.

Even frequent and mundane rituals such as daily prayer can tie in with positive and negative emotions. I conjecture that such performances can serve to dampen the effects of anxiety about the vicissitudes of life, in the same way as transcendental meditation. Dampening can work by fostering hope for the future through divine providence, or simply by providing calm and distraction that can change the physiological inputs that are part of the brain's process of generating emotional reactions.

Evolutionary Irrelevance

It has become fashionable in recent years to try to use biological evolution to explain various aspects of culture, including religion (Atran 2002; Boyer 2001). I will now review some ways in which evolutionary psychology might be applied to explaining religious belief and practice, and argue that there is no good reason to apply any of them.

We can distinguish several possible ways in which evolutionary biology and psychology might be applied to religion.

1. Religion is an adaptation, built into the human brain as the result of natural selection for religious beliefs and practices.
2. Religion is not an adaptation, but it is natural given special-purpose adaptations that have been selected for.
3. Religion is a spandrel, an accidental by-product of psychological features that have been selected for.
4. Religion is an exaptation, which is the use of a structure or feature for a function other than which it was developed for by natural selection.
5. Religion is independent of evolution by natural selection.

None of these views seems right to me, so let me now say more about the evolutionary status of emotional cognition.

It is easy to make the case that emotion is part of human cognition because of biological evolution by natural selection. There is much more to this case than simply generating "just so stories" about how humans with joys and fears might have been more likely to survive and reproduce. First, neurophysiology and psychology indicate that there are special brain areas such as the amygdala dedicated to emotional processing. Moreover, the anatomical interconnections with cognitive areas such as the prefrontal cortex have also been thoroughly investigated. Second, these emotional brain areas are not unique to humans, but have been largely carried over from our evolutionary predecessors. For example, the neural pathways for fear conditioning in rats are similar to the corresponding pathways in humans (Le Doux 1996). Even fish have amygdalas, and there are behavioral reasons for thinking that higher mammals, at least, have many of the emotions that people do. Third, we know from studies of people with damage to emotional brain areas that their ability to function well in natural and social environments is impaired (Damasio 1994). For example, people with damage to the amygdala are limited in learning to avoid and flee dangerous situations.

Contrast the situation with what is known about the evolution of religion. There are no known brain areas dedicated specifically to religious beliefs and practices, and no animal precursors of these areas. Being deficient in religiosity does not seem, at least in the current world environment, to impede the ability of people to survive and reproduce. (There does seem to be a correlation in Europe between a decrease in religiosity and a decline in birth rates, but both factors are probably caused by increases in education and economic security.) There is no evidence that religiosity is heritable, or that religiosity favored individuals while our species was evolving. Hence there is no reason to believe that religion is an adaptation.

We could perhaps say that religion is a by-product or exaptation of emotional cognition. Animals such as humans naturally approach what is emotionally positive to them and avoid what is emotionally negative, so it might be possible to say that religion arises indirectly as the result of the natural selection of emotions: evolution leads to emotional cognition which leads to religion. The problem with this sequence is that the second "leads to" is much weaker biologically and psychologically than the first one. We know little about the psychological origins of religion in preliterate cultures. A substantial portion of humans (15%) manages to get by without religious beliefs and practices. In technologically advanced cultures such as the United States, religion is less universal than watching television or using the telephone. Watching television depends on our evolved psychological abilities such as seeing and hearing, but no one would say it is a necessary by-product of evolution.

The tightest relation that one can plausibly posit between emotional cognition and religion is perhaps that the former *encourages* the latter. But the connection between emotionality and religion is no greater than the connection between emotionality and other widespread aspects of human culture such as art, music, cooking, sports, politics, technology, and science. Biological evolution is not completely irrelevant to understanding these cultural developments, since they all depend on cognitive-emotional representations and processes that are wired into human brains. But, given how little is known about the early biological and social development of our species, the dependency relation is so speculative that it is best to say that evolutionary biology has little current role to play in the explanation of the prevalence and nature of religion. Talk of "evolutionary origins" and "evolutionary landscapes" adds nothing to psychological and sociological explanations. Our evolved cognitive-emotional capacities make human beings susceptible to religion, but they also make us susceptible to myriad other cultural developments; so the explanatory connection between evolution and religion is very weak.

As Richardson (1996) has argued, theorizing in evolutionary psychology on such topics as the origins of language and social behavior has fallen well below the standards of good evolutionary explanations. Evolutionary psychology has generally failed to provide evidence that: (1) selection of psychological capacities has occurred; (2) ecological factors explain strength of selection; (3) differences between individuals have been heritable; (4) evolution was affected by ancient environments, population structure, gene flow, interbreeding, and mutation rates; and (5) psychological traits are primitive and ancestral. Unless there is a dramatic increase in historical and biological knowledge about the evolution of *Homo sapiens*, evolutionary conjectures will remain uninformative.

Conclusion

There is an old joke about a Jewish man stranded alone on a desert island who builds two synagogues, one that he happily attends, and one that he scorns to enter. This story illustrates the positive and negative emotions that accompany religious cognition. I have described some of the emotions that attend religious beliefs and practices, and explained the prevalence of religious beliefs in part by a theory of emotional coherence that shows how emotion and cognition intersect. This chapter has also outlined the role that emotions and emotional coherence play in religious rituals, and argued that evolutionary biology has little to tell us about why and how people are religious. Emotional cognition is central to religion, and emotional cognition derives from brain structures that are the product of biological evolution, but evolution currently sheds little light on the structures and content of religious beliefs and practices.

15 | Critique of Emotional Reason

Introduction

In the title of her 1998 book, Susan Haack describes herself as a *passionate* moderate. With eloquence and verve, she ably defends the rationality of science and philosophy against a host of postmodernist critics. Haack (1998, p. 49) approvingly quotes Peirce's descriptions of the scientific attitude as "a craving to know how things really are," "an intense desire to find things out," and "a great desire to learn the truth." But despite the passion evident in her own arguments and in her citations of Peirce, Haack's explicit epistemology is emotion free: the word "emotion" does not appear in the index of her treatise on epistemology (Haack 1993). She does however remark in her later book on the "misconception of the emotions as brutally irrational" (Haack 1998, p. 142).

In this chapter I want to address the question of how emotions are relevant to rationality. Answering this question should further the development of theories of theoretical and practical reason that take seriously the pervasive role of emotions in human thinking. I want to reject both the *classical* view that emotions are primarily an impediment to reason and the *romantic* view that emotionality is inherently superior to reason. Instead, I develop a *critical* view that delineates the ways in which emotions contribute to reason as well as the ways in which emotions can impede reason. My title uses the term "critique" to mean not criticism but assessment. I will argue that emotional cognition can provide a useful supplement to Haack's "foundherentist" epistemology, and also extend her discussion of the practical question of affirmative action.

Theoretical and Practical Reason

Emotion is relevant to theoretical reason, which concerns what to believe, and to practical reason, which concerns what to do. The main kind of theoretical reason I want to discuss is what Peirce called *abduction*, the formation and acceptance of explanatory hypotheses. Abductive inference has two phases: the *generation* of hypotheses and then their *evaluation*, ideally leading to the acceptance of hypotheses that are part of the best explanation of the evidence. Abduction is common in everyday life, for example when I make inferences about why my car fails to start or why a friend is in a bad mood; but it is also central to scientific theorizing, for example in the generation and evaluation of hypotheses concerning the causes of disease. My aim is to lay out ways in which emotions affect the generation and evaluation of scientific hypotheses.

Practical reasoning also has two phases: the generation of possible actions and their evaluation, ideally leading to the choice of those actions that best satisfy the goals relevant to the decision. For example, when members of an academic department make a hiring decision, they have to choose whom to appoint from the typically large number of candidates for the position. I will discuss how emotions affect both the generation and evaluation of actions. Finally, I will try to generalize concerning how emotions do and should affect theoretical and practical reason.

Theoretical Reason: Generation

As Peirce (1931–1958, 5.591) noted, and as Fodor (2000) recently reiterated, it is a puzzle why and how abductive inference is ever successful. There is a huge range of facts that people might try to explain, and for each fact there is a huge range of hypotheses that might explain it. Fodor throws up his hands and says that abduction is a terrible problem for cognitive science, while Peirce postulates an innate ability, derived by evolution, for forming and choosing good hypotheses. Preferable to both these rather desperate conclusions is the attempt to specify the cognitive mechanisms by which explanatory hypotheses are generated (see, e.g., Thagard 1988; Josephson and Josephson 1994). Little noticed has been the fact that these mechanisms are in part emotional.

Consider first the problem of deciding what to attempt to explain. As Peirce observed, abductive inference is usually prompted by surprise, the emotional reaction that occurs when our expectations are violated. Most of the facts that we encounter are not surprising, in that they fit perfectly well with what we already believe. Occasionally, however, we encounter facts that do not fit with our beliefs, generating surprise by a process of emotional incoherence (Thagard 2000, p. 194). Hence we substantially focus our abductive activity by narrowing it down to events that have the emotional character of being surprising. Other emotions that stimulate explanatory activity include curiosity, in which people have the emotional drive to find out answers to questions that interest them. For example, Watson and Crick had a passion to find out the structure of DNA (see chap. 10). In addition to surprise and curiosity, abductive inference can be emotionally prompted by practical need, for example when a doctor urgently tries to find a diagnosis that explains the symptoms of a seriously sick patient. Thus we do not try to explain everything, just those events and facts that we care about.

Once emotion initiates the attempt to generate explanatory hypotheses, it can also serve to focus the search for them. Scientists often get excited about particular lines of thinking and as a result pursue them intensively. As Peirce noticed, there is no way that a person could do an exhaustive search of all possible explanatory hypotheses for a set of data. Moreover, it has been proven that abduction is computationally intractable, in the sense that the time required to assemble a set of hypotheses to explain data grows exponentially with the number of propositions involved (Bylander et al. 1991), so no computer could do an exhaustive search either. However, human thinking and current computational models use heuristic techniques such as backward chaining of rules and spreading activation of concepts to narrow the search for hypotheses.

I conjecture that emotion is a valuable part of heuristic search in humans. Once a fact to be explained is tagged as emotionally important, then concepts and rules relevant to explaining it can also be tagged as emotionally important. For example, when Watson and Crick were working to find the structure of DNA, they got excited about ideas such as the double helix that seemed most relevant to divining the structure. Abduction is sometimes described as having the structure:

E is to be explained.
H could cause E.
So maybe H.

This structure obscures the fact that considerable thinking goes into putting together the hypothesis H. To take a simple example, the ancient Greeks came up with the wave theory of sound to explain various properties of sound, such as propagation and echoing. The hypothesis that sound consists of waves requires the linkage of three concepts: *sound*, *waves*, and *consists*. For these concepts to be assembled into a proposition, they need to be simultaneously active in working memory. Emotion may help to bring potentially useful combinations into juxtaposition. Chrysippus, the Greek stoic who first constructed the wave theory of sound, was probably puzzled by the behaviors of sounds. When something about water waves caught his attention, he was able to generate the hypothesis that sound consists of waves. Emotional involvement with a concept, either moderately as interest or more passionately as excitement, focuses attention on it. When interest in one concept gives rise to interest in another relevant one, as when *sound* gets linked to *wave*, there emerges the powerful excitement that signals a discovery.

Emotions are also relevant to guiding the finding of analogies that often contribute to scientific discovery (see Holyoak and Thagard 1995, chap. 8). For example, if the fact to be explained F1 is analogous to another fact F2 that has already been explained, and if scientists have a positive emotional attitude toward the kind of hypothesis H2 that explains F2, then they may get excited about finding an analog of H2 to explain F1. Thus analogy can transfer positive emotions from one theory to another similar one that is judged to be promising (see chap. 3 above). Analogy can also transfer negative emotions, for example when a potential research program is compared to cold fusion and thereby discouraged.

Thus emotion seems to be an important part of the generation of explanatory hypotheses, both in selecting what is to be explained and in guiding the search for useful hypotheses. On the negative side, emotions may unduly narrow the search for fruitful explanations. If scientists become obsessed with a particular kind of hypothesis, they may be blinded from discovering a very different kind of hypothesis needed to explain some particularly puzzling fact. Emotions serve a valuable cognitive function in narrowing the search for hypotheses, but like any heuristic mechanism they can take the search in undesirable directions. Misdirection can occur especially if the goals that provoke emotional excitement are personal rather than intellectual ones. If scientists get excited about a particular kind of hypothesis because it might make them rich and famous, they may be blinded from searching for less lucrative hypotheses that have greater explanatory potential.

Theoretical Reason: Evaluation

Someone who wants to maintain the classical position that emotion should not be part of theoretical reason might respond to the previous section as follows: *Granted, emotion has a useful role to play in the context of discovery, but it must be kept out of the context of justification, which it can only distort.* To be sure, there are a variety of ways that emotions can distort theoretical reason in general and abductive inference in particular, as I will shortly describe. But there is an argument consistent with Haack's epistemology that shows a crucial role for emotion in the evaluation of explanatory hypotheses.

Haack (1993) defended a powerful and plausible epistemological position she dubbed *foundherentism*. It combines the foundationalist insight that empirical evidence has a special role to play in justifying theories with the coherentist insight that such evidence cannot be taken as given but must be assessed with respect to overall explanatory integration. Haack uses the apt analogy of a crossword puzzle, in which there must be an integration of entries and clues, to indicate how in abductive inference there must be a coherence of hypotheses and evidence. She does not, however, provide a method or algorithm for assessing the success of such integration in particular cases. How do people judge that they have a good fit in their answers to a crossword puzzle, and how do scientists decide that one theory fits better with the evidence than its competitors?

I have developed a theory of explanatory coherence that shows how the best explanation can be efficiently computed with artificial neural networks (Thagard 1992). I have also argued that this theory, which gives a degree of priority to empirical evidence while maintaining a coherentist perspective, implements and naturalizes Haack's foundherentism (Thagard 2000). I will not repeat that argument here, but want to draw a conclusion concerning the role of emotions.

Suppose I am right that foundherentist abductive inference is accomplished in humans by a neural network that performs parallel constraint satisfaction in a way that maximizes explanatory coherence. People have no conscious access to this process: when you realize you prefer one theory over another, you do not really know why, although you may be able to retrace your intellectual history of acquiring the various hypotheses and evidence that contributed to your preference. All you can say is that one theory "makes more sense" to you than the other. This is not to say that inferences based on explanatory coherence are irrational, since they may well involve maximization of coherence with respect to the available hypotheses and evidence. But given the limited access to mental processes, there is no way you can directly know that you have maximized coherence.

This is where emotions are crucial. According to my recent theory of emotional coherence, the way you know that you have achieved explanatory coherence is by a feeling of happiness that emerges from the satisfaction of many constraints in your neural network (Thagard 2000, pp. 194ff.). Highly coherent theories are praised by scientists for their elegance and beauty. Because we cannot extract from our brains judgments such as "Acceptance of theory T1 satisfies .69 of the relevant constraints," we have to fall back on the overall emotional judgment such as "T1 just makes sense." Thus the feeling of happiness that emerges from a coherence judgment is part of our ability to assess scientific theories. Ideally, a good theory generates a kind of emotional gestalt that signals its coherence with the evidence and the rest of our beliefs. Negative emotions attached to a theory signal that it does not fit with our other beliefs, and a general feeling of anxiety may signal that none of the available theories is very coherent. Such anxiety may trigger a search for new hypotheses.

So a gut feeling that represents an emotional gestalt may be a valid sign of a highly coherent evaluation of competing hypotheses. The problem is that such a feeling may instead signal a different kind of coherence based on wishful thinking or motivated inference rather than fit with the evidence. I once got a letter from someone urging me to send my explanatory coherence computer program to him right away, because he had a theory of the universe that no one else believed, and my program might help him convince other people. Presumably his attachment to his theory was based more on its satisfying personal goals than on its providing the best explanation of all the evidence. Noting the role of emotion in appreciating coherence may seem to endorse the romantic view: if it feels good, believe it.

I know of no psychological way of distinguishing between the positive emotion of emotional coherence and the similar emotion of self-promotion. Here it is important that science is a social as well as an individual process. Scientists know that the fact that they like their own theories cuts no ice with other scientists with different personal motivations. In order to publish their work or to get grants to continue it, scientists' hypotheses must stand up to peer review, where the peers are people familiar with the relevant hypotheses and evidence and not moved by the personal goals of the submitting scientist. Awareness of this scrutiny requires scientists to calibrate their coherence judgments against what the scientific community is likely to accept, and influences them to make their own assessments on the basis of explanatory coherence rather than personal expedience. In everyday life, people encounter less social pressure to reason in accord with evidence and explanatory coherence, so they are more likely to succumb to evidence-poor but personally coherent hypotheses such as conspiracy theories. Even in science there is the danger that the emotional bias of one individual may spread to associates by a kind of emotional contagion.

I will use the term *emotional skewer* for a factor that is so vivid and affectively intense that it can produce an emotional gestalt that does not reflect the maximal satisfaction of the relevant and appropriate constraints. Such factors skew the coherence calculation by placing too much weight on epistemically irrelevant factors such as self-promotion. We will see that emotional skewers also are a threat to rational judgment in practical reasoning.

Practical Reason: Generation

In order to decide what to do, we need to generate a set of possible actions and then choose the best. Bazerman (1994, p. 4) says that rational decision making should include the following six steps:

1. Define the problem, characterizing the general purpose of your decision.
2. Identify the criteria, specifying the goals or objectives that you want to be able to accomplish.
3. Weight the criteria, deciding the relative importance of the goals.
4. Generate alternatives, identifying possible courses of action that might accomplish your various goals.
5. Rate each alternative on each criterion, assessing the extent to which each action would accomplish each goal.
6. Compute the optimal decision, evaluating each alternative by multiplying the expected effectiveness of each alternative with respect to a criterion times the weight of the criterion, then adding up the expected value of the alternative with respect to all criteria.

Then pick the alternative with the highest expected value.

But experts on decision making usually take for granted step 4, in which alternative actions are generated. Creative decision making often involves not just choosing the best among available alternatives, but in expanding the range of alternatives. Consider, for example, hiring decisions in academic departments. The usual course of action is something like:

1. Assess the needs of the department and establish the area or areas in which to hire. Then advertise a position in these areas.
2. Examine all applications and choose a short list for further discussion.
3. Choose a few applicants to invite to campus.
4. Select a candidate to receive a job offer.

Emotions play a major role in all of these stages.

When departments decide in which areas to hire, there is often a conflict based on the differing goals of individual members (see chap. 5 above). Professors typically value their own specialties over those of their colleagues, so they often have an emotional bias toward hiring in their own areas. But a thorough assessment of the pedagogical and research needs of a department should lead to a more reasonable choice of areas. No data are available on the role of emotions in generating alternatives for decision making, but I expect that the cognitive process is similar to that involved in generating hypotheses in abductive reasoning. There are routine cognitive processes such as backward chaining that use rule-like knowledge of action–goal connections. For example, if the department members know that there is a ethics course that needs teaching, then they might think of hiring someone in ethics. But hiring priorities might also be based on more amorphous considerations, such as ideas about what areas are emerging as important. Diffuse mechanisms such as spreading activation among concepts may contribute, but would be of little use in focusing the search for good ideas.

As with the search for hypotheses, emotions are a useful way to focus the search for decision alternatives. Certain ideas may get high positive valence and suggest other ideas with positive valence. For example, my own department recently learned that Waterloo is getting a very well-funded new institute in theoretical physics, so it occurred to some of us that it might be desirable to hire someone in the philosophy of physics to provide a connection with this institute. The occurrence was based on excitement about the new institute which spurred excitement about connecting philosophy with it which spurred excitement about the possibility of adding a department member with the relevant specialty.

In academic hiring, the set of applicants is usually determined by the advertisement, so at this stage the range of alternatives is fixed. But more creative hiring often involves actively searching out candidates rather than just passively waiting for the applications to come in. Once again emotions play a role: people tend to think of potential candidates whose work they like or whom they like personally. Of course, emotions can also work negatively, ruling out people whose work is not respected or whose personalities are suspect. But emotions can be useful in the process of headhunting, i.e., trying to identify candidates to urge to apply rather than simply waiting to see who applies. Of course, emotions can also prevent options from being generated, as when a name evokes an "over my dead body" response.

Practical Reason: Evaluation

Once a range of alternative actions is identified, for example a list of job applicants, then the department must decide whom to hire. In contrast to the systematic approach to decision making recommended by Bazerman, department members usually proceed in a quite haphazard fashion. Members of the hiring committee look over the applications, and select a small number to comprise a short list. This selection is both an individual and a group process, as committee members first make their own short lists and then meet to agree upon a common short list. Ideally, the members individually and cooperatively work with a set of criteria, such as:

1. Research quality, as shown by publications and letters of reference.
2. Teaching ability, as shown by experience and student course evaluations.

However, such objectivity may go out the window when candidates come to campus for personal interviews. Then personal interactions and quality of performance in the job talk may swamp the more extensive information contained in the applicant's dossier. A candidate with a charming personality may win out over an introvert with a better academic record. On the other hand, the department hiring may make a rational decision to choose the candidate who best fits their reasonably established criteria.

In either case, I conjecture, the individuals in the department reach their decisions by means of a kind of emotional gestalt that summarizes how they feel about particular candidates (see chaps. 4 and 5 above). They choose to hire candidates that they feel good about, and reject candidates that they do not feel good about. As with hypothesis evaluation in science, we have no direct access to the unconscious mental processes that integrate various criteria to produce a coherent decision. Decision making is a coherence process similar in structure and processing to hypothesis evaluation (see the DECO model of decision making in Thagard and Millgram 1995, and Thagard 2000). One might try working with pencil-and-paper models that implement the kind of decision-making procedure described by Bazerman above, but doing so is difficult because it is hard to ensure that the numerical weightings one applies actually correspond to the importance one attaches to the various criteria. Moreover, if one went through this exercise and found that it suggested hiring someone with a negative emotional gestalt, it would not be unreasonable to think that the numerical process had gone astray.

However, it must be admitted that practical reason is even more susceptible to emotional skewers than is theoretical reason. For example, a person trying to decide what to have for dinner may want to make the decision based on a strong aim to eat healthy foods, but be seduced by a menu into ordering a cheeseburger with French fries. Here the momentary but intense desire for high-fat food swamps the long-term interests of the eater and serves as an emotional skewer. The familiar phenomena of weakness of will and self-deception can be best understood as the result of emotional skewers.

Hiring decisions are unquestionably susceptible to emotional skewers. Faced with hundreds of applicants for a job, it is natural for members of a philosophy department to eliminate individuals on the basis of solitary criteria: this one hasn't published, that one has no teaching experience, and so on. There is nothing wrong with such elimination if the criteria are the ones appropriate for the position, but stereotypes and prejudices operating consciously or unconsciously can have the same effect in normatively inappropriate ways. They can lead, for example, to the summary rejection of women with young children, or to gay or lesbian candidates who just would not "fit in" with the department. Members of an academic department may have an unconscious schema of the appropriate sort of colleague to have, a schema that is based in substantial part on themselves. Someone who does not fit that schema because of features that are irrelevant to job performance may nevertheless be considered just not right for the job.

The operation of emotional skewering shows why preferential hiring is sometimes necessary. Like Haack (1998, chap. 10), I would much prefer a hiring process in which the best candidate for a job is hired, which, given the plausible assumption that women are as academically talented as men, would over time lead to the elimination of gender bias in academic hiring. But there have undoubtedly been departments where emotional skewers are so pronounced that fair hiring is very unlikely. An American philosopher once told me about the difficulties that his illustrious department had had in placing their female candidates. For example, the chair of one hiring department told him: "Don't bother telling us about your women students—we don't have to hire a woman yet." In such cases, administrative action to enforce the hiring of women is the only way to change the department in ways that allow the development of fair hiring practices.

Haack (1998, p. 173) is well aware of the role of emotions in hiring decisions, describing the hiring process as a combination of greed and fear:

Greed: we want someone who will improve the standing of the department, who has contacts from which we might benefit, who will willingly do the teaching we'd rather not do, who will publish enough so the tenure process will go smoothly. Fear: we don't want someone so brilliant or energetic that they make the rest of us look bad, or compete too successfully for raises and summer money, or who will vote with our enemy on controversial issues.

Any of these greed factors and fear factors, alone or in combination, can serve as emotional skewers that contribute to an emotional gestalt that produces an unfair and suboptimal hiring decision. So should we just try to turn off the emotional contribution to decision making and proceed in as analytical a manner as possible using something like Bazerman's procedure?

I doubt that it is possible or even desirable to turn hiring and other decisions into matters of cold calculation (see chap. 2 above). Our brains are wired with many interconnections between cognitive areas such as the neocortex and emotional areas such as the amygdala (Damasio 1994). There is no way we can shut down the amygdala, which contributes to emotional assessments via dense connections with bodily states. Moreover, if Damasio's patients (who have brain damage that interferes with neocortex–amygdala connections) are a good indication, then shutting down the amygdala would worsen rather than improve decision making. These patients have normal verbal and mathematical abilities, but tend to be ineffective and even irresponsible in their personal and social decisions. Hence I do not think that we can write emotions out of the practical reasoning process.

Still, there is lots of room for improvement in decisions based on emotional intuitions. Chapter 2 advocated the process of *informed intuition*:

1. Set up the decision problem carefully. This requires identifying the goals to be accomplished by your decision and specifying the broad range of possible actions that might accomplish those goals.

2. Reflect on the importance of the different goals. Such reflection will be more emotional and intuitive than just putting a numerical weight on them, but should help you to be more aware of what you care about in the current decision situation. Identify goals whose importance may be exaggerated because of emotional distortions.

3. Examine beliefs about the extent to which various actions would facilitate the different goals. Are these beliefs based on good evidence? If not, revise them.

4. Make your intuitive judgment about the best action to perform, monitoring your emotional reaction to different options. Run your decision past other people to see if it seems reasonable to them.

This procedure is obviously applicable to hiring decisions and would, I hope, lead to the hiring of the best person for the job.

This model of decision making applies to individual thinkers, but much decision making is social, involving the need to accommodate the views and preferences of various members in a group. Emotions can definitely be a hindrance to social decision making, if some members are irrationally exuberant about or obstinately resistant to particular options. But emotions can also be valuable in communicating people's preferences and evaluations. If I am trying to coordinate with people and see that they are getting very upset by a potential action such as hiring a candidate, I can realize that their strong emotions signal a strong preference against the action. Alternatively, if they are as enthusiastic as I am, then together we can achieve a kind of group emotional coherence that is very good for social solidarity (see chap. 5 above).

Conclusion

In sum, both theoretical and practical reason involve processes of generating alternatives and evaluating them in order to select the best. Both generation and evaluation involve emotions, and the involvement is often positive, when emotions guide the search for attractive alternatives and when they signal a gestalt that marks the achievement of a maximally coherent state of mind. There is no realistic prospect of stripping these emotional contributions from generation and evaluation. I would not want it otherwise, since passion adds much to science, philosophy, and everyday life. But the involvement of emotions can also be negative, when emotional skewers impede the generation of attractive alternatives and distort the evaluation of which alternatives are the best. To overcome these negative effects of emotions, we need to adopt procedures such as informed intuition that recognize and encourage the contributions of affect to theoretical and practical reason, while watching for the presence of distortions. In addition to being passionately moderate, one should aim to be moderately passionate.

To conclude this book, I will briefly review some of my related research: past, present, and future. The first section describes published research on emotion that complements the work presented in this book, and then summarizes several papers currently in progress which extend my account of the different mechanisms involved in emotional cognition. The second section is much more speculative, pointing to some exciting prospects for new developments in the theory and applications of emotional cognition. It also muses on the prospects for the illumination of philosophical problems concerning rationality and reduction.

Related Research

The chapters in this book include only some of the research on emotion that my collaborators and I have conducted over the past decade. I will now point to some related work that did not quite fit into the mechanisms-and-applications theme of this book; most is available on my Web site: http:// cogsci.uwaterloo.ca/. My interest in emotional cognition began with Allison Barnes's work on empathy as a form of analogical reasoning. Our paper, "Analogy and Empathy," used the multiconstraint theory of analogy of Holyoak and Thagard (1995) to argue that empathy is best viewed as a kind of analogical thinking (Barnes and Thagard 1997). In another philosophical paper on emotion, Jing Zhu and I argued on the basis of recent research in cognitive neuroscience that emotion has a much greater role in human action than philosophers have traditionally recognized (Zhu and Thagard 2002).

In a more applied paper, Mike Poznanski and I included moods and emotions as part of a neural network theory of personality and personality change (Poznanski and Thagard 2005). The purpose of this theory is to suggest ways in which computer programs such as games and human–machine interfaces can be made more interesting and natural by virtue of incorporating some understanding of the human personality.

Additional aspects of emotions are discussed in three papers currently under revision. In a paper on the moral psychology of conflicts of interest, I show the practical relevance of the GAGE model presented above in chapter 6 (Thagard forthcoming b). The result is an explanation of why conflicts of interest are so common in business, politics and other fields, and why people rarely recognize their own conflicts of interest. This paper expands the account of self-deception given in chapter 13 by showing the relevance of neural mechanisms for cognitive-affective interaction.

Similarly, the issues about scientific discovery discussed in chapters 10 through 12 are deepened by a neurocomputational account of abduction, which is the generation and evaluation of explanatory hypotheses (Thagard forthcoming a). I argue that abductive inference is not a purely verbal process, but rather involves multimodal representations including emotions. Abduction involves emotional reactions both as input to indicate a target is worthy of explanation and as output to signal satisfaction with an inferred hypothesis. See also Thagard and Litt forthcoming.

Another paper on the procedural knowledge required for scientific collaboration continues the social perspective applied in chapter 5 (Thagard forthcoming b). I argue that knowing how to collaborate involves understanding and sharing emotions crucial to scientific research, including curiosity, excitement, and the potential joy of discovery. Such knowledge is rarely translatable into conscious rules.

Planned Extensions

Several additional research projects are now underway aimed at developing new ideas about emotional cognition. When I developed the HOTCO model in the 1990s, computational models of emotional thinking were rare, although others are emerging (e.g., Moore and Oaksford 2002). There is much more to be done to increase understanding of the mechanisms of emotional cognition.

Expanding GAGE

Chapter 6 presented the GAGE neurocomputational model of decision making. I am now working with Abninder Litt to expand the GAGE model and to apply it to new psychological applications concerning decision making and explanation. The first task required is to identify an additional set of brain areas that should be incorporated into the model. The relevant areas include the insula, the anterior cingulate cortex, the dorsolateral prefrontal cortex, and the thalamus; these are discussed below in the particular applications to different aspects of emotional decision making and explanation. The second task is to redesign the GAGE model within the neural computing framework of Eliasmith and Anderson (2003), who have developed a powerful general account of how the brain encodes, decodes, and transforms information. The third task is to use the computational tools that Eliasmith and Anderson have developed to implement the expanded GAGE model, including simulations of brain areas that go beyond the original GAGE simulations.

The fourth task is to incorporate into the model representations of complex relations of the sort needed for describing contexts of decision making and explanation (see below). In order to represent relations between objects, I want to employ a rich kind of vector structure called holographic reduced representations (HRRs), which Eliasmith and Thagard (2001) applied to the problem of analogical thinking. An HRR is a vector of real numbers that in its simplest form can represent a basic feature. HRRs use a number of different mathematical operations to build up vectors that can represent complex relations between vectors, such as (CAUSE (CHASE (DOG BOY)) (FLEE BOY DOG)), i.e., the boy fled from the dog because the dog chased the boy. Eliasmith and Anderson (2003) show how vectors can be encoded and decoded in spiking neural networks, and Eliasmith has recently developed a way to encode and transform HRRs using his neural engineering techniques.

Once the expanded GAGE model, GAGE II, is designed and implemented, it will be possible to apply it to numerous important psychological phenomena that involve the integration of cognition and affect, including aspects of decision making, explanation, mathematical thinking, and possibly even consciousness.

The current GAGE model applies only to simple, unconscious decisions, but I plan to apply the GAGE II to encompass much more general kinds of decision making in economics, politics, and ethics. The aim is to give a deep and broad account of the cognitive, affective, and neural mechanisms that underlie financial decisions, political judgments, and ethical conclusions. I conjecture that all of these kinds of decision making involve the integration of cognition and affect along the lines described by the original GAGE model, but with greater cognitive complexity and wider involvement of brain areas, including the insula and dorsolateral prefrontal cortex.

For application to economic decision making, I plan to develop GAGE II into a general theory of preference. Microeconomic theory is currently based on a set of assumptions about the behavior of individual consumers (e.g.,

Kreps 1990). One of the most basic assumptions is that preferences are asymmetric: If a consumer prefers X to Y, then the consumer does not prefer Y to X. However, Kahneman and Tversky (1979) devised examples in which people frequently violate asymmetry when choices are framed in different ways. For instance, if people are asked to choose between an action that will save 400 people out of 600 with certainty and an action that will save no one with probability 1/3 and 600 with probability 2/3, they usually prefer the first action. But if people are asked to choose between an action that will have 200 people out of 600 die with certainty and an action that will have a 2/3 chance that no one will die and 1/3 chance that 600 will die, then they usually prefer the second action. Mathematically, all four actions are equivalent, but framing them in terms of saving people versus people dying has a crucial impact on people's choices. One natural interpretation of this widely replicated phenomenon is that people's decisions are based on their emotional reactions to the different options, and the GAGE II model should be able to generate hypotheses about the brain areas involved in positively valenced concepts such as saving lives versus those involved in negatively valenced concepts such as dying.

GAGE II may also be relevant to explaining other well-known paradoxes of behavioral choice such as the Allais paradox, in which people show a mathematically puzzling preference for sure things. Certainty is much more emotionally satisfying than even small amounts of uncertainty. As Loewenstein et al. (2001) show, many of the experimental results on economic behavior involving risk can be understood on the hypothesis that people's evaluation of risk is based on emotional feelings. Slovic et al. (2002) interpret many findings about people's judgments concerning risks and benefits in terms of an "affect heuristic." GAGE II should provide a comprehensive explanation of these phenomena.

Another well-documented phenomenon in which people violate the norms of microeconomic theory is the ultimatum game (Sanfey et al. 2003). In this game, two players can split a sum of money if one player proposes a division of the sum and the other player accepts the division. From an economic perspective, the proposer should offer the smallest sum of money possible, with the expectation that the accepter will judge any amount of money preferable to none. Experimenters have found, however, that proposers typically offer around 50 percent of the sum, and that low offers are often rejected by the accepters. Sanfey et al. (2003) used fMRI scanning to determine that unfair offers elicited activity in brain areas related to both emotion (anterior insula) and cognition (dorsolateral prefrontal cortex). Extension of the GAGE model to include the insula and the dorsolateral prefrontal cortex should make possible a neurocomputational explanation of this result. The natural interpretation of people's performance in the ultimatum game is that the proposer reasonably expects that the accepter would respond to an unfair offer with negative emotional reactions such as anger and disgust. Another economically relevant brain area is the anterior cingulate cortex, which has neurons that encode reward expectancy (Peoples 2002).

I hope to contribute both to the development of the cognitive psychology of decision making, and also to the rapidly emerging field of neuroeconomics (Camerer, Loewenstein, and Prelec 2005). I envision *computational neuroeconomics* as an emerging field at the intersection of psychology, neuroscience, economics, and computer modeling. See also Litt, Eliasmith, and Thagard forthcoming.

It should also be possible to apply GAGE II to political judgment. I am already collaborating on this topic with Drew Westen of the Departments of Psychology and Psychiatry at Emory University. He has collected extensive data about political judgments in American political controversies, for example, the sexual behavior of Bill Clinton and the Florida vote in the 2000 U.S. election. In general, Democrats have very different cognitive-emotional reactions to events from Republicans. I have already used my HOTCO (hot coherence) model to simulate some of Westen's experimental results (see chap. 8 above; Westen et al. forthcoming), and want to develop a much more neurologically deep account using GAGE II.

GAGE II should also apply to another important kind of cognitive-affective decision: ethical judgment. When people judge that an act is right or wrong, the assessment is based both on cognitive inferences, such as that the act violates ethical principles, and on emotional reactions. The emotional reactions could involve highly positive ones such as that a perceived act of kindness invokes pleasure, or highly negative ones such as that an act is disgusting, with a full range of intermediate possibilities. There is recent experimental evidence that such emotional reactions are a key part of ethical judgments (Greene and Haidt 2002). However, there is not yet available a detailed theoretical account of how cognitive and emotional processes interact to produce such judgments. I hope that the GAGE II model, expanded to include brain areas known to be involved in ethical judgments, such as the medial frontal gyrus, will contribute to a theoretical understanding of the neural basis of ethical judgments.

Greene et al. (2001) have reported fMRI studies of people making decisions that involve moral dilemmas. Consider two problems much discussed by ethical theorists, the trolley problem and the footbridge problem. In the first, people have to choose between turning a trolley in order to save five people, at the indirect cost of killing one. In the second, people have to choose between pushing a person off a footbridge in order to save five people. Just as in Kahneman and Tversky's framing examples, the choices are mathematically equivalent, but people's preferences are dramatically affected by how they are described. Most people choose saving five lives over losing one in the trolley example, but recoil from directly causing a death in the footbridge example. Greene et al. (2001) argue that the crucial difference between the two dilemmas is that the latter engages people's emotions. Their fMRI data revealed that people presented with the footbridge dilemma had increased activation in several brain areas previously identified with emotional processing, including the medial frontal gyrus and the posterior cingulate gyrus. I hope to use the GAGE II model to account for these data, as well as other brain scanning data that show that moral emotions involve brain areas such as the amygdala and the thalamus (Moll et al. 2002).

My most ambitious hope for the GAGE II model is to use it as a stepping stone to the development of a neurocomputational theory of emotional consciousness. There have been philosophical arguments that no scientific theory of consciousness is possible, on the grounds that science cannot address questions about the nature of qualitative experience such as "What is it like to feel happy?" But the prospects seem bright for providing a mechanistic explanation of key aspects of emotional consciousness: how emotions begin and end, and why they have qualitative features such as positive or negative value and greater or lesser intensity.

Morris (2002) conjectures that emotional feelings emerge from complex interactions of numerous brain areas, including the prefrontal cortex, amygdala, insula, and thalamus. How this works will require further expanding GAGE to include neural representations that summarize and integrate other neural representations from all these areas and others. I hope to see a GAGE III model that will mechanistically explain the emergence of positive versus negative emotions in terms of the interaction of two processes: the cognitive appraisal of perceptual stimuli carried out by the prefrontal cortex, and the assessment of bodily states carried out by the insula and the amygdala. Positive emotional states most likely arise from activity in reward centers such as the nucleus accumbens, whereas negative emotional states may derive from activity in fear centers such as the amygdala. It should be comparatively simple to explain the varying intensity of emotional experience mechanistically, in terms of the varying spiking rates of the many regions involved in emotional experience, particularly the regions that represent the activity of other regions that represent cognitive and somatic states. GAGE III may not tell us what it is like to be happy, a question as misleading as how many hours there are in a kilogram. But I hope the model will be able to describe the mechanisms that produce the onset, positive/negative character, and intensity of emotional experience.

Rationality

GAGE II and III are planned projects in computational neuropsychology, but they will also have implications for philosophical problems such as the nature of rationality and the problem of reduction, which concerns the relation between the different levels of explanation I have been discussing: social, cognitive, neural, and molecular. I hope that the development of richer theories of emotional cognition will aid in the philosophical project of assessing the rationality of emotions. Chapter 15 rejected both the traditional view that emotions are impediments to rationality, and the romantic view that emotions are somehow superior to rationality. Rather, effective human thinking requires the smooth integration of cognition and emotion, enabling people to acquire beliefs and other representations that achieve truths, explanations, and decisions about things that matter.

It may be useful to think about rationality and its breakdowns in terms of the malfunction of the mechanisms of emotional cognition, just as in medicine diseases are explained in terms of the malfunction of biological mechanisms (Thagard 2003). In an organism, normal functioning is produced by mechanisms consisting of a complex of components, relations, and changes that accomplish biologically useful goals such as digestion, respiration, and reproduction. Diseases occur because of defects in or interference with organs or cells. For example, diabetes develops because of problems in the pancreas and in cells that produce or process insulin.

Analogously, it may be useful to think of breakdowns in rationality such as motivated inference (chap. 8) and self-deception (chap. 13) in terms of malfunctioning mechanisms of emotional cognition. The relevant mechanisms may include all of those discussed in chapters 1 through 7, including social, cognitive, neural, and molecular mechanisms. The end of chapter 5 described how deformed social mechanisms such as propaganda and coercion can undermine the desirable results of emotional consensus. In chapter 8, I showed how motivated inference about legal guilt can arise from illegitimate influences of emotional evaluation on belief assessment, as did the self-deception of Dimmesdale in chapter 13.

There is nothing wrong with emotional evaluation, and in fact it is crucial to decision making as many of the above chapters show, but irrationality can arise when emotions have inappropriate effects. Compare the situation in medicine with the immune system, which is a crucial part of the body's defense against bacteria and other pathogens. Sometimes the immune system malfunctions and begins to attack the organs it is supposed to protect, resulting in autoimmune diseases such as lupus, multiple sclerosis, and rheumatoid arthritis. Similarly, irrationality can arise when the emotional system goes beyond its proper biological function of focusing attention and effort, producing inappropriate interference with belief evaluation.

Relation between Levels of Explanation

Another important philosophical problem concerns the relation between the different levels of explanation that are required to understand emotional cognition. Table 1.1 summarized the social, cognitive, neural, and molecular mechanisms that are discussed in this book. If I am right that explanations at each level are in terms of mechanisms, then the problem of interlevel relations can be understood as the problem of describing the relations between mechanisms consisting of components, relations, interactions, and changes.

The easiest part of this description concerns components, which naturally fit into a part–whole hierarchy. Social groups consist of persons, who have mental representations. Persons consist of bodies, including brains, which consist of neurons. Neurons consist of proteins and other molecules, which consist of atoms and so on. However, this hierarchy of parts tells us nothing about the causal processes that are crucial to the explanatory role of mechanisms.

We can also give a hierarchical account of the nature of relations between components that operate at each mechanistic level. To take the most obvious case, consider a social group of two persons who sit next to each other. The relation *next to* has an approximate decomposition: each person's body is physically near the other's. Such spatial relations are only interesting if there are also temporal relations involving interactions, for example, one person talking to another. Such interactions also decompose: talking consists of two or more persons engaged in their own bodily behaviors of speaking and listening. At the cognitive level, these activities are explained in terms of mental representations, whose interactions can in principle be understood in terms of the interactions of the neural structures that are the basis for their mental representations. At the next level, interactions between neurons such as excitation and inhibition can be understood in terms of interactions between molecules, for example, the production, movement, and reception of neurotransmitters such as dopamine and serotonin.

The reason that scientists do research on all these levels of components, relations, and interactions is to explain how changes are caused, and this is where the crux of the problem of reduction lies. To what extent are the changes at one level to be explained in terms of changes at the lower levels? The major social change discussed in chapter 5 was consensus, when the group as a whole acquires a shared belief or decision. This change was directly related to changes at the cognitive level, as consensus came about through changes in the preferred decisions of the individual decision makers. But the social mechanisms are not replaceable by the cognitive mechanisms operating in individuals, because a crucial aspect of the social process is interaction at the social level, including emotional contagion, empathy, and altruism. Similarly, we can see the relevance of neural changes to changes in mental representations at the cognitive level, but it is still valuable to consider changes at the cognitive level, such as the inferences that people make. Interactions between mental representations cause inferences, providing explanations of the desired phenomena that neural matters do not directly address, just as interactions between neurons produce changes in brain activity in ways that are usually best described in terms of neural interactions rather than molecular transformations.

The appropriate picture for the connections between mechanistic explanations at two different levels is sketched in figure 16.1. At each level, the interactions between components lead to changes, with identifiable connections between the two sets of objects, interactions, and changes. But these connections are not tight enough to render the top level redundant with respect to the lower one, nor are they loose enough to render the top level independent of the bottom one. What matters for understanding the research on emotions and other topics is seeing the systematic connections between each pair of levels.

It should not be supposed, however, that the only connections are between one level and those immediately above and below it. There is now a burgeoning field called *social cognitive neuroscience* that ties social psychology, not

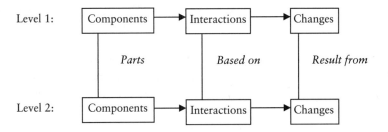

Figure 16.1
Relations between two levels of explanation. At each level, components have interactions that cause changes in the system of objects.

just to cognitive psychology as has been the case for several decades, but all the way down to neural and even molecular levels (Cacioppo et al. 2002). For example, the formation of marriages, which are social groups, may partly need to be explained in terms of the molecular mechanisms involved in pair bonding, such as expression of the hormones vasopressin and oxytocin. (Prairie voles are monogamous but mountain voles are not, and the relevant genetic differences involve these two chemicals.) Similarly, a recent study found that oxytocin affects people's willingness to trust each other (Kosfeld et al. 2005). Hence a fuller, more accurate version of figure 16.1 would portray several levels of mechanisms with connections that skip over one or more levels.

In accord with the *explanatory pluralism* of McCauley and Bechtel (2001), my view of research on emotion is neither reductionist nor antireductionist. Antireductionists claim that theories at one level are autonomous from theories at the lower level. This view is clearly incompatible with developments in psychology and neuroscience, for there are many cases where social theories are being informed by cognitive theories, and where cognitive theories are being informed by neural theories, and where neural theories are being informed by molecular theories. Equally implausible is the reductionist view that there is just one fundamental level of explanation, say the neurological one. Neuroscience is currently the greatest source of new insights about how emotions work, but its success depends in part on how well it meshes with social, cognitive, and molecular explanations. The ultimate reductionist fantasy would be that everything would be explained in terms of even more fundamental objects, like atoms, quarks, or quantum loops. Currently atoms are not totally irrelevant to explaining emotional cognition, because the structure and behavior of atoms is pertinent to explaining chemical reactions, which are pertinent to molecular biology, which is pertinent to understanding the behavior of neurons, and so on. But reductionism that privileges a particular level of explanation over others neglects the fact that mechanisms of different scale are most appropriate for explaining different phenomena. For example, consensus is a social phenomena mostly explained in terms of social mechanisms such as emotional contagion (chap. 5), even if emotional contagion might itself be understood in terms of neural processes. Quantum theory has little relevance to psychology (Litt et al. forthcoming).

An ongoing understanding of the relationships between the different levels of mechanisms relevant to producing emotions will depend, not on abstract philosophical reflection, but on the course of scientific development. Current trends suggest that explanations of emotional cognition will continue to benefit from the interpenetration and integration of multiple levels, including social, cognitive, neural, and molecular mechanisms. Advances in understanding this development will benefit from considering not only the general topic of emotional cognition discussed in this book, but by a finer-grained analysis of scientific developments concerning particular emotions. It would be very useful to have thorough multidisciplinary case studies of the current state of social, cognitive, neural, and molecular understanding of emotions such as happiness, fear, and love. I expect they will support my preference for explanatory pluralism over reductionism and antireductionism, but only decades of continuing research will reveal the most plausible answer to the question of the nature of the relations between different explanatory levels.

This chapter has outlined some current and future lines of scientific and philosophical research on how emotions influence thinking. Undoubtedly other lines will emerge as progress continues on understanding the mechanisms and applications of emotional cognition.

References

Abelson, R. (1963). Computer simulation of "hot" cognition. In S. Tomkins and S. Messick (eds.), *Computer Simulation of Personality* (pp. 277–298). New York: John Wiley and Sons.

Adherents (2003). *Adherents.com.* Retrieved Nov. 26, 2003, from http://www.adherents.com/.

Adleman, L. M. (1994). Molecular computation of solutions to combinatorial problems. *Science* 266: 1021–1024.

Aggleton, J. (2000). *The Amygdala: A Functional Analysis.* Oxford: Oxford University Press.

AHFMR. (1999). Reovirus: Cancer fighter. Retrieved May 18, 2005, from http://www.ahfmr.ab.ca/publications/reports/Tri99/lee.shtml/.

Allen, R. J. (1991). The nature of juridical proof. *Cardozo Law Review* 373: 373–422.

Allen, R. J. (1994). Factual ambiguity and a theory of evidence. *Northwestern University Law Review* 88: 604–660.

Anderson, J. R. (1993). *Rules of the Mind.* Hillsdale, N.J.: Lawrence Erlbaum Associates.

Arabsheibani, G., D. de Meza, J. Maloney, and B. Pearson (2000). And a vision appeared unto them of a great profit: Evidence of self-deception among the self-employed. *Economics Letters* 67: 35–41.

Ashby, F. G., A. M. Isen, and A. U. Turken (1999). A neuropsychological theory of positive affect and its influence on cognition. *Psychological Review* 106: 529–550.

Atran, S. (2002). *In Gods We Trust: The Evolutionary Landscape of Religion.* Oxford: Oxford University Press.

Barnes, A. (1997). *Seeing through Self-Deception.* Cambridge: Cambridge University Press.

Barnes, A., and P. Thagard (1997). Empathy and analogy. *Dialogue: Canadian Philosophical Review* 36: 705–720.

Barsade, S. (2002). The ripple effect: Emotional contagion in group behavior. *Administrative Science Quarterly* 47: 644–675.

Bazerman, M. H. (1994). *Judgment in Managerial Decision Making*. New York: John Wiley and Sons.

Bechara, A., A. R. Damasio, H. Damasio, and S. Anderson (1994). Insensitivity to future consequences following damage to human prefrontal cortex. *Cognition* 50: 7–15.

Bechara, A., H. Damasio, D. Tranel, and A. R. Damasio (1997). Deciding advantageously before knowing the advantageous strategy. *Science* 275: 1293–1295.

Bechtel, W., and A. A. Abrahamsen (2005). Explanation: A mechanistic alternative. *Studies in History and Philosophy of Science* 36: 421–441.

Bechtel, W., and R. C. Richardson (1993). *Discovering Complexity*. Princeton, N.J.: Princeton University Press.

Berns, G., S. McClure, G. Pagnoni, and P. Montague (2001). Predictability modulates human brain response to reward. *Journal of Neuroscience* 21: 2793–2798.

Bhalla, U. S., and R. Iyengar (1999). Emergent properties of networks of biological signaling pathways. *Science* 283: 381–387.

Bischoff, J. R., D. H. Kirn, A. Williams, C. Heise, S. Horn, M. Muna, L. Ng, J. A. Nye, A. Sampson-Johannes, A. Fattaey, and F. McCormick (1996). An adenovirus mutant that replicates selectively in p53-deficient human tumor cells. *Science* 274: 373–376.

Black, I. B. (1991). *Information in the Brain: A Molecular Perspective*. Cambridge, Mass.: MIT Press.

Blanchette, I., and K. Dunbar (2001). Analogy use in naturalistic settings: The influence of audience, emotion, and goals. *Memory and Cognition* 29: 730–735.

Bosanquet, B. (1920). *Implication and Linear Inference*. London: Macmillan.

Bower, G. H. (1981). Mood and memory. *American Psychologist* 36: 129–148.

Bower, G. H. (1991). Mood congruity of social judgments. In J. P. Forgas (ed.), *Emotion and Social Judgments* (pp. 31–53). Oxford: Pergamon Press.

Boyer, P. (2001). *Religion Explained: The Evolutionary Origins of Religious Thought*. New York: Basic Books.

Bray, D. (1995). Protein molecules as computational elements in living cells. *Nature* 376: 307–312.

Breiter, H., I. Aharon, D. Kahneman, A. Dale, and P. Shizgal (2001). Functional imaging of neural responses to expectancy and experience of monetary gains and losses. *Neuron* 30: 619–639.

Brink, D. O. (1989). *Moral Realism and the Foundations of Ethics*. Cambridge: Cambridge University Press.

Brown, R. E. (1994). *An Introduction to Neuroendocrinology*. Cambridge: Cambridge University Press.

Brown, S. (1996). *Buzz: The Science and Lore of Alcohol and Caffeine*. New York: Penguin.

Bugliosi, V. (1997). *Outrage: The Five Reasons Why O. J. Simpson Got Away with Murder*. New York: Island Books.

Bylander, T., D. Allemang, M. Tanner, and J. Josephson (1991). The computational complexity of abduction. *Artificial Intelligence* 49: 25–60.

Byrne, M. D. (1995). The convergence of explanatory coherence and the story model: A case study in juror decision. In J. D. Moore and J. F. Lehman (eds.), *Proceedings of the Seventeenth Annual Conference of the Cognitive Science Society* (pp. 539–543). Mahwah, N.J.: Lawrence Erlbaum Associates.

Cacioppo, J. T., G. G. Berntson, R. Adolphs, C. S. Carter, R. J. Davidson, M. K. McClintock, B. S. McEwen, M. J. Meaney, D. L. Schacter, E. M. Sternberg, S. S. Suomi, and S. E. Taylor (eds.). (2002). *Foundations in Social Neuroscience*. Cambridge, Mass.: MIT Press.

Calabresi, P., M. de Murtas, and G. Bernardi (1997). The neostriatum beyond the motor function: Experimental and clinical evidence. *Neuroscience* 78: 39–60.

Camerer, C., G. F. Loewenstein, and D. Prelec (2005). Neuroeconomics: How neuroscience can inform economics. *Journal of Economic Literature* 34: 9–64.

Campanario, J. M. (1996). Using *Citation Classics* to study the incidence of serendipity in scientific context. *Scientometrics* 37: 3–24.

Churchland, P. S. (1996). Feeling reasons. In A. R. Damasio, H. Damasio, and Y. Christen (eds.), *Neurobiology of Decision Making* (pp. 181–199). Berlin: Springer-Verlacht.

Churchland, P. S., and T. Sejnowski (1992). *The Computational Brain*. Cambridge, Mass.: MIT Press.

Clore, G., N. Schwarz, and M. Conway (1994). Affective causes and consequences of social information processing. In R. Wyer and T. Srull (eds.), *Handbook of Social Cognition*, vol. 1 (pp. 323–417). Hillsdale, N.J.: Lawrence Erlbaum.

Coady, C. A. J. (1992). *Testimony: A Philosophical Study*. Oxford: Clarendon Press.

Cochran, J. L., Jr. (1997). *Journey to Justice*. New York: One World.

Coffey, M. C., J. E. Strong, P. A. Forsyth, and P. W. K. Lee (1998). Reovirus therapy of tumors with activated Ras pathway. *Science* 282: 1332–1334.

Cohen, S., and S. Bersten (1990). Probability out of court: Notes on "Guilt beyond reasonable doubt." *Australasian Journal of Philosophy* 68: 229–240.

Cooke, R. (2001). *Dr. Folkman's War: Angiogenesis and the Struggle to Defeat Cancer*. New York: Random House.

Cooley, A., C. Bess, and M. Rubin-Jackson (1995). *Madam Foreman: A Rush to Judgment?* Beverly Hills, Calif.: Dove Books.

Cooper, J., and R. H. Fazio (1984). A new look at dissonance theory. In L. Berkowitz (ed.), *Advances in Experimental Social Psychology*, vol. 17. New York: Academic Press.

Cozman, F. J. (2001). JavaBayes: Bayesian networks in Java. Http://www-2.cs .cmu.edu/~javabayes/.

Crick, F. (1988). *What Mad Pursuit: A Personal View of Scientific Discovery.* New York: Basic Books.

Crossin, K. L., and L. A. Krushel (2000). Cellular signaling by neural cell adhesion molecules of the immunoglobulin superfamily. *Developmental Dynamics* 218: 260–279.

Dalgleish, T., and M. J. Power (eds.). (1999). *Handbook of Cognition and Emotion.* New York: John Wiley and Sons.

Damasio, A. R. (1994). *Descartes' Error.* New York: G. P. Putnam's Sons.

Damasio, H., T. Grabowski, R. Frank, A. M. Galburda, and A. R. Damasio (1994). The return of Phineas Gage: Clues about the brain from the skull of a famous patient. *Science* 264: 1102–1104.

Darley, J. M., M. P. Zanna, and H. L. Roediger (2004). *The Compleat Academic: A Career Guide.* Washington, D.C.: American Psychological Association.

Davidson, B., and B. Pargetter (1987). Guilt beyond reasonable doubt. *Australasian Journal of Philosophy* 65: 182–187.

Davidson, D. (1985). Deception and division. In E. LePore and B. P. McLaughlin (eds.), *Actions and Events: Perspectives on the Philosophy of Donald Davidson.* Oxford: Blackwell.

de Sousa, R. (1988). *The Rationality of Emotion.* Cambridge, Mass.: MIT Press.

Demos, N. F. (1960). Lying to oneself. *Journal of Philosophy* 57: 588–595.

Dennett, D. (1991). *Consciousness Explained.* Boston: Little, Brown.

Dershowitz, A. M. (1997). *Reasonable Doubts: The Criminal Justice System and the O. J. Simpson Case.* New York: Touchstone.

Descartes, R. (1964). *Philosophical Writings.* E. Anscombe and P. T. Geach, trans. London: Nelson.

Dunbar, K. (1995). How scientists really reason: Scientific reasoning in real-world laboratories. In R. J. Sternberg and J. Davidson (eds.), *Mechanisms of Insight* (pp. 365–395). Cambridge, Mass.: MIT Press.

Dunbar, K. (2001a). The analogical paradox: Why analogy is so easy in naturalistic settings, yet so difficult in the laboratory. In D. Gentner, K. Holyoak, and B. K. Kokinov (eds.), *The Analogical Mind* (pp. 313–334). Cambridge, Mass.: MIT Press.

Dunbar, K. (2001b). What scientific thinking reveals about the nature of cognition. In K. Crowley, C. D. Schunn, and T. Okada (eds.), *Designing for Science: Implications from Everyday, Classroom, and Professional Settings* (pp. 115–140). Mahwah, N.J.: Lawrence Erlbaum.

Edwards, J. (2003/1746). *A treatise concerning religious affections.* Retrieved Nov. 26, 2003, from http://www.ccel.org/e/edwards/affections/religious_affections.html.

Ekman, P. (1992). An argument for basic emotions. *Cognition and Emotion* 6: 169–200.

Eliasmith, C., and C. H. Anderson (2003). *Neural Engineering: Computation, Representation, and Dynamics in Neurobiological Systems.* Cambridge, Mass.: MIT Press.

Eliasmith, C., and P. Thagard (2001). Integrating structure and meaning: A distributed model of analogical mapping. *Cognitive Science* 25: 245–286.

Elster, J. (1983). *Sour Grapes.* New York: Cambridge University Press.

Engel, A. K., P. Fries, P. König, M. Brecht, and W. Singer (1999). Temporal Binding, Binocular Rivalry, and Consciousness. *Consciousness and Cognition* 8: 128–151.

Ephrati, E., and J. S. Rosenschein (1996). Deriving consensus in multiagent systems. *Artificial Intelligence* 87: 21–74.

Erez, A., D. E. Johnson, and T. A. Judge (1995). Self-deception as a mediator of the relationship between dispositions and subjective well-being. *Personality and Individual Differences* 19(5): 597–612.

Everitt, B., S. Landau, and M. Leese (2001). *Cluster Analysis.* 4th ed. New York: Oxford University Press.

Falkenhainer, B., K. D. Forbus, and D. Gentner (1989). The structure-mapping engine: Algorithms and examples. *Artificial Intelligence* 41: 1–63.

Faust, J. (2000a). Proof beyond a reasonable doubt: An annotated bibliography. *The APA Newsletters (American Philosophical Association)* 99(2): 229–235.

Faust, J. (2000b). Reasonable doubt jury instructions. *The APA Newsletters (American Philosophical Association)* 99(2): 226–229.

Fazio, R. H. (2001). On the automatic activation of associated evaluations: An overview. *Cognition and Emotion* 15: 115–141.

Feist, G. J. (1993). A structural model of scientific eminence. *Psychological Science* 4: 366–371.

Feist, G. J., and M. E. Gorman (1998). The psychology of science: Review and integration of a nascent discipline. *Review of General Psychology* 2: 3–47.

Fenno, R. F. (1978). *Home Style: House Members in Their Districts.* Boston: Little, Brown.

Festinger, L. (1957). *A Theory of Cognitive Dissonance*. Stanford, Calif.: Stanford University Press.

Feynman, R. (1999). *The Pleasure of Finding Things Out*. Cambridge, Mass.: Perseus Books.

Fingarette, H. (1969). *Self-Deception*. London: Routledge and Kegan Paul.

Finucane, M. L., A. S. Alhakami, P. Slovic, and S. M. Johnson (2000). The affect heuristic in judgements of risks and benefit. *Behavioral Decision Making* 13: 1–17.

Fiske, S., and M. Pavelchak (1986). Category-based versus piecemeal-based affective responses: Developments in schema-triggered affect. In R. Sorrentino and E. Higgins (eds.), *Handbook of Motivation and Cognition*, vol. 1 (pp. 167–203). New York: Guilford.

Fodor, J. (2000). *The Mind Doesn't Work That Way*. Cambridge, Mass.: MIT Press.

Forgas, J. P. (1995). Mood and judgment: The Affect Infusion Model (AIM). *Psychological Bulletin* 117: 39–66.

Frank, R. H. (1988). *Passions within Reason*. New York: Norton.

Galarreta, M., and S. Hestrin (2001). Spike transmission and synchrony detection in networks of GABAergic interneurons. *Science* 292: 2295–2299.

Galison, P. (1997). *Image and Logic: A Material Culture of Microphysics*. Chicago: University of Chicago Press.

Gallagher, S. (2000). Philosophical conceptions of the self: Implications for cognitive science. *Trends in Cognitive Science* 4(1): 14–21.

Gentner, D. (1983). Structure-mapping: A theoretical framework for analogy. *Cognitive Science* 7: 155–170.

Giere, R. N. (1999). *Science without Laws*. Chicago: University of Chicago Press.

Gilovich, T. (1991). *How We Know What Isn't So*. New York: Free Press.

Goldbeck, R. (1997). Denial in physical illness. *Journal of Psychosomatic Research* 43(6): 575–593.

Goldberg, S. C. (1997). The very idea of computer self-knowledge and self-deception. *Minds and Machines* 7: 515–529.

Goldman, A. (1999). *Knowledge in a Social World*. Oxford: Oxford University Press.

Gooding, D. (1990). *Experiment and the Nature of Meaning*. Dordrecht: Kluwer.

Gooding, D., T. Pinch, and S. Schaffer, eds. (1989). *The Uses of Experiments*. Cambridge: Cambridge University Press.

Gopnik, A. (1998). Explanation as Orgasm. *Minds and Machines* 8: 101–118.

Grace, A., and H. Moore (1998). Regulation of information flow in the nucleus accumbens: A model for the pathophysiology of schizophrenia. In M. F. Lenzenweger and R. H. Dworkin (eds.), *Origins and Development of Schizophrenia: Advances in*

Experimental Psychopathology (pp. 123–157). Washington, D.C.: American Psychological Association.

Greene, J., and J. Haidt (2002). How (and where) does moral judgment work? *Trends in Cognitive Sciences* 6: 517–523.

Greene, J. D., R. B. Sommerville, L. E. Nystrom, J. M. Darley, and J. D. Cohen (2001). An fMRI investigation of emotional engagement in moral judgment. *Science* 293: 2105–2108.

Grice, H. P. (1989). *Studies in the Way of Words*. Cambridge, Mass.: Harvard University Press.

Gross, M. (1998). Molecular computation. In T. Gramß, S. Bornholdt, and S. Groß (eds.), *Non-Standard Computation* (pp. 15–58). Weinheim: Wiley-VCH.

Haack, S. (1993). *Evidence and inquiry: Towards Reconstruction in Epistemology*. Oxford: Blackwell.

Haack, S. (1998). *Manifesto of a Passionate Moderate*. Chicago: University of Chicago Press.

Hacking, I. (1975). *The Emergence of Probability*. Cambridge: Cambridge University Press.

Hacking, I. (1983). *Representing and Intervening*. Cambridge: Cambridge University Press.

Haight, M. R. (1980). *A Study of Self-Deception*. Sussex: Harvester Press.

Harman, G. (1986). *Change in View: Principles of Reasoning*. Cambridge, Mass.: MIT Press/Bradford Books.

Harris, K. M. (1988). *Hypocrisy and Self-Deception in Hawthorne's Fiction*. Charlottesville: University Press of Virginia.

Hatfield, E., J. T. Cacioppo, and R. L. Rapson (1994). *Emotional Contagion*. Cambridge: Cambridge University Press.

Hawthorne, N. (1850). *The Scarlet Letter: A Romance*. Boston: Ticknor and Fields.

Hick, J. (1967). Faith. In P. Edwards (ed.), *The Encyclopedia of Philosophy*, vol. 3 (pp. 165–169). New York: Macmillan.

Hitchcott, P., and G. Phillips (1997). Amygdala and hippocampus control dissociable aspects of drug associated conditioned rewards. *Psychopharmacology* 131: 187–195.

Holyoak, K. J., L. R. Novick, and E. R. Melz (1994). Component processes in analogical transfer: Mapping, pattern completion, and adaptation. In K. J. Holyoak and J. A. Barnden (eds.), *Advances in Connectionist and Neural Computation theory*, vol. 2, *Analogical Connections* (pp. 113–180). Norwood, N.J.: Ablex.

Holyoak, K. J., and B. A. Spellman (1993). Thinking. *Annual Review of Psychology* 44: 265–315.

Holyoak, K. J., and P. Thagard (1989). Analogical mapping by constraint satisfaction. *Cognitive Science* 13: 295–355.

Holyoak, K. J., and P. Thagard (1995). *Mental Leaps: Analogy in Creative Thought.* Cambridge, Mass.: MIT Press.

Hummel, J. E., and K. J. Holyoak (1997). Distributed representations of structure: A theory of analogical access and mapping. *Psychological Review* 104: 427–466.

Hurley, S. L. (1989). *Natural Reasons: Personality and Polity.* New York: Oxford University Press.

Hutchins, E. (1995). *Cognition in the Wild.* Cambridge, Mass.: MIT Press.

Isen, A. M. (1993). Positive affect and decision making. In M. Lewis and J. M. Haviland (eds.), *Handbook of Emotions* (pp. 261–277). New York: Guilford Press.

Jacob, F. (1988). *The Statue Within.* F. Philip, trans. New York: Basic Books.

James, W. (1948). *Essays in Pragmatism.* New York: Hafner.

James, W. (1958). *Varieties of Religious Experience.* New York: New American Library.

Johnson, N. R., and W. E. Feinberg (1989). Crowd structure and process: Theoretical framework and computer simulation model. In E. Lawler and B. Markovsky (eds.), *Advances in Group Processes,* vol. 6 (pp. 49–86). Greenwich, Conn.: JAI Press.

Johnston, M. (1988). Self-deception and the nature of mind. In B. P. McLaughlin and A. O. Rorty (eds.), *Perspectives on Self-Deception* (pp. 63–91). Berkeley: University of California Press.

Josephson, J. R., and S. G. Josephson (eds.). (1994). *Abductive Inference: Computation, Philosophy, Technology.* Cambridge: Cambridge University Press.

Judson, H. F. (1979). *The Eighth Day of Creation: Makers of the Revolution in Biology.* New York: Simon and Schuster.

Just, D. (1998). *Excluding prejudicial evidence from criminal juries.* Retrieved May 6, 2005, from http://www.justd.com/prejev.htm/.

Kahneman, D. (1999). Objective happiness. In D. Kahneman, E. Diener, and N. Schwarz (eds.), *Well-Being: Foundations of Hedonic Psychology* (pp. 3–25). New York: Russell Sage Foundation.

Kahneman, D., P. Slovic, and A. Tversky (1982). *Judgment under Uncertainty: Heuristics and Biases.* New York: Cambridge University Press.

Kahneman, D., and A. Tversky (1979). Prospect theory: An analysis of decision under risk. *Econometrica* 47: 263–291.

Kitcher, P. (1993). *The Advancement of Science.* Oxford: Oxford University Press.

Knutson, B., C. Adams, G. Fong, and D. Hommer (2001). fMRI visualization of brain activity during a monetary incentive delay task. *NeuroImage* 12: 20–27.

Koch, C. (1999). *Biophysics of Computation: Information Processing in Single Neurons*. New York: Oxford University Press.

Koch, C. M., and D. J. Devine (1999). Effects of reasonable doubt definition and inclusion of a lesser charge on jury verdicts. *Law and Human Behavior* 23: 653–674.

Kolodner, J. (1993). *Case-Based Reasoning*. San Mateo, Calif.: Morgan Kaufmann.

Kosfeld, M., M. Heinrichs, P. J. Zak, U. Fischbacher, and E. Fehr (2005). Oxytocin increases trust in humans. *Nature* 435: 673–676.

Koza, J. R. (1992). *Genetic Programming*. Cambridge, Mass.: MIT Press.

Kreps, D. M. (1990). *A Course in Microeconomic Theory*. Princeton, N.J.: Princeton University Press.

Kubovy, M. (1999). On the pleasures of the mind. In D. Kahneman, E. Diener, and N. Schwarz (eds.), *Well-being: Foundations of Hedonic Psychology* (pp. 134–154). New York: Russell Sage Foundation.

Kunda, Z. (1990). The case for motivated inference. *Psychological Bulletin* 108: 480–498.

Kunda, Z. (1999). *Social Cognition*. Cambridge, Mass.: MIT Press.

Kunda, Z., and P. Thagard (1996). Forming impressions from stereotypes, traits, and behaviors: A parallel-constraint-satisfaction theory. *Psychological Review* 103: 284–308.

Kurzweil, R. (1999). *The Age of Spiritual Machines*. New York: Viking.

Lajunen, T., A. Corry, H. Summala, and L. Hartley (1996). Impression management and self-deception in traffic behavior inventories. *Personality and Individual Differences* 22(3): 341–353.

Lazar, A. (1999). Deceiving oneself or self-deceived? On the formation of beliefs "under the influence." *Mind* 108: 265–290.

Lazarus, R. S. (1991). Cognition and motivation in emotion. *American Psychologist* 46: 352–267.

LeDoux, J. (1996). *The Emotional Brain*. New York: Simon and Schuster.

Lempert, R. (1986). The new evidence scholarship: Analyzing the process of proof. *Boston University Law Review* 66: 439–477.

Lerner, J. S., and D. Keltner (2000). Beyond valence: Toward a model of emotion-specific influences on judgement and choice. *Cognition and Emotion* 14: 473–493.

Lerner, J. S., and D. Keltner (2001). Fear, anger, and risk. *Journal of Personality and Social Psychology* 81: 146–159.

Lerner, J. S., D. A. Small, and G. F. Loewenstein (2004). Heart strings and purse strings: Carryover effects of emotions on economic decisions. *Psychological Science* 15: 337–341.

Levine, D. S. (2000). *Introduction to Neural and Cognitive Modeling*, 2nd ed. Mahwah, N.J.: Lawrence Erlbaum.

Lewin, K. (1951). *Field Theory in Social Science*. New York: Harper and Row.

Lieberman, M. D. (2000). Intuition: A social cognitive neuroscience approach. *Psychological Bulletin* 126: 109–137.

Litt, A., C. Eliasmith, F. W. Kroon, S. Weinstein, and P. Thagard (forthcoming). Is the brain a quantum computer? *Cognitive Science.*

Litt, A., C. Eliasmith, and P. Thagard (forthcoming). A large-scale neural model of human reward processing.

Lockwood, P., and Z. Kunda (1997). Superstars and me: Predicting the impact of role models on the self. *Journal of Personality and Social Psychology* 73: 91–103.

Lodge, M., and P. Stroh (1993). Inside the mental voting booth: An impression-driven process model of candidate evaluation. In S. Iyengar and W. J. McGuire (eds.), *Explorations in political psychology* (pp. 225–295). Durham, N.C.: Duke University Press.

Lodish, H., A. Berk, S. L. Zipursky, P. Matsudaira, D. Baltimore, and J. Darnell (2000). *Molecular Cell Biology,* 4th ed. New York: W. H. Freeman.

Loewenstein, G. (1994). The psychology of curiosity: A review and reinterpretation. *Psychological Bulletin* 116: 75–98.

Loewenstein, G. F., E. U. Weber, C. K. Hsee, and N. Welch (2001). Risk as feelings. *Psychological Bulletin* 127: 267–286.

Lucretius. (1969). *On the Nature of Things*. London: Sphere Books.

Maass, W., and C. M. Bishop (eds.). (1999). *Pulsed Neural Networks*. Cambridge, Mass.: MIT Press.

Machamer, P., L. Darden, and C. F. Craver (2000). Thinking about mechanisms. *Philosophy of Science* 67: 1–25.

Macmillan, M. (2000). *An Odd Kind of Fame: Stories of Phineas Gage*. Cambridge, Mass.: MIT Press.

Magnasco, M. O. (1997). Chemical kinetics is Turing universal. *Physical Review Letters* 78: 1190–1193.

Marshall, B. J., and J. R. Warren (1984). Unidentified curved bacilli in the stomach of patients with gastritis and peptic ulceration. *Lancet* 1(8390): 1311–1315.

McAllister, J. W. (1996). *Beauty and Revolution in Science*. Ithaca, N.Y.: Cornell University Press.

McCauley, R. N., and W. Bechtel (2001). Explanatory pluralism and the heuristic identity theory. *Theory and Psychology* 11: 736–760.

McCauley, R. N., and E. T. Lawson (2002). *Bringing Ritual to Mind: Psychological Foundations of Cultural Forms*. Cambridge: Cambridge University Press.

McGuire, W. J. (1999). *Constructing Social Psychology: Creative and Critical Processes*. New York: Cambridge University Press.

McLaughlin, B. P. (1988). Exploring the possibility of self-deception in belief. In B. P. McLaughlin and A. O. Rorty (eds.), *Perspectives on Self-Deception* (pp. 29–62). Berkeley: University of California Press.

McLaughlin, B. P. (1996). On the very possibility of self-deception. In R. T. Ames and W. Dissanayake (eds.), *Self and Deception: A Cross-Cultural Philosophical Enquiry*. New York: SUNY Press.

Medawar, P. B. (1979). *Advice to a Young Scientist*. New York: Harper and Row.

Meichenbaum, D. (1994). *A Clinical Handbook/Practical Therapist Manual for Assessing and Treating Adults with Post-Traumatic Stress Disorder (PTSD)*. Waterloo, Ont.: Institute Press.

Mele, A. R. (2001). *Self-Deception Unmasked*. Princeton, N.J.: Princeton University Press.

Mill, J. S. (1970). *A system of logic*, 8th ed. London: Longman.

Millgram, E. (1997). *Practical Induction*. Cambridge, Mass.: Harvard University Press.

Millgram, E., and P. Thagard (1996). Deliberative coherence. *Synthese* 108: 63–88.

Minsky, M. (2003). *The emotion machine*. Retrieved Dec. 4, 2003, from http://web.media.mit.edu/~minsky/E2/eb2.html/.

Mischel, W., and Y. Shoda (1995). A cognitive-affective system theory of personality: Reconceptualizing situations, dispositions, dynamics, and the invariance in personality structure. *Psychological Review* 102: 246–268.

Mitchell, J. (2000). Living a lie: self-deception, habit, and social roles. *Human Studies* 23: 145–156.

Mitroff, I. I. (1974). *The Subjective Side of Science*. Amsterdam: Elsevier.

Mogenson, G., D. Jones, and C. Yim (1980). From motivation to action: Functional interface between the limbic system and the motor system. *Progress in Neurobiology* 14: 69–97.

Moll, J., R. de Oliveira-Souza, P. Eslinger, I. E. Bramati, J. Mourao-Miranda, P. A. Andreiuolo, and L. Pessoa (2002). The neural correlates of moral sensitivity: A functional magnetic resonance imaging investigation of basic and moral emotions. *Journal of Neuroscience* 22: 2730–2736.

Moore, S., and M. Oaksford (eds.). (2002). *Emotional Cognition*. Amsterdam: John Benjamins.

Moravec, H. (1998). *Robot: Mere Machine to Transcendent Mind*. Oxford: Oxford University Press.

Morris, J. S. (2002). How do you feel? *Trends in Cognitive Sciences* 6: 317–319.

Moss, S. (2002). Challenges for agent-based social simulation of multilateral negotiation. In K. Dautenhaum, A. Bond, L. Canamero, and B. Edmonds (eds.), *Socially Intelligent Agents: Creating Relationships with Computers and Robots* (pp. 251–258). Norwell, Mass.: Kluwer.

Neapolitan, R. (1990). *Probabilistic Reasoning in Expert Systems*. New York: John Wiley and Sons.

Nerb, J., and H. Spada (2001). Evaluation of environmental problems: A coherence model of cognition and emotion. *Cognition and Emotion* 15: 521–551.

Nerb, J., H. Spada, and K. Lay (2001). Environmental risk in the media: Modeling the reactions of the audience. *Research in Social Problems and Public Policy* 9: 57–85.

Nersessian, N. (1992). How do scientists think? Capturing the dynamics of conceptual change in science. In R. Giere (ed.), *Cognitive Models of Science*, vol. 15 (pp. 3–44). Minneapolis: University of Minnesota Press.

Newell, A. (1990). *Unified Theories of Cognition*. Cambridge, Mass.: Harvard University Press.

Newman, E. A., and K. R. Zahs (1998). Modulation of neuronal activity by glial cells in the retina. *Journal of Neuroscience* 18: 4022–4028.

Newman, L. S., K. Duff, N. Schnopp-Wyatt, and B. Brock (1997). Reactions to the O. J. Simpson verdict: "Mindless tribalism" or motivated inference processes? *Journal of Social Issues* 53: 547–562.

O'Donnell, P. (1999). Ensemble coding in the nucleus accumbens. *Psychobiology* 27: 187–197.

O'Donnell, P., and A. Grace (1995). Synaptic interactions among excitatory afferents to nucleus accumbens neurons: Hippocampal gating of prefrontal cortical input. *Journal of Neuroscience* 15: 3622–3639.

Oatley, K. (1992). *Best Laid Schemes: The Psychology of Emotions*. Cambridge: Cambridge University Press.

Olby, R. (1974). *The Path to the Double Helix*. London: Macmillan.

Olson, J. S. (1989). *The History of Cancer: An Annotated Bibliography*. New York: Greewood Press.

Ortony, A., G. L. Clore, and A. Collins (1988). *The Cognitive Structure of Emotions*. Cambridge: Cambridge University Press.

Paluch, S. (1967). Self-deception. *Inquiry* 10: 268–278.

Panksepp, J. (1993). Neurochemical control of moods and emotions: Amino acids to neuropeptides. In M. Lewis and J. M. Haviland (eds.), *Handbook of Emotions* (pp. 87–107). New York: Guilford Press.

Panksepp, J. (1998). *Affective Neuroscience: The Foundations of Human and Animal Emotions*. Oxford: Oxford University Press.

Parks, R. W., D. S. Levine, and D. L. Long (eds.). (1998). *Fundamentals of Neural Network Modeling*. Cambridge, Mass.: MIT Press.

Parsons, G. G., and A. Rueger (2000). The epistemic significance of appreciating experiments aesthetically. *British Journal of Aesthetics* 40: 407–423.

Paulhus, D. L., and D. B. Reid (1991). Enhancement and denial in social desirable responding. *Journal of Personality and Social Psychology* 60: 307–317.

Pearl, J. (1988). *Probabilistic Reasoning in Intelligent Systems*. San Mateo, Calif.: Morgan Kaufmann.

Pears, D. (1986). The goals and strategies of self-deception. In J. Elster (ed.), *The Multiple Self* (pp. 59–78). Cambridge: Cambridge University Press.

Peirce, C. S. (1931–1958). *Collected Papers*. Cambridge, Mass.: Harvard University Press.

Peirce, C. S. (1958). *Charles S. Peirce: Selected Writings*. New York: Dover.

Pennington, N., and R. Hastie (1992). Explaining the evidence: Tests of the story model for juror decision making. *Journal of Personality and Social Psychology* 51: 189–206.

Pennington, N., and R. Hastie (1993). Reasoning in explanation-based decision making. *Cognition* 49: 125–163.

Peoples, L. L. (2002). Will, anterior cingulate cortex, and addiction. *Science* 296: 1623–1624.

Petrocelli, D. (1998). *Triumph of Justice: The Final Judgment of the Simpson Saga*. New York: Crown.

Pfrieger, F. W., and B. A. Barres (1997). Synaptic efficacy enhanced by glial cells in vitro. *Science* 277: 1684–1687.

Plato (1961). *The Collected Dialogues*. Princeton, N.J.: Princeton University Press.

Polanyi, M. (1958). *Personal Knowledge*. Chicago: University of Chicago Press.

Popkin, R. H. (1979). *The History of Scepticism from Erasmus to Spinoza*. Berkeley: University of California Press.

Popper, K. (1959). *The Logic of Scientific Discovery*. London: Hutchinson.

Port, R., and T. van Gelder (eds.). (1995). *Mind as motion: Explorations in the Dynamics of Cognition*. Cambridge, Mass.: MIT Press.

Posner, R. A. (1999). Emotion versus emotionalism in law. In S. A. Blandes (ed.), *The Passions of Law* (pp. 309–329). New York: New York University Press.

Poznanski, M., and P. Thagard (2005). Changing personalities: Towards realistic virtual characters. *Journal of Experimental and Theoretical Artificial Intelligence* 17: 221–241.

Ramón y Cajal, S. (1999). *Advice for a Young Investigator*. N. S. Swanson and L. W. Swanson, trans. Cambridge, Mass.: MIT Press.

Read, S. J., E. J. Vanman, and L. C. Miller (1997). Connectionist, parallel constraint satisfaction, and Gestalt principles: (Re)Introducing cognitive dynamics to social psychology. *Personality and Social Psychology Review* 1: 26–53.

Reichenbach, H. (1938). *Experience and Prediction*. Chicago: University of Chicago Press.

Reisenzein, R. (1983). The Schachter theory of emotion: Two decades later. *Psychological Review* 94: 239–264.

Rey, G. (1988). Toward a computational account of akrasia and self-deception. In B. P. McLaughlin and A. O. Rorty (eds.), *Perspectives on Self-Deception* (pp. 264–296). Berkeley: University of California Press.

Richardson, R. C. (1996). The prospects for an evolutionary psychology: Human language and human reasoning. *Minds and Machines* 6: 541–557.

Roberts, R. M. (1989). *Serendipity: Accidental Discoveries in Science*. New York: John Wiley and Sons.

Rolls, E. T. (1999). *The Brain and Emotion*. Oxford: Oxford University Press.

Rorty, A. O. (1988). The deceptive self: Liars, layers, and lairs. In B. P. McLaughlin and A. O. Rorty (eds.), *Perspectives on Self-Deception* (pp. 11–28). Berkeley: University of California Press.

Rorty, A. O. (1996). User-friendly self-deception: A traveler's manual. In R. T. Ames and W. Dissanayake (eds.), *Self and Deception: A Cross-Cultural Philosophical Enquiry*. New York: SUNY.

Rottenstreich, Y., and C. K. Hsee (2001). Money, kisses, and electric shocks: On the affective psychology of risk. *Psychological Science* 12: 185–190.

Rudner, R. (1961). Value judgments in the acceptance of theories. In P. G. Frank (ed.), *The Validation of Scientific Theories* (pp. 31–35). New York: Collier Books.

Rumelhart, D. E., and J. L. McClelland (eds.). (1986). *Parallel Distributed Processing: Explorations in the Microstructure of Cognition*. Cambridge Mass.: MIT Press/ Bradford Books.

Russell, B. (1984). *Theory of Knowledge (Collected Papers*, vol. 7). London: George Allen and Unwin.

Russo, J. E., and P. J. H. Schoemaker (1989). *Decision Traps*. New York: Simon and Schuster.

Sackeim, H. A., and R. C. Gur (1978). Self-deception, self-confrontation, and consciousness. In G. E. Schwartz and D. Shapiro (eds.), *Consciousness and Self-Regulation: Advances in Research*, vol. 2 (pp. 139–197). New York: Plenum.

Salmon, N. (1995). Being of two minds: Belief with doubt. *Noûs* 29: 1–20.

Salmon, W. (1984a). *Logic.* 3rd ed. Englewood Cliffs, N.J.: Prentice-Hall.

Salmon, W. (1984b). *Scientific Explanation and the Causal Structure of the World.* Princeton, N.J.: Princeton University Press.

Sanfey, A. G., J. K. Rilling, J. A. Aronson, L. E. Nystrom, and J. D. Cohen (2003). The neural basis of economic decision making in the ultimatum game. *Science* 300: 1755–1758.

Sanitioso, R., Z. Kunda, and G. T. Fong (1990). Motivated recruitment of autobiographical memories. *Journal of Personality and Social Psychology* 59: 229–241.

Sartre, J.-P. (1958). *Being and Nothingness.* H. E. Barnes, trans. London: Methuen.

Schacter, S., and J. Singer (1962). Cognitive, social, and physiological determinants of emotional state. *Psychological Review* 69: 379–399.

Scheffler, I. (1991). *In Praise of the Cognitive Emotions.* New York: Routledge.

Scherer, K. R. (1993). Studying the emotion-antecedent appraisal process: An expert system approach. *Cognition and Emotion* 7: 325–355.

Scherer, K. R., A. Schorr, and T. Johnstone (2001). *Appraisal Processes in Emotion.* New York: Oxford University Press.

Schick, T., Jr., and L. Vaughn (1999). *How to Think about Weird Things*, 2nd ed. Mountain View, Calif.: Mayfield.

Schiller, L., and J. Willwerth (1997). *American Tragedy: The Uncensored Story of the Simpson Defense.* New York: Avon Books.

Sears, D., L. Huddy, and L. Schaffer (1986). A schematic variant of symbolic politics theory, as applied to racial and gender equality. In R. Lau and D. Sears (eds.), *Political Cognition* (pp. 159–202). Hillsdale, N.J.: Lawrence Erlbaum.

Shapiro, R. L. (1996). *The Search for Justice.* New York: Warner Books.

Shastri, L., and V. Ajjanagadde (1993). From simple associations to systematic reasoning: A connectionist representation of rules, variables, and dynamic bindings. *Behavioral and Brain Sciences* 16: 417–494.

Shelley, C. P. (2001). The bicoherence theory of situational irony. *Cognitive Science* 25: 775–818.

Shelley, C. P. (1999). Multiple analogies in evolutionary biology. *Studies in History and Philosophy of Science*, pt. C, *Studies in History and Philosophy of Biological and Biomedical Sciences* 30: 143–180.

Shultz, T. R., and M. R. Lepper (1996). Cognitive dissonance reduction as constraint satisfaction. *Psychological Review* 103: 219–240.

Sinclair, L., and Z. Kunda (1999). Reactions to a black professional: Motivated inhibition and activation of conflicting stereotypes. *Journal of Personality and Social Psychology* 77: 885–904.

Sinclair, L., and Z. Kunda (2000). Motivated stereotyping of women: She's fine if she praised me but incompetent if she criticized me. *Personality and Social Psychology Bulletin* 26: 1329–1342.

Sindermann, C. J. (1985). *The Joy of Science*. New York: Plenum.

Slovic, P., M. L. Finucane, E. Peters, and D. G. MacGregor (2002). The affect heuristic. In T. Gilovich, D. Griffin, and D. Kahneman (eds.), *Heuristics and Biases: The Psychology of Intuitive Judgement* (pp. 397–420). Cambridge: Cambridge University Press.

Snodgrass, J., G. Levy-Berger, and M. Haydon (1985). *Human Experimental Psychology*. New York: Oxford University Press.

Song, J. Y., K. Ichtchenko, T. C. Sudhof, and N. Brose (1999). Neuroligin 1 is a postsynaptic cell-adhesion molecule of excitatory synapses. *Proceedings of the National Academy of Sciences* 96: 1100–1105.

Starek, J. E., and C. F. Keating (1991). Self-deception and its relationship to success in competition. *Basic and Applied Social Psychology* 12: 145–155.

Strong, J. E., M. C. Coffey, D. Tang, P. Sabinin, and P. W. K. Lee (1998). The molecular basis of viral oncolysis: Usurpation of the Ras signaling pathway by reovirus. *EMBO Journal* 17: 3351–3362.

Strong, J. E., and P. W. K. Lee (1996). The v-erbB oncogene confers enhanced cellular susceptibility to reovirus infection. *Journal of Virology* 70: 612–616.

Strong, J. E., D. Tang, and P. W. K. Lee (1993). Evidence that the epidermal growth factor receptor on host cells confers reovirus infection efficiency. *Virology* 197: 405–411.

Surbey, M. K., and J. J. McNally (1997). Self-deception as a mediator of cooperation and defection in varying social contexts described in the iterated prisoner's dilemma. *Evolution and Human Behavior* 18(6): 417–435.

Swinburne, R. (1990). *The Existence of God*, 2nd ed. Oxford: Oxford University Press.

Talbott, W. J. (1995). Intentional self-deception in a single coherent self. *Philosophy and Phenomenological Research* 55(1), 27–74.

Tang, D., J. E. Strong, and P. W. K. Lee (1993). Recognition of the epidermal growth factor receptor in reovirus. *Virology* 197: 412–414.

Taylor, S. E. (1989). *Positive Illusions: Creative Self-Deception and the Healthy Mind*. New York: Basic Books.

Thagard, P. (1988). *Computational Philosophy of Science*. Cambridge, Mass.: MIT Press.

Thagard, P. (1989). Explanatory coherence. *Behavioral and Brain Sciences* 12: 435–467.

Thagard, P. (1992). *Conceptual Revolutions*. Princeton, N.J.: Princeton University Press.

Thagard, P. (1996). *Mind: Introduction to Cognitive Science*. Cambridge, Mass.: MIT Press.

Thagard, P. (1999). *How Scientists Explain Disease*. Princeton, N.J.: Princeton University Press.

Thagard, P. (2000). *Coherence in Thought and Action*. Cambridge, Mass.: MIT Press.

Thagard, P. (2003). Pathways to biomedical discovery. *Philosophy of Science* 70: 235–254.

Thagard, P. (2004). Causal inference in legal decision making: Explanatory coherence versus Bayesian networks. *Applied Artificial Intelligence* 18: 231–249.

Thagard, P. (2005). *Mind: Introduction to Cognitive Science*, 2nd ed. Cambridge, Mass.: MIT Press.

Thagard, P. (forthcoming a). Abductive inference: From philosophical analysis to neural mechanisms. In A. Feeney and E. Heit (eds.), *Inductive reasoning: Cognitive, mathematical, and neuroscientific approaches*. Cambridge: Cambridge University Press.

Thagard, P. (forthcoming b). How to collaborate: Procedural knowledge in the cooperative development of science. *Southern Journal of Philosophy*.

Thagard, P. (forthcoming c). The moral psychology of conflicts of interest: Insights from affective neuroscience. *Journal of Applied Philosophy*.

Thagard, P. (forthcoming d). Testimony, credibility, and explanatory coherence. *Erkenntnis*.

Thagard, P., D. Gochfeld, and S. Hardy (1992). Visual analogical mapping. In *Proceedings of the Fourteenth Annual Conference of the Cognitive Science Society* (pp. 522–527). Hillsdale, N.J.: Lawrence Erlbaum Associates.

Thagard, P., and A. Litt (forthcoming). Models of scientific explanation. In R. Sun (ed.), *The Cambridge Handbook of Computational Cognitive Modeling*. Cambridge: Cambridge University Press.

Thagard, P., and E. Millgram (1995). Inference to the best plan: A coherence theory of decision. In A. Ram and D. B. Leake (eds.), *Goal-Driven Learning* (pp. 439–454). Cambridge, Mass.: MIT Press.

Thagard, P., and K. Verbeurgt (1998). Coherence as constraint satisfaction. *Cognitive Science* 22: 1–24.

Thagard, P., and J. Zhu (2003). Acupuncture, incommensurability, and conceptual change. In G. M. Sinatra and P. R. Pintrich (eds.), *Intentional Conceptual Change* (pp. 79–102). Mahwah, N.J.: Lawrence Erlbaum.

Thelen, E., and L. B. Smith (1994). *A dynamic systems approach to the development of cognition and action.* Cambridge, Mass.: MIT Press.

Tversky, A., and D. J. Koehler (1994). Support theory: A nonextensional representation of subjective probability. *Psychological Review* 101: 547–567.

Vallacher, R. R., S. J. Read, and A. Nowak (2002). The dynamical perspective in personality and social psychology. *Personality and Social Psychology Review* 6: 274–282.

van Andel, P. (1994). Anatomy of the unsought finding, serendipity: Origin, history, domains, traditions, appearances, patterns, and programmability. *British Journal for the Philosophy of Science* 45: 631–648.

van Gelder, T. (1995). What might cognition be, if not computation? *Journal of Philosophy* 92: 345–381.

Wagar, B. M., and P. Thagard (2003). Using computational neuroscience to investigate the neural correlates of cognitive-affective integration during covert decision making. *Brain and Cognition* 53: 398–402.

Wagar, B. M., and P. Thagard (2004). Spiking Phineas Gage: A neurocomputational theory of cognitive-affective integration in decision making. *Psychological Review* 111: 67–79.

Ward, T. B., S. M. Smith, and J. Vaid (eds.). (1997). *Creative Thought: An Investigation of Conceptual Structures and Processes.* Washington, D.C.: American Psychological Association.

Watson, J. D. (1969). *The Double Helix.* New York: New American Library.

Watson, J. D. (2000). *A Passion for DNA: Genes, Genomes, and Society.* Cold Spring Harbor, N.Y.: Cold Spring Harbor Laboratory Press.

Weiner, B. (1995). *Judgments of Responsibility: A Foundation for a Theory of Social Conduct.* New York: Guilford Press.

Westen, D., A. Feit, J. Arkowitz, P. Blagov, and P. Thagard (forthcoming). On selecting and impeaching presidents: Emotional constraint satisfaction in motivated political reasoning.

White, D. O., and F. J. Fenner (1994). *Medical Virology.* San Diego, Calif.: Academic Press.

Whitehouse, H. (2000). *Arguments and Icons: Divergent Modes of Religiosity.* Oxford: Oxford University Press.

Wilkins, J. (1969). *Of the Principles and Duties of Natural Religion.* New York: Johnson Reprint Corp.

Wilson, T. D., and J. W. Schooler (1991). Thinking too much: Introspection can reduce the quality of preferences and decisions. *Journal of Personality and Social Psychology* 60: 181–192.

Wolpert, L., and A. Richards (1997). *Passionate Minds: The Inner World of Scientists*. Oxford: Oxford University Press.

Wooldridge, M. (2002). *An Introduction to Multiagent Systems*. Chichester: John Wiley and Sons.

Wrangham, R. (1999). Is military incompetence adaptive? *Evolution and Human Behavior* 20: 3–17.

Zerbe, W. J., and D. L. Paulhus (1987). Socially desirable responding in organized behavior: A reconception. *Academy of Management Review* 12: 250–264.

Zhu, J., and P. Thagard (2002). Emotion and action. *Philosophical Psychology* 15: 19–36.

Index